CW00552475

FASHION MEDIA

FASHION MEDIA

PAST AND PRESENT

edited by
djurdja bartlett, shaun cole
and agnès rocamora

Bloomsbury Academic
An imprint of Bloomsbury Publishing Plc

B L O O M S B U R Y

LONDON · NEW DELHI · NEW YORK · SYDNEY

Bloomsbury Academic

An imprint of Bloomsbury Publishing Plc

50 Bedford Square	1385 Broadway
London	New York
WC1B 3DP	NY 10018
UK	USA

www.bloomsbury.com

BLOOMSBURY and the Diana logo are trademarks of Bloomsbury Publishing Plc

First published 2013
Reprinted by Bloomsbury Academic 2014

© Djurdja Bartlett, Shaun Cole, Agnès Rocamora and contributors, 2013

Djurdja Bartlett, Shaun Cole, Agnès Rocamora and contributors have asserted
their right under the Copyright, Designs and Patents Act, 1988,
to be identified as Authors of this work.

British Library Cataloguing-in-Publication Data
A catalogue record for this book is available from the British Library.

ISBN: HB:	978-0-8578-5306-6
PB:	978-0-8578-5307-3
ePDF:	978-0-8578-5308-0
ePub:	978-0-8578-5309-7

Library of Congress Cataloging-in-Publication Data
A catalog record for this book is available from the Library of Congress.

Typeset by Apex CoVantage, LLC, Madison, WI, USA
Printed and bound in Great Britain

CONTENTS

LIST OF ILLUSTRATIONS

FIGURES

PLATES

ACKNOWLEDGEMENTS

We are grateful to London College of Fashion, University of the Arts London for its support on this project, particularly Frances Corner, director of the college; Helen Thomas, then director of research; and Tony Kent, the associate dean of research, all of whom were encouraging and supportive of both the original conference and this book. We are particularly grateful for the support of the London College of Fashion Research Fund, which assisted with image rights and production of our book.

We would like to thank Penny Martin for her role in the conference and editing the round-table discussion and photographer Ben Hassett for allowing us to use his wonderful image on the cover. Our special appreciation goes towards all the contributors of this book for their enthusiastic work on their texts, as well as for their dedication in securing the images for this publication. We would also like to thank all those people who were so generous in allowing us to use photographs and images in the book: photographer Tim Walker for his kind permission to use his photographs accompanying Sarah Cheang's chapter; artist Flavio Lucchini for allowing us to publish images of two of his artworks referred to in Barbara Vinken's chapter, and to Prada and *Vogue*, whose logotypes appear in Lucchini's art work; David Abbott from IPC for his generosity in approving the publication of the images from the magazine *Nova* within Alice Beard's chapter; SHOWstudio and Simon Foxton for the Thirty Men image in Nilgin Yusuf's chapter; artist and filmmaker Sasa Kovacevic for images in Friedrich Weltzien's chapter; Jockey, Courtaulds and Sunspel for underwear images; Roberto Baldassari, Quentin Shih and Carlo Chionna for permission to use their images in Simona Segre Reinach's chapter; Susie Lau for the image from her blog, Style Bubble; and Nina Cohen, Jana Kossaibati, Ghaida Tsurayya, Hana Tajima-Simpson and H2O Pink Label, whose images visually support Reina Lewis's argument.

We would also like to thank Anna Wright, fashion book editor at Bloomsbury Academic, for believing in the subject enough to commission the book, and Hannah Crump, assistant editor at Bloomsbury Academic, for her tireless engagement with permissions.

Editors and authors have tried to trace and secure rights for all the images in this book. Any omissions will be acknowledged and corrected in future editions.

CONTRIBUTORS

Dr Djurdja Bartlett is senior research fellow at the London College of Fashion, University of the Arts London. She has published widely on the theme of fashion during socialism and post-socialism. Bartlett is author of *FashionEast: the Spectre That Haunted Socialism* (MIT Press, 2010; Novoe literaturnoe obozrenie, 2011) and editor of a volume on East Europe, Russia and the Caucasus in the *Berg Encyclopedia of World Dress and Fashion* (Berg, 2010). Bartlett's recent research project under the title *Translating Fashion: East Europe West Europe, 1910–2010,* funded by the Arts and Humanities Research Council UK, explores the relationship between East European and Western fashion.

Alice Beard is senior lecturer in design history at Kingston University. Her teaching and research is focused on fashion media and the intersections between fashion, design, text and photography. She is particularly interested in magazine cultures and uses oral history to reconstruct production and consumption histories. Her published work includes 'Put in Just for Pictures' (*Fashion Theory,* 2002) and 'Hairstyling in the Fashion Magazine: Nova in the 1970s' in *Hair: Styling, Culture and Fashion* (Berg, 2008). At The Women's Library (London) Beard curated *Beauty Queens: Smiles, Swimsuits and Sabotage* (2004) and *Remembering Nova Magazine 1965–1976* (2006).

Dr Sarah Cheang is senior tutor in the history of design programme, where she leads the Modern Specialism. Her research interests centre on fashion, the body and cultural exchange between East and West. She has a special interest in the role of Chinese material culture within histories of Western fashionable dress and domestic interiors, a subject on which she has published widely and lectures frequently. Cheang co-edited *Hair: Styling, Culture and Fashion* (Berg, 2008) and has prepared two new books for publication: *Fashion and Ethnicity* (Bloomsbury Academic, forthcoming) and *Sinophilia: Fashion, Western Modernity and Things Chinese After 1900* (I.B. Tauris, 2014).

Shaun Cole is a writer, lecturer and curator, and currently the programme director for curation and culture and course leader for MA History and Culture of Fashion at London College of Fashion, UAL. He was formerly head of contemporary programmes at the Victoria and Albert

Museum, where he curated several exhibitions, most notably *Graphic Responses to AIDS* (1996), *Dressing the Male* (1999) and *Black British Style* (2004). Cole's published work includes *'Don We Now Our Gay Apparel': Gay Men's Dress in the Twentieth Century* (Berg, 2000); *Dialogue: Relationships in Graphic Design* (V&A Publishing, 2005); and *The Story of Men's Underwear* (Parkstone International, 2010).

Dr Reina Lewis is Artscom Centenary Professor of Cultural Studies at the London College of Fashion, University of the Arts London. Her books are *Re-fashioning Orientalism: New Trends in Muslim Style* (Duke University Press, 2014); *Rethinking Orientalism: Women, Travel and the Ottoman Harem* (I.B. Tauris, 2004); and *Gendering Orientalism: Race, Femininity and Representation* (Routledge, 1996). She is editor of *Modest Fashion: Styling Bodies, Mediating Faith* (I.B. Tauris, 2013); and, with Zeynep Inankur and Mary Roberts, *The Poetics and Politics of Place: Ottoman Istanbul and British Orientalism* (Suna and İnan Kıraç Foundation, 2011); with Nancy Micklewright, *Gender, Modernity and Liberty: Middle Eastern and Western Women's Writings* (I.B. Tauris, 2006); with Sara Mills, *Feminist Postcolonial Theory: A Reader* (Edinburgh University Press, 2003); with Peter Horne, *Outlooks: Lesbian and Gay Visual Cultures* (Routledge, 1996).

Dr Sanda Miller is research fellow at Southampton Solent University and visiting lecturer at Istituto Marangoni, London. At present she is working on a book entitled *The New History of Fashion* commissioned by Thames and Hudson and two other books, on fashion criticism and fashion journalism, in collaboration with Peter McNeil, commissioned by Bloomsbury.

Dr Agnès Rocamora is a reader in social and cultural studies at the London College of Fashion, University of the Arts London. She is the author of *Fashioning the City: Paris, Fashion and the Media* (I.B. Tauris, 2009). Her writing on the field of fashion, on the fashion media and on fashion blogging has appeared in various journals, including *Fashion Theory*, *Sociology* and the *Journal of Consumer Culture*. She is a co-editor of *The Handbook of Fashion Studies* (Bloomsbury Academic, 2013) and *Thinking Through Fashion: A Guide to Key Thinkers* (I.B. Tauris, 2014), and she is a contributor to *Fashion's World Cities* (Berg, 2006) and *Fashion as Photograph* (I.B. Tauris, 2008). She is currently developing her work on fashion and digital media.

Simona Segre Reinach is cultural anthropologist and professor of fashion studies at Bologna University. She has written on fashion from a global perspective in the books *Berg Encyclopedia of World Dress and Fashion* (Berg, 2010) and *The Fashion History Reader* (Routledge, 2010), and in the journals *Fashion Theory*, *Fashion Practice*, *Business and Economic History* and *Critical Studies in Fashion and Beauty*. Segre Reinach's fieldwork on Sino-Italian joint ventures within a collaborative project, The New Silk Road (conducted in China, 2002–10), will be published by Chicago University Press (2014). She is a founding partner of Misa, Associazione Italiana Studi di Moda. Segre Reinach's latest book is *Un Mondo di mode* (Laterza, 2011).

Dr Eugénie Shinkle is senior lecturer in photographic theory and criticism at the University of Westminster. She is the editor of *Fashion as Photograph* (I.B. Tauris, 2008) and has written widely on the notion of embodiment in fashion photography. More recent writing builds on her earlier research into digital games to explore the body–technology interface in emerging fashion media. Her work is included in publications such as *Carnal Aesthetics: Transgressive Imagery and Feminist Politics* (I.B. Tauris, 2012) and *Images in Time* (Wunderkammer Press, 2011).

Dr Änne Söll is research fellow at the Institut für Künste und Medien at the University of Potsdam. She is an art historian specializing in modern and contemporary art, concentrating on gender and media theory. She has written two books on the art of Pipilotti Rist and edited three interdisciplinary books: one on the theory of materiality, another on the subject of friendship and, most recently, a book on the aesthetics of 'coolness'. Other publications include work on contemporary photography and fashion photography. Her current research concerns images of masculinity in portraiture of the 1920s.

Marketa Uhlirova is senior research fellow in fashion history and theory at Central Saint Martins College of Arts and Design. Since 2006 she has been director of Fashion in Film, an exhibition, research and education project with an international touring programme. Alongside editing Fashion in Film's own publications (including *If Looks Could Kill: Cinema's Images of Fashion, Crime and Violence* [2008] and *Birds of Paradise: Costume as Cinematic Spectacle* [2013], both Koenig Books), Uhlirova has contributed writing to the journals *Fashion Theory, Art Monthly, The Measure* and the *Berg Encyclopedia of World Dress and Fashion* (Berg, 2010) among others.

Professor Dr Barbara Vinken (master's, Dr. phil. [Konstanz], PhD [Yale], Dr. phil. habil. [Jena]) holds the chair for French and comparative literature at Ludwig-Maximilians-University, Munich, Germany. She previously held professorships at the universities of Hamburg and Zurich. As visiting scholar, she has taught at the EHESS (Paris), New York University, the Humboldt University (Berlin), the Johns Hopkins University and Chicago University. Her books include *Fashion Zeitgeist: Trends and Cycles in the Fashion System* (Berg, 2005); *Die deutsche Mutter—Der lange Schatten eines Mythos* (Fischer, 2007); and *Flaubert Postsecular* (Stanford University Press, 2013).

Professor Dr Friedrich Weltzien studied art history, archaeology and philosophy at the Universities of Freiburg, Vienna, Cologne and the Free University Berlin, and gained a PhD in 2001 with research on the image of the human body between 1945 and 1955. He has authored several publications on contemporary art, media theory in the nineteenth and twentieth centuries and aesthetics of production. In 2011 he published a book on autopoietical practices in art and science covering the German romantic period in the nineteenth century. Weltzien is interested in fashion as a cultural practice, incorporating and influencing all other forms of communication and expression.

Dr Elizabeth Wissinger is an associate professor of sociology at BMCC/City University of New York and a fashion studies instructor in the Masters of Liberal Studies at the Graduate Center of CUNY and has written and spoken frequently about modelling and fashion. Recent publications include 'Modeling Consumption: Fashion Modeling Work in Contemporary Society' in the *Journal of Consumer Culture* and 'The Top Model Life' in *Contexts,* the magazine of the American Sociological Association. Wissinger co-edited, with Joanne Entwistle, an anthology entitled *Fashioning*

Models: Image, Text, and Industry (Berg, 2012). She also co-edited the upcoming special issue on fashion for the journal *WSQ* (May 2013).

Nilgin Yusuf is director of programmes in media in the school of graduate studies and course leader for MA Fashion Media Production at London College of Fashion. Formerly fashion editor of the *Sunday Times,* she also worked as a fashion writer for the *Daily Telegraph* and *Elle* magazine. Since completing a master's in fashion history and culture at London College of Fashion, she has been developing her own research, which deconstructs and explores the sartorial genres of criminal dress.

INTRODUCTION

Since their first appearance in the seventeenth century—indeed Jean Donneau de Visé's 1672 *Le Mercure Galant* is generally credited as being the ancestor of fashion magazines (see Vincent 2005)—fashion media platforms have proliferated. This is testament not only to the popularity of fashion as a topic of news but also to the crucial role of the media in the field of fashion, for fashion words and images are central to the production, circulation and dissemination of fashion (Barthes 1990; Jobling 1999; Rocamora 2009).

By mapping key changes in fashion and commodity culture, the fashion media have also captured and produced modernity in all its contradictions. Art and commerce, elite and ordinary cultures, spaces, times, professional and amateur practices meet and intertwine in the field of the fashion media. Today this field is in the midst of deep social and technological changes. Its present, as well as its past, offer a unique opportunity to explore the complex, multilayered nature of the processes that bind design, technology, society and identity together. Yet, and in spite of the now well-established presence of fashion as a topic of academic enquiry, the fashion media remain relatively underexplored. *Fashion Media: Past and Present* attends to this gap.

Like the conference that inspired it, this book aims to shed light on past and current shifts in the fashion media.[1] More fundamentally, it interrogates key social and cultural issues through the empirical analyses of a variety of textual platforms from different historical times and cultures. Fashion advertisements, magazines, fashion films, websites and photography are among the media sites discussed as a way of engaging with a range of topics central to the understanding of not only fashion but of society and culture, too.

The book is divided into three sections. The first addresses the fashion magazine. This is followed by an investigation of how painting, photography and film all act as fashion media. The third section engages with digital media, and the book concludes with a roundtable discussion on contemporary development and issues in the fashion media.

Section I starts with the early history of the fashion magazine. In her essay entitled 'Taste, Fashion and the French Fashion Magazine', Sanda Miller discusses the early period of the fashion press. Based on an analysis of fashion titles from the time—Melchior von Grimm's *Le courier de la mode ou Journal du goût* (1768–70) and *Le Journal des Dames et des Modes* (1797–1839)—Miller's chapter argues for the centrality of the concept of taste in the context of the newly emerging world of the French fashion magazines. Continuing on the theme of taste and its presence in fashion magazines, Miller brings her essay into the twentieth century with a discussion of the use of fine artists' work to illustrate the French fashion journal *Gazette du Bon Ton*.

Throughout the twentieth century, fashion magazines addressed and nurtured the interests of their readership within rapidly changing social, cultural and commercial practices. Yet, the concepts of femininity and masculinity were changing in line with the changing social and cultural circumstances. In the United Kingdom, *Nova* magazine captured at the same time as it created a new type of fashionable femininity, one aimed at reconciling some of the feminist agenda with fashionable appearance. The contribution Caroline Baker made to this magazine as fashion editor is the object of Alice Beard's chapter. Baker was employed in this role at *Nova* in 1967 'in order to style a different fashion to the one published on the pages of *Vogue, Queen* and *The Times*'. Based on an examination of her fashion spreads and drawing on information and ideas from interviews Beard conducted with Baker, this chapter reveals that Baker's styling operated as an intrinsic part of both achieving a particular look and as a signifier of the new young fashionable woman who consumed these images.

In the third chapter of this volume, Sarah Cheang also engages with images of women in high-fashion magazines, only this time not to unpack the idea of femininity but to interrogate the idea of the Other by challenging the depiction of fashion 'out of place'. Through a close analysis of fashion shoots in exotic, non-Western spaces, such as dusty Palestine, rural India or mountainous Peru, she explores how particular concepts of fashion and fashion's Other—ethnic dress—have been reproduced in British *Vogue* in the last five years. Discussing the work of photographers Mario Testino, Patrick Demarchelier and Tim Walker, Cheang examines important debates of globalization and cultural imperialism but also considers the opportunities for fashion photography to challenge or interrogate racial and ethnic stereotypes.

Fashion, of course, is not the preserve of the Western world (Eicher 1995; Rabine 2002) as Djurdja Bartlett's chapter reminds us. Indeed, in 'Coco Chanel and Socialist Fashion Magazines' she investigates East European socialist women's magazines and emphasizes that they were informed by the conventions of both fashion journals and more or less sophisticated political bulletins. In that sense, all the ideologically imposed changes in socialist fashion and the concept of gender were mediated through women's and fashion magazines but imposed through a 'chatty' writing style resembling that of their Western counterparts. Along with the conventional concept of femininity, socialist good taste was promoted as well. As an official aesthetics and style guide for the emerging middle classes, socialist good taste incorporated the concepts of elegance and prettiness but insisted that only simplicity is elegant and beautiful.

Although the majority of fashion magazines have traditionally been targeted at women, there have been, and still are, fashion media that are produced for consumption by men. In his essay 'Advertising Men's Underwear', Shaun Cole considers the ways in which men's underwear was presented and sold to both male and female consumers in the period following the Second World War. He explores ideas around the presentation of the clothed and unclothed body, as well as the complete omission of men's bodies, in relation to acceptable representations of post-war masculinity and sexuality. In addressing the textual element of the advertisements as well as the imagery used, Cole addresses technological developments in textiles and design of underwear and relates this to the concept of 'masculine comfort' presented in many of these advertisements.

Section 2 of this volume engages with dress, clothes and fashion through their presentation in image form, be that painted, photographic or filmic. Indeed, as Hollander reminds us, 'The history of dress or the study of clothes has no real substance other than in *images* of clothes' (1993: 454). However, as Malcolm Barnard observes, 'The visual has remained relatively neglected in fashion studies' (2012: 416). This book goes someway to reddressing this imbalance.

To raise the notion of the relationship between fashion and art is to open up a complex and much-debated arena that includes such questions as: Is fashion art? Are fashion designers artists? Can artists create fashion? It has been well documented (cf. Breward 1998; Cumming 2004; Taylor 2002, 2004) that it was within the discipline of art history that historic dress was first seriously used within academia in the post-war period to date clothing and its representation in paintings. This use of paintings that depict 'fashion' is sometimes problematic as artists used props, drapery, historic or stage costume or allegorical references and so could cast doubts upon the authenticity of the fashions depicted therein. 'A portrait is not merely a mechanical image,' dress historian Aileen Ribeiro pointed out. 'It is a likeness of the sitter and his or her character seen through the temperament of the artist' (1995: 14).

It is the notion of the authentic versus the allegorical that is raised by Änne Söll in her essay 'Fashion, Media and Gender in Christian Schad's Portraiture of the 1920s', which interrogates the 'fashionable' clothing in a pair of portraits and a self-portrait by German painter Christian Schad. Söll unpacks the ways in which Schad made comments upon questions of gendered and sexual identities expressed through the choice of clothes and accessories of the characters in the three paintings examined in detail. However, it is not just through painting that art and fashion come together. In her essay on the Muslim headscarf and the modern woman, Barbara Vinken ventures between law, fine arts, film, fashion magazines and catwalk shows, both in their historical and current contexts, in order to examine how modern women negotiate questions of eroticization, modesty and legality in their adoption of the hijab. Friedrich Weltzien, meanwhile, addresses the performance art of Marina Abramovic and her comments on the uncredited referencing of artistic practice to discuss the similarities between Jana Sterbak's 1987 *Vanitas—Flesh Dress for an Albino Anoretic* and the performative attendance of Lady Gaga dressed in a meat dress at the 2010 MTV Music Video Awards.

The inclusion of photography and fashion film in this section of the book also raises questions about the boundaries of what we might consider art. The collection and exhibition of fashion photographs by fine art and decorative art museums such at Museum of Modern Art in New York, the San Francisco Museum of Modern Art and the Victoria and Albert Museum, as well as the opening in 2012 of The Tanks at the Tate Modern in London, the world's 'first museum galleries permanently dedicated to exhibiting live art', furthers the debate on the intersection and increasingly blurred lines of the definition between art and what might previously have been described as media or lesser forms of visual culture with a commercial imperative.[2]

Longhurst and colleagues (2008: 278) note that 'as subsequent history has shown, both motion and still photography can serve diverse purposes'—as scientific instruments, as entertainment, as forms of art, as methods of surveillance, for example. Three of the authors within this section consider photography through a variety of purposes that it can serve. The inclusion of moving image/film within three of the essays, and as a particular focus for Marketa Uhlirova, can also be considered within the bounds of Longhurst and colleagues' consideration and proposition for photography. The invention of photography in the early nineteenth century changed the way that dress and the dressed body could be presented and viewed. Although photography did not make a major impact in printed media until the middle of the twentieth century, it did serve as a means of recording fashion. Michael Boordro made an interesting point in relation to this when he noted, 'Ironically just when photography usurped the role of painting in documenting clothing, clothing came to play a different role in art' (2007: 258). He points out how impressionists were particularly concerned with the everyday life of the middle classes and thus gave 'unprecedented importance to ordinary clothes' (2007: 258).

Walter Benjamin (1999) has discussed the way a confrontation occurred between painting and photography. Vicki Karaminas (2012) draws on this idea to explore how photography was the start of a development that led to moving film and later to digital imagery. In Chapter 8, Nilgin Yusuf covers this very transition through the lens of fashion and crime imagery and media. It is also this point of the introduction of 'moving' imagery to represent and 'play' with movement in dress and its transformative nature that Marketa Uhlirova addresses in her chapter.

The idea of comparison between forms of media is one that is addressed by all of the authors in the section. Vinken compares artist Flavio Lucchini's images of the veil presented at the Venice Biennale in 2011, in which eroticism has been erased, with fashion shoots in *Vogue* in which there is an element of the 'fetishes of eroticism' of Western fashion, thus raising questions about the role and place of the veil in contemporary life and fashion representation. Vinken also compares the roots of the words *fashion* and *modern,* addressing the complexity of the historical and ongoing relationship between the two.

Yusuf's use of comparison is perhaps the most blatant in one respect—in that it draws an analogy between fashion and crime and the ways in which photography is utilized to present fashion and dress and to record the criminal and his or her behaviour. Yusuf addresses the development of photography and how photographs are used as a form of representational media to show developments in fashion and dress and in the ways in which crime and the dressed criminal body is captured and presented to a range of audiences. Following Karaminas's notion that photography led to film and digital technology, Yusuf debates how Hollywood film and particularly presentations of gangsters and criminals in film impacted upon fashion whilst at the same time making a strong case for the criminal as a follower (and perhaps unconscious leader) of fashion. She brings her discussion up to date by looking at the ways in which the voyeurism that can be attributed to CCTV and 'happy slapping' can be compared to the viewing of certain types of fashion film, especially as presented on the originally groundbreaking and now well-established website SHOWstudio.

SHOWstudio, originally the brainchild of fashion photographer Nick Knight and graphic designer Peter Saville, pioneered fashion film and has become internationally recognized as *the* site in/ on which fashion and its relationship with moving image in the digital age is produced, discussed and disseminated. As such, it features in the discussion in three of the essays in the chapter: Weltzin uses it to situate the moving image as a fashion and political showcase, Yusuf highlights how it allows the viewers to see the processes and practices behind the creation of still and moving fashion imagery, and, in her fashion film specific exploration, Uhlirova discusses its role as an 'archive' of fashion film and the place it played in the reintroduction of movement through fashion film that was perhaps lost in still fashion photography.

Both Weltzien and Uhlirova make fashion film a central focus of their essays. Weltzien situates fashion film within the context of art touching upon the much debated concept of fashion as art and how within Marshal McLuhan's theorization of medium, fashion takes on a role as a vehicle of communication as, and similar to that of, artistic output as a presentation of creativity. As well as discussing Yugoslav-born designer Sadak's use of fashion film as a means of presenting both a fashion collection and a political statement, Weltzien unpacks Lady Gaga's and Jana Sterbak's meat dresses in light of McLuhan's discussion of the hybrid (here of art and fashion). Uhlirova situates the recent explosion of fashion film in the context of the development of presentations of fashion within film in early cinema. She is particularly concerned with the way in which movement is interjected into the presentations of fashion and so perhaps here makes an unconscious comparison with the still images that are discussed by Söll and Yusuf. Uhlirova presents an argument that there is a painterly quality in digital cinema and many of the non-narrative fashion films that have been produced. This sits alongside her more obvious comparison of more traditional forms of cinema and the contemporary fashion film.

Discussing fashion film in the context of other media formats is something that Weltzien also addresses in his essay. Unlike Uhlirova, who is particularly concerned with the aesthetic qualities of fashion (and other forms of) film, Weltzien addresses his chosen media through a much more political lens. His invocation of certain radical political groups' actions against fashion shops in the early 1970s, as a response to the demeaning of women by fashion, relates to the gendered ideas that have been promoting the contradiction between the masculine nature of art and creative productivity and the femininity or 'feminization of fashion and consumption.

The confrontation that occurred between photography and painting in the early twentieth century is raised and discussed by Änne Söll in her essay on Christian Schad. By discussing the way in which Schad used photography to inform his painting style, Söll investigates the interstices between fashion, photography and painting to inspect the dressed gendered body through what she calls 'the embodiment of fashion in paint'. The notion of the presentation of gender and sexuality within forms of fashion media also permeates this section of the book. Both Söll and Vinken specifically address these ideas: Söll through the gender ambiguity in Schad's character portraits and Vinken through contemporary catwalk shows and fashion advertising that highlight notions of male masculinity or female femininity in the displayed body. Fashion has been used as a means of making statements about the wearer's identity and the complexities of the elements that make up each individual's identity.

Although the field of fashion has been comparatively slow to embrace new digital technologies since the years 2009 and 2010, in particular fashion producers and consumers have embraced new media platforms in a manner theretofore unparalleled. Thus *Women's Wear Daily* argued, 'For fashion companies, 2009 is turning out to be the year of social media' (Corcoran 2009), and in 2010 the *Business of Fashion* noted, 'Fashion media is embracing digital technology like never before' (Kansara 2010).

All media have at some point in their history been new: the telegraph has been a new medium and so have the radio, TV and smart phones. The term *new media* then refers to an ever-changing reality, with the new media of yesterday becoming today's old or traditional media. Levinson (2009) captures this temporal relativity in what he terms *new new media,* in contrast with old new media, to refer to those media users and consumers can engage with as producers or content creators, a distinction crucial to the development of new fashion media such as blogs, as Chapters 13 and 14 show.

Though it acknowledges that novelty is not an absolute value, in discussing new media the third section of this book is referring to the range of platforms that proliferated in the 1990s and 2000s and are, in common parlance as well as in much of the academic literature on the subject (see, for instance, Fuery 2009; Lister et al. 2009), the textual platforms that rely on digital technologies for their flourishing, are computer-mediated and, often, circulated on the Internet. In the field of fashion, these include Facebook, fashion films, Instagram, Twitter, YouTube, blogs and apps as well as all the fashion websites more generally that are now increasingly part of the fashion media landscape.

While Section 2 addresses the increasingly popular genre of the fashion film, drawing attention to the role of Internet in its mediation, the third and final section of the book pursues this investigation of fashion on the Internet by turning towards some of its other manifestations. Simona Segre Reinach, Reina Lewis and Agnès Rocamora focus on fashion blogs, a form that appeared in the early 2000s (see Rocamora 2011; Rocamora and Bartlett 2009); Eugenie Shinkle looks at fashion interactives—'digital content which users can select and control via a computer interface'; and Elizabeth Wissinger interrogates the Internet's contribution to the circulation of new bodily ideals. All five authors draw attention to the importance of new media in new practices of production, circulation and consumption of fashion.

For Lewis and Segre Reinach, an interrogation of processes of identity construction is at the heart of their investigations of the significance of new fashion media, blogs in particular. Indeed, in 'The Modest Fashion Blogosphere' Lewis addresses the relation between fashion and faith identities through an analysis of blogs devoted to modest fashion. She looks at the way 'new conventions of modesty are created, communicated, contested and co-opted by practitioners from different denominations and religions'. Whilst Lewis discusses the tensions at play in the formation of religious identity, Segre Reinach's 'Fashion Films, Blogs and E-Commerce' interrogates those at work in the representational enactment of national identity, here that of the Chinese. She contrasts the communication strategy of established Western fashion brands in China with the discourse of Chinese fashion bloggers. Where the former tend to reproduce existing stereotypes on China, the latter, she argues, offers an alternative vision of fashion in China. Privileging the banal and the mundane, Chinese fashion bloggers revisit stereotypes, which forces a reinterpretation of the relation between China and the West and allows for Chinese fashion to gain agency. A process of adaptation takes place, she contends, that allows for the voice of 'creative China' to come through.

In 'Fashion Modelling, Blink Technologies and New Imaging Regimes', Wissinger also pays attention to the idea of identity, that of models, caught between a realm of images increasingly shaped by the forces of commerce and new technologies, and the reality of everyday life, uncertain and brutal. She argues that the harsh constraints placed on models to leave a precarious life and work on their body to conform to the industry's requirements are glamourized to serve the interest of business. Models' work has become a sort of humanware that supports the shift towards a biopolitics of power geared towards a market logic of profit. This is a logic Lewis also attends to when she conceptualizes the modest fashion blogosphere as a space of crossovers between faiths, between religious and secular women and between commerce and spiritual integrity. Indeed Lewis shows that modest fashion bloggers, like many fashion bloggers more generally, are having to face the difficult negotiation of the relation between independence and co-optation.

Both Lewis and Wissinger are interested in uncovering the new discourses that emerge out of new fashion media. Whilst the former draws attention to the role of blogs in the creation of 'new types of spiritual, social and religious discourse', Wissinger argues that the shift towards cable television and the Internet has resulted in the creation of 'a new imaging regime'. She draws on Patricia

Cough's post-structuralist theory and Malcolm Gladwell's concept of the blink to unpack the changes that have informed our images and practices of the body. New media technologies and the 'regime of the blink', Wessinger argues, have supported the shrinking of models' bodies and what journalist Guy Trebay calls a 'bleaching of the catwalks'. In a context of the rapid circulation of images and shortened attention spans, models have to be read quickly as models. Their normalizing into extremely white and thin figures satisfies this need.

Fashion discourse, Segre Reinach, Wissinger and Lewis show, then, cannot be seen outside of the capitalist forces that structure contemporary society. It is first and foremost a discourse aimed at selling commodities and a commodity itself but also a practice that takes in its commercializing stride both material and symbolic entities: the bodies of models as in the work of Wissinger, the religion of bloggers as in the work of Lewis, and the imagined identity of China as in the work of Segre Reinach.

The relation between the material and the symbolic, a tension between the phenomenological and the representational, is also at the heart of Shinkle's 'Fashion's Digital Body'. Indeed, in this chapter, Shinkle looks at the role of fashion interactives in promoting a dialogue between representation and embodied action. She reminds us that the body is not just a discursive construction, but it is also a material thing. In addressing the tactile body, the fashion media become meaningful and relevant to human subjects as embodied subjects. With fashion interactives, she asks, is this privilege mode of address 'enabled'? Thus drawing on the work of media theorist Mark B. N. Hansen, new media images, she argues, demand a kind of interactivity that is premised on users 'bringing their own sensory memories and physical presence to bear on the act of perception'. However, looking at the case of Burberry's fashion interactives she shows that 'representation and embodied action' are divorced from one another. In contrast, Virtual Dressing Room (VDR) applications allow for the creation of a relationship between the user's 'own affectively sensed body, and its onscreen image'. The distinction between the real and the virtual is broken down. Also discussing wearable computers—wearables—she contends that by dissolving the boundary between technology and the body, they offer a privileged relation between the two that no other interfaces can match.

In 'How New Are New Media? The Case of Fashion Blogs', Rocamora problematizes the idea of the newness of new media in the light of the fashion blogosphere. She looks at some of its characteristics in contrast with the traditional printed press. In particular, she mobilizes the notion of hypertextuality to discuss some of the ways blogs part with traditional models or representations, allowing for a decentralizing of the field of fashion. Thus, like Lewis and Segre Reinach, she attends to the ways new fashion media open up fashion media discourse to subjects and ideas traditionally excluded from it, whilst also paying attention, like Shinkle, to the textual specificity of fashion on the Web and the implication this textuality—a hypertextuality—has for practices of fashion. Whilst Shinkle shows that it forces one to reconsider the traditional opposition between the virtual and the real, Rocamora shows that, in the case of fashion bloggers, it challenges the distinction between amateur and experts, which Lewis also problematizes by discussing the professionalization of faith-based fashion media roles in blogging.

Moreover, drawing on the concept of remediation Rocamora also looks at some of the borrowings and exchanges that inform the relation between blogs and print magazines. She shows in what ways new media can be perceived as new whilst at the same time reproducing existing conventions of fashion discourse. New media may well be spaces where new values and ideals of fashion can be conveyed, but they are also platforms for the reproduction or strengthening of existing visions—as Segre Reinach and Wissinger also remind us: Segre Reinach by drawing attention to the stereotypes on China that can be challenged but also reproduced on new fashion media sites; Wissinger by showing how new technologies and the Internet participate in pushing the feminine bodily ideal to an extreme of thinness and whiteness.

Finally, the book concludes with an edited transcript of the roundtable discussion that took place at the Fashion Media Yesterday Today Tomorrow conference. This panel brought together four key players involved with new fashion media to consider and reflect upon current issues facing fashion media.

NOTES

1. The book is based on the Fashion Media Yesterday Today Tomorrow conference that took place at the London College of Fashion, 21–22 October 2010, and was organized by Dr Djurdja Bartlett and Penny Martin, who was a professor at the London College of Fashion at that time.
2. See 'New Tate Modern Tanks Open to the Public' (2012), 16 July, http://www.tate.org.uk/about/press-office/press-releases/new-tate-modern-tanks-open-public, accessed 12 November 2012. The Museum of Modern Art in New York held the *Fashioning Fiction in Photography since 1990* exhibition in 2004 and the San Francisco Museum of Modern Art, the Richard Avedon exhibition in 2009. Also, the Victoria and Albert Museum, which holds the national collection of the art of photography, has held various fashion photography exhibitions including *Imperfect Beauty,* in 2000.

BIBLIOGRAPHY

Barnard, M. (2012), 'Looking Sharp: Fashion Studies', in I. Heywood and B. Sandywell (eds), *The Handbook of Visual Culture,* London: Berg, 405–25.

Barthes, R. (1990), *The Fashion System,* Berkeley: University of California Press.

Benjamin, W. (1999), *Illuminations,* London: Pimlico.

Boordro, M. (2007), 'Art and Fashion', in L. Welters and A. Lillethun (eds), *The Fashion Reader,* Oxford: Berg, 256–60.

Breward, C. (1998), 'Cultures, Identities, Histories: Fashioning a Cultural Approach to Dress', *Fashion Theory: The Journal of Dress, Body and Culture,* 2/4: 301–13.

Corcoran, C. T. (2009), 'Everyone's Doing It: Brands Take On Social Media', 28 September, http://wwd.com/media, accessed 5 January 2010.

Cumming, V. (2004), *Understanding Fashion History,* London: Batsford.

Eicher, J. B., ed. (1995), *Dress and Ethnicity: Change across Space and Time,* Oxford: Berg.

Fuery, K. (2009), *New Media,* New York: Palgrave.

Hollander, A. (1993), *Seeing through Clothes,* Berkeley: University of California Press.

Jobling, P. (1999), *Fashion Spreads: Word and Image in Fashion Photography since 1980,* Oxford: Berg.

Kansara, V. A. (2010), 'Jaime Perlman Tests the Future of Fashion Editorial', *Business of Fashion,* 18 January, www.businessoffashion.com, accessed 2 February 2010.

Karaminas, V. (2012), 'Image', in A. Geczy and V. Karaminas (eds), *Fashion and Art,* London: Berg, 177–89.

Levinson, P. (2009), *New New Media,* Boston: Pearson.

Lister, M., J. Dovey, S. Giddings and K. Kelly (2009), *New Media: A Critical Introduction,* London: Routledge.

Longhurst, B., G. Smith, G. Crawford, M. Ogborn, E. Baldwin and S. McCracken (2008), *Introducing Cultural Studies,* Harlow: Pearson Education.

Rabine, L. W. (2002), *The Global Circulation of African Fashion,* Oxford: Berg.

Ribeiro, A. (1995), *The Art of Dress: Fashion in England and France, 1750–1820,* New Haven, CT: Yale University Press.

Rocamora, A. (2009), *Fashioning the City: Paris, Fashion and the Media,* London: I.B. Tauris.

Rocamora, A. (2011), 'Personal Fashion Blogs: Screens and Mirrors in Digital Self-Portraits', *Fashion Theory,* 15/4: 407–24.

Rocamora, A. and D. Bartlett (2009), 'Blogs de mode: Les nouveaux espaces du discours de mode', *Sociétés,* 104/2: 105–14.

Taylor, L. (2002), *The Study of Dress History,* Manchester: Manchester University Press.

Taylor, L. (2004), *Establishing Dress History,* Manchester: Manchester University Press.

Vincent, M. (2005), *Le Mercure Galant: Présentation de la première revue féminine d'information et de culture, 1672–1710,* Paris: Champion.

Williams, V., ed. (1998), *Look at Me: Fashion Photography in Britain 1960 to the Present,* London: British Council.

Section 1

MAGAZINES

1

TASTE, FASHION AND THE FRENCH FASHION MAGAZINE
sanda miller

Ever since their emergence in seventeenth-century France during the reign of Louis XIV (1638–1715), fashion magazines have been truthful mirrors of their time. They have functioned not only as repositories of the progress of sartorial fashion and the most up-to-date social, cultural and artistic developments but also as self-styled barometers of taste.

The point of inception for the emergence of the fashion magazine is generally accepted to be 1672, when the journalist, royal historian and playwright Jean Donneau de Visé (1638–1710) published *Le Mercure Galant,* which was initially conceived as a gazette aimed to cover the arts, theatre and literature, as well as society reports and a gossip column. Its content—modest by modern standards—consisted of articles and illustrations, but its special contribution was that, by publishing the addresses of the *marchandes de modes,* it pioneered an early form of advertising, and for that reason it could arguably be regarded as the first modern form of publicity in this sector (Morini 2006: 29). Its short-lived existence of one year, however, may well be an indication that during the seventeenth century, *Le Mercure Galant* was very likely ahead of its time. By 1724, however, when it re-emerged as *Mercure de France,* its survival was assured.

It was also during the eighteenth century that by transcending their initial informative and commercial remit, fashion magazines gradually acquired the wider intellectual profile which conferred upon them the status of worthy by-products of the Enlightenment. One such example materialized in 1768 when the distinguished publisher Friedrich Melchior von Grimm (1723–1807) proudly announced to his readers the publication of '*le première journal des modes*', by which he meant the *Courrier de la mode ou le Journal du goût* (published 1768–70). Compared to all its antecedents, this was an altogether different type of publication. Moreover, it could be argued that the emphatic linking of the words *fashion* and *taste* in its title testifies to the unexpected role the concept of taste was to play within the newly emerging context of the fashion magazine. The moot question to be asked at this point is whether this unprecedented link was the result of the ideological revolution brought about by the Enlightenment or simply an attempt to elevate fashion above its existing status—hitherto relegated to the world of merchants, tailors and shopkeepers—to a subject worthy of intellectual pursuit.

TASTE AND THE EMERGENCE OF THE CRITIC

Philosophical aesthetics as a new branch of philosophy emerged during the Enlightenment and central to its enquiry was the concept of taste; in order to deal with the shift in interest from the object of aesthetic contemplation (e.g. the work of art) to its subjective appreciation (our psychological response; e.g. how fantastic is this!), it was necessary to postulate an enabling faculty or ability through which such an aesthetic response was made possible. Instead of looking for objective defining qualities that make an object beautiful, philosophical aesthetics sought to understand how our experience of beauty transcended personal opinion—'I like this painting'—and thus establish intersubjectively valid (public) criteria of taste: 'This painting is beautiful.' But why would we wish to perform such a shift in the first place? The answer is simple: the interrelation between the object deemed aesthetic (the work of art) and the subjective aesthetic experience (the feelings of pleasure/displeasure such an object induced in the person experiencing it) requires an explanation. Thus, the concept of taste—defined as an inborn special evaluative faculty—was postulated to perform this task. Taste then was the answer to Immanuel Kant's famous antimony which states that, on the one hand, our subjective experience—perfectly summed up in the popular saying, 'Beauty is in the eyes of the beholder'—affirms that there is no common denominator in our likes and dislikes and, on the other, that, yes, there must be such a common denominator, otherwise intersubjectively valid judgements of taste such as, 'This is a good/beautiful painting,' would be without rational foundation and as such not different from personal avowals of the kind: 'I like/ dislike this.' The concept of 'taste' was the creation of the British Empiricist philosophers, starting with Anthony Ashley-Cooper, Third Earl of Shaftesbury (1671–1713), and followed by David Hume (1711–76) and Edmund Burke (1729–97), among others, who sought to provide a rational foundation for a seemingly subjective, emotional response to the aesthetic experience by postulating a special faculty—taste—which provided a rational basis on which such response could be regarded as universal. They postulated an inborn faculty of taste which enables us to discern a beautiful object—where beauty is used as an aesthetic category—from a not-so-beautiful or not-at-all-beautiful object and to share in this experience together, rather like we share our understanding of logical definitions such as, 'This is a red, spherical object.' By acquiring a rational basis, our appreciation of beauty, instead of being a matter of personal preference, becomes an intersubjectively valid aesthetic judgement.

In his seminal essay 'Of the Standard of Taste', David Hume argued that 'the great variety of Taste, as well as of opinion, which prevails in the world, is too obvious not to have fallen under every one's observation' (Hume 1965: 3), but equally 'it is natural to seek a standard of Taste; a rule by which the various sentiments of men may be reconciled; at least a decision afforded confirming one sentiment, and condemning another' (Hume 1965: 5). Thus he established a basis for the rational discourse needed for determining intersubjectively valid criteria of aesthetic evaluation. This was made possible by taste.

According to Edmund Burke, however, taste is simply 'no more than that faculty or those faculties of the mind which are affected with or form a judgement of the works of the imagination and the elegant arts' (Burke 1990: 13).

A by-product of philosophical aesthetics was the emergence of the art critic, whom David Hume identified as a special person endowed with a 'delicacy of the imagination'. Hume undertook to provide 'a more accurate definition … than has hitherto been attempted' with an example from Miguel de Cervantes's masterpiece, *Don Quixote*. The story is told by the *hidalgo*'s valet, Sancho, who boasted a superior judgement in wine which he said was hereditary. He proceeded to tell a story involving two of his kinsmen. Called to give their opinion of an excellent hogshead, one of them tasted it and found it wanting because of a 'small taste of leather', whilst the second criticized it because he 'found a taste of iron'. They were derided for their verdicts, but when the hogshead was emptied, there was found at the bottom an old key with a leather thong tied to it (Hume 1965: 10–11). Apart from a 'delicacy of the imagination', the real critic must 'practice in a particular art' and 'must preserve his mind free from all prejudice' (Hume 1965: 13–14), for only a qualified observer is in a position to provide a proper verdict of the true standard of taste and beauty. But even the critical criteria of such a privileged person could be disqualified on empirical grounds such as insensibility, prejudice or lack of experience. Thus Hume's proposed system has a non-relativist basis, whereby 'the general principles of taste are uniform in human nature', but, nevertheless, 'There is room for a good deal of explainable variability since different works of art will appear to different temperaments or at different stages of life. Hence there is a residual range of un-resolvable disagreements' (Beardsley 1966: 191).

The *Académie royale de peinture et sculpture* was officially inaugurated in 1648 but did not start to function properly until 1661, when Louis XIV's minister of finance, Jean-Baptiste Colbert (1619–83), became its official patron (Wilenski 1973: 77). Among its most important innovations was the founding of the Salons held at the Louvre palace inaugurated during the seventeenth century, albeit sporadically. They became regular events during the eighteenth century; between 1737 and 1751, they were held annually and, thereafter, biennially, until the start of the Revolution in 1789. The Salons created a public 'which had contact with art for a few hours every two years and which formed its standards from the casual contact and they induced the artists to cover the approbation of this ill-educated public' (Wilenski 1973: 77). The art critic emerged to serve as a mediator between the largely uneducated public and the Academy, so that those who came to the Salons would not only enjoy the art on display but also understand the complex iconographical programme imposed by Academic requirements on the painters who were expected to deal with grand and noble subjects rather than everyday experience (realism was not acceptable).

One of the pioneers of art criticism was Friedrich Melchior von Grimm's friend, the *philosophe* Denis Diderot (1713–84). The Salons provided the public space which gave birth to this new profession. Diderot's critical career was in fact prompted by von Grimm, whose task as a confidential correspondent of King Friedrich II of Prussia was to report about the latest intellectual and cultural developments in Paris. Von Grimm's reports took the form of a private journal which circulated in the form of a manuscript entitled *Correspondence littéraire*, *philosophique et critique* in which he reviewed the Salons of 1753, 1755 and 1757. In 1759 he invited Diderot to take over (Harrison, Wood and Grainger 2000: 592). Between 1759 and 1767, Diderot reviewed the Salons regularly. His reviews grew in length and verbosity in direct proportion with his confidence; by 1767, Diderot produced a text thirty-five times the length of that of 1759. Between 1769 and 1781, Diderot began his European travels, and his contributions became more sporadic, with his last review as an homage to Jacques Louis David dated 1781 (Delon 2008).

The critic provided not only a detailed description, which can almost be summed up as a rhetorical exercise in *ekphrasis,* but also attempted to engage in judicial criticism—which Diderot certainly did when it came to his contemptuous disapprobation of François Boucher's erotic paintings. It is therefore instructive here to compare Diderot's disparaging review of Boucher's (1703–70) gallery of voluptuous courtesans and hedonistic representations of shepherds and shepherdesses frolicking in Arcadian landscapes with the sycophantic praise he lavished on the work of Jean-Baptiste Greuze (1725–1805), both of which were included in the 1765 Salon. In reviewing them side by side, Diderot can also be regarded as having assumed 'a role similar to a journalistic critic', in as much as he expressed the current opinion in France that 'it was the chief business of art to touch and to move' by 'getting close to nature' (Holt 1958: 311).

The composition of Greuze's *The Beloved Mother* (whose sentimentality is paradigmatic of the kind of moralizing representation of the uncomplicated country life which brought Greuze popularity) appeared so simple, Diderot explained, 'that the careless observer might think that he could have done as well himself and that it did not require much thought or cleverness' (cited in Holt 1958: 316). Diderot, however, argued that was not the case because Greuze's drawing is 'excellent as a work of art and a truthful portrait of what a happy home should be', the reason, Diderot tediously proposed, being that 'it preaches this lesson to every man: keep your family in comfort and take care to have a happy home to which to return' (Holt 1958: 317). By contrast, his scathing review of Boucher's paintings revealed Diderot's contempt and venom for everything that invoked the ancien régime and its artistic taste:

> The degradation of taste, of colour, composition, dramatis *personae* … followed the depravation of manners … I am telling you that he never understood truth; I am telling you that ideas about delicacy, honesty, innocence, simplicity have become estranged to him; I am telling you that he did not look at nature even for one instance, at least the one aspect that would have interested my soul, yours. (Holt 1958: 139–40)

But whilst taste was indeed borrowed from aesthetic discourse, its application to fashion was, we could say, revolutionary, for these fashion magazines became—as pointed out at the beginning—more than mere repositories of taste; rather, they prescribed it. Thus the magazines' distinguished readership were told how to dress, how to furnish their elegant interiors and how to entertain, as well as everything they needed to know about manners and mores and examples abound. It could therefore be argued that we witness the beginning of what is now referred to as 'life and style'. When von Grimm welcomed the publication of the *Courier de la mode ou journal du goût* as the premier journal of fashion in France, his approbation may have implied that the concepts of fashion and taste were employed interchangeably, but this could not have been the case. Rather, what was being implied here is the centrality of the concept of taste for the emergence of a new type of intellectual fashion magazine fit for the Enlightenment.

THE FASHION MAGAZINE

The fashion magazine *La Gallerie des modes* consisted of albums with engravings printed in colour as well as in black and white, published on a regular basis by Jean Esnauts and Michel Rapilly between 1778 and 1787. In 1779, they produced a new volume which contained ninety-six prints selected from the first seventeen portfolios, published under the grandiose title *La Gallerie des modes et des costumes français dessinés d'après nature, Gravés par les plus Célèbres Artistes en ce genre et colorés avec le plus gran soin par Madame Le Beau. Ouvrage commencé en l'année 1778. A Paris, chez les S.rs Esnauts et Rapilly, rue St. Jacques, à la Ville de Coutances. Avec Priv. Du Roi* (Morini 2006: 29). What was on offer here were 'fashions' and 'costumes' drawn 'after nature' (*d'après nature*) in a manner analogous to that of the curriculum of the Academy of Fine Arts. Moreover, these fashion images were produced by artists described as 'the most famous artists specialized in this *genre*', generally fine artists (as the professional fashion illustrator was yet to emerge), among them Claude-Louis Desrais, Pierre-Thomas LeClerc and Antoine Watteau's grandnephew, François-Louis-Joseph Watteau (Morini 2006: 32).

Although their primary aim was to represent the latest outfits worn at the French court and in aristocratic circles, what makes these plates special is that they were also representations of 'real life'. Whilst the majority of the plates concentrate on the wasteful elegance of the aristocracy during the Rococo period, in some instances we catch a glimpse of women from the middle or working classes: one example, signed by Pierre-Thomas LeClerc, represents a dressmaker accompanied by a little girl, probably her daughter, delivering a pair of *paniers* to her client, but the curious caption which accompanies it describes her as a 'couturière élègante', delivering her 'ouvrage'. Another plate, also signed by Pierre-Thomas LeClerc, represents an intimate scene in which a seated, fashionably dressed aristocratic lady is suckling her baby, attended by her servant standing in a humble position to her right and slightly behind her. The contrast between their attire and body language is masterfully captured by the artist, reinforcing the idea that indeed these plates would have been made 'after nature'—and it reminds us of Diderot's complementing of Greuze. In this respect, they provide a fascinating insight into a society about to disappear, destroyed by the bloodiest revolution in European history: the French Revolution.

In his seminal book *A Concise History of Costume*, James Laver considers *La Gallerie des modes* to be a 'pioneer in the field of the fashion plate', observing that 'considerable variation in female attire is now possible' (Laver 1969: 144). Most importantly, Laver quotes the radical distinction made by Vyvyan Holland in his *Hand-coloured Fashion Plates, 1770–1899* between what he called the 'fashion plate' and the 'costume plate', whereby the latter attempts to show clothes 'after the event', as Wenceslas Hollar did, for example, in his *Ornatus Muliebris Anglicanus*, published in 1640, or as Jean Dieu de Saint-Jean did in France in his admirable engravings of male and female costume at the Court of Louis XIV (Laver 1969: 145–6)

Vyvyan Holland's distinction according to Laver then hinges on the historical rather than actual character of the dress. In that sense he argued even *Le Monument du Costume* of Freudenberg and Moreau le Jeune, published in Paris between 1775 and 1783, consisted of 'costume plates' (Laver 1969: 146). The 'real' fashion plate, Laver argued patriotically, perhaps started with the English *The Lady's Magazine,* in which they were published from 1770. Laver continued: 'suddenly similar plates were being published all over Europe' (Laver 1965: 146–7).

Laver then compares *La Gallerie des modes* with *The Gallery of Fashion,* published between 1794 and 1803 by the Swiss-born painter and publisher Nicholas Wilhelm von Heideloff, who left Paris during the Revolution to seek refuge in London. Von Heideloff's lovingly hand-coloured fashion plates documented the new 'Directory' style, which replaced the ornate rococo style of dress reproduced in *La Gallerie des modes*. Laver makes the point that

> although a gap of a mere ten years separates these two publications, the clothes depicted in them are entirely different. What had happened in the meantime, of course was the French Revolution. (Laver 1969: 148)

The exact historical location of the emergence of the phenomenon we call fashion is less important than establishing how it was understood in its proper historical and cultural context. As James Laver pointed out, it was the fashion plate as distinct from the costume plate that provided the answer, ultimately rooted in the notion of 'contemporaneity', as Charles Baudelaire pointed out in his definition of modernity as 'the transient the fleeting, the contingent: it is one half of art, the other being the eternal and the immovable' (Baudelaire 1972: 403).

The first proper women's fashion magazine was *Le Cabinet des Modes* (Gaudriault in Morini 2006: 31) published by Jean Antoine Brun (aka Le Brun Tossa) from 1785 until 1795, when it was renamed *Le Magazine des Modes nouvelles françaises et anglaises;* it was published under this title between 1796 and 1789, when it finally acquired the significant title *Le journal de la mode et du goût*. The latter's short existence (1790–93) coincided with the French Revolution, and against this horrendous backdrop we wonder how concerns about taste and fashion were possible at all. There is little doubt that Le Brun Tossa's choice of the last title of his magazine replicates that of the 1768 *Courrier de la mode ou Journal du goût,* with one important difference. At the beginning of this chapter, I asked whether when von Grimm described the *Courrier de la mode ou Journal du gout* as France's first fashion magazine, it served as a fashion magazine (*Courrier de la mode*) or a journal of taste (*Journal du goût*)—that is whether it was regarded not just as a record of style but also as a barometer of taste whose influence extended to a prescriptive function. Le Brun Tossa, however, eliminated this distinction with a stroke—replacing 'ou' (or) with 'et' (and)—in the simplified title *Le journal de la mode et du goût*. Le Brun Tossa intended the concepts of fashion and taste to be regarded as fulfilling the same function: if fashion could be aligned with taste, it could also—very conveniently—be regarded as a form of art, and if fashion could indeed be regarded as a form of art, then it would also legitimately become the proper remit of the faculty of taste. *Le journal de la mode et du goût* was also not a 'simple presentation of objects'; rather, what it proposed was a new kind of fashion plate, which 'through a succession of different types of attire as well as social practices and prescriptions to which the clothes corresponded … represented the new rules of a new lifestyle more accustomed to luxury, caprice and the seduction of fashion' (Morini 2006: 31)

The proliferation of fashion magazines during the second half of the eighteenth century has been attributed to 'an increasingly well-informed, provincial as well as urban, female readership eager for the latest news in fashion' (Blackman 2007: 6). The common denominator that linked these magazines as a new type of publication was their editors' ambition to enlarge their function of reporting the latest developments in sartorial dress, in itself no mean feat, and transform them into repositories of the cultural, intellectual and artistic developments of their period.

An interesting historical overview of the emergence of the fashion magazines can be found in the poet Henri Bidou's introduction for the first issue of the *Gazette du Bon Ton: art, modes et frivolities,* in November 1912 (Plate 1). The journal was the brainchild of Lucien Vogel, an important French editor in the fine arts and fashion publishing. Inspired by some earlier examples, Vogel wanted to blur the distinction between the arts and fashion, and towards that goal, he invited contemporary artists to contribute to the *Gazette du Bon Ton*. As further elaborated in Bidou's introductory essay, the aim was to 'renew the charming and illustrious tradition of fashion anthologies of yesteryear' (Bidou 1912: 2). The first proper fashion magazine in the modern sense, Bidou argues, was Le Brun Tossa's *Le Cabinet des Modes*, which he noted included 'plates after Desrais et Deframe, philosophical varieties, anecdotes, literary productions, comparisons between French and English fashions, which extended also to jewellery and furniture' (Bidou 1912: 2). Its success was swift, and as a consequence, Bidou stated, similar magazines started to be published in Weimar and Liège, London, Florence, Leipzig, Haarlem and Prague. 'All of Europe was paying attention to fashion' ('Toute l'Europe était attentive aux modes') (Bidou 1912: 3). But however charming these fashion plates were, Bidou deemed them old fashioned, and he proposed a radical transformation, with new approaches and new techniques that would yield a very different kind of fashion plate. What Henri Bidou wanted to see was not that new, however. Rather, he wanted a return to the late eighteenth-century approach when the public was paying attention to fashion and painters were collaborating with the couturiers, which for him was not only understandable but highly desirable because, he charmingly argued, 'women's finery is a pleasure for the eye which must not be judged in any way as inferiour to the other arts' (Bidou 1912: 3). This was an audacious statement because, although Bidou does not equate fashion with art, he considers fashion worthy of the painters' attention, which is why they were collaborating with the fashion designers. Moreover, he argued, 'the attire of a woman is a leisure for the eye which must not be judged in any way inferious to the other arts' (Bidou 1912: 3).

The *Gazette du bon ton* continued this noble tradition, Bidou argued, and 'in the same way as Mésangère had previously published his delicious suite of *Merveilleuses* and his *Incroyables*' (Bidou 1912: 4), so too would each issue of *Gazette du bon ton* contain two sets of watercolours. One set was meant to represent ideas of 'outfits invented by the artists', where artists such as Bakst, Iribe and Lepape, as well as the illustrious artist Maurice Boutet de Monvel would in fact design the silhouettes which would become the true trendsetters for the seasons and years to come. Another set of watercolours would represent the outfits invented and realized by the couturiers, but even these watercolours would initially be executed by the hands of the same artists, thus becoming in a manner of speaking 'portraits' of these clothes as interpreted by the painters (Bidou 1912: 4). Bidou, it seems, was not prepared to leave anything either to chance or indeed to the couturiers. Moreover, in mentioning Mésangère's suite of *Merveilleuses and Incroyables*, Bidou was in fact referring to *Le Journal des Dames et des Modes*, which was founded in 1797 by Jean-Baptiste Selléque and then taken over in 1801 by Pierre-Antoine Leboux de la Mésangère. When Mésangère became its chief editor, he proceeded to establish it as the uncontested arbiter of taste 'en matière du goût et de mode' (in matters of taste and style) at the Napoleonic court because, on its pages, fashion and taste met.

Le Journal des Dames et des Modes also captures an important moment in the turbulent history of France, when one of the most totalitarian regimes in Europe was brutally brought to an end and replaced by an equally brutal period of transition: that of the Directory period (1794–9), followed by the period of Napoleon Bonaparte's rise from consul (1799–1804) to emperor (1804–15). The political, social, cultural and artistic changes brought about by these events were captured in fashion magazines whose illustrated plates became a unique, and at times even humorous, way of reporting these gruesome events, as we glean from the pages of *Le Journal des Dames et des Modes*. Two examples have a particular resonance because they emulate 'the victims' of the Revolution in ways which may well appear somewhat gruesome to our modern sensibilities. In one instance (19 May 1798), we find a young lady seen from the back wearing a white muslin dress with victim-style crossed bands ('croissures à la victime'). In another (4 March 1798), a lady wearing fashionable flat pumps, her body wrapped in a wide cape, wears her hair in the style called *en porc-epic* (porcupine) or 'hairstyle of the victim' ('coiffure à la victime'), which was created in solidarity with those condemned to the guillotine. Even more revealing is the accompanying caption: drawn from nature on the boulevard des Capucines ('dessinée d'après nature sur le boulevard des Capucines'). So like Esnauts and Rapilly's *Les Galleries des Modes,* the most important aim for *Le Journal des Dames et des Modes* in reproducing the fashionable dresses on its pages was that they were drawn 'from nature'.

One of the consequences of the Revolution was that the court of Versailles ceased to be the European arbiter of taste and the stage for the display of the sumptuous rococo fashions. Instead, the latest fashionable clothes were paraded in public places for all to see: the theatre, the promenade, festivities, celebrations and balls. This is illustrated in a charming aquatint by Philibert-Louis Debucourt (1755–1822) entitled *Promenade de la galerie du Palais Royal* (1787), in which we see people milling about against the background of the famous neoclassical portico. The Palais Royal also provided space for shops and Debucourt shows an interior of a fashion merchant's shop (*marchande des modes*), filled with all the accessories required by the latest fashions. In the shop we see elegant young ladies dressed in neoclassical attire complemented by Grecian hairstyles surveying the tempting merchandise. In the middle ground, a man dressed in the black outfit introduced as the new uniform of the middle classes contrasts with the figure of a dandy dressed in a sophisticated Parisian costume consisting of a white shirt and cravat tied under his chin and a collared redingote completed by breeches and soft boots. There is no doubt that this image captures the street atmosphere which provided artists with inspiration for their fashion plates.

By the mid-nineteenth century, fashion magazines were well-established in their new role. Thus we read in the list of contents of the weekly *La Vie Parisienne* founded in 1863 by Emile Marcelin (1825–87) that it included 'contes, nouvelles, sports, théâtre et musique et les arts' (stories, news, sports, theatre, music, and the arts). Marcelin succeeded in enlisting the collaboration of some of the finest writers and poets Paris had to offer, so that the list of contributors read like the who's who of nineteenth-century Parisian intelligentsia. As haute couture was still in its infancy (the first *maison de couture* was opened by Charles Frederick Worth in 1858), reporting or writing about sartorial fashion was not introduced until 1912, with a regular column entitled '*Élégances*', signed by Iphis, charmingly introduced by Marcelin as the 'melancholic spectator of the eternal Parisian comedy'.

In conclusion, the dramatic volte-face in the style of dress which marked the transition from the *ancien régime* to the modern era testifies to a very special transformation which did not only consist in its look but went deeper to encompass all the changes which ensued: political, social, economic and cultural. We see this wider picture captured uniquely on the pages of the fashion magazines published during the Enlightenment, and as such they can justifiably be regarded not only as repositories of taste, manners and mores but also mirrors of their time.

BIBLIOGRAPHY

Baudelaire, C. (1972), *Selected Writings on Art and Artists,* London: Penguin Books.
Beardsley M. (1966), *Aesthetics: From Classical Greece to the Present,* New York: Macmillan.

Bidou, H. (1912), 'Introduction', *Gazette du bon ton,* November: 1–4.

Blackman, C. (2007), *100 Years of Fashion Illustration,* London: Laurence King Publishing.

Burke, E. (1990), *A Philosophical Enquiry into the Origin of Our Ideas of the Sublime and Beautiful,* Oxford: Oxford University Press.

Delon, M., ed. (2008), *Diderot: Salons,* Paris: Gallimard.

Harrison, C., P. Wood and J. Grainger, eds. (2000), *Art in Theory: 1648–1815,* Oxford: Blackwell.

Holt, E., ed. (1958), *A Documentary History of Art,* vol. 2, New York: Doubleday Anchor Books.

Hume, D. (1965), *Of the Standard of Taste and Other Essays,* New York: Bobbs-Merrill.

Laver, J. (1969), *A Concise History of Costume,* London: Thames and Hudson.

Morini, E. (2006), *Storia della Moda (XVIII–XX secolo),* Milan: Skira.

Wilenski, H. R. (1973), *French Painting,* New York: Dover Publications.

2

FUN WITH PINS AND ROPE
HOW CAROLINE BAKER STYLED
THE 1970s
alice beard

INTRODUCTION

> You know, every now and again I think that probably a stylist does come out with a vision
> and a strength which might come from her own experience, to then inspire you to change
> the way you're wearing your clothing. (Baker 2007)

A double-page photographic spread from *Nova* magazine picturing a host of fashion editors arriving at the 1969 autumn/winter Paris collections suggests an interest in fashion's 'backstage' that perhaps pre-empts today's mood of fascination, where stylists are held up as celebrities and fashion editors are the subjects of feature films (see Figure 2.1). The recognisable names are there—among them, Diana Vreeland (American *Vogue*), Ernestine Carter (*Sunday Times*) and a young Grace Coddington (British *Vogue*)—and maybe less well-known, editors, such as Meriel McCooey, who were working for a new generation of fashion media: the Sunday newspaper colour supplements. Caroline Baker from the then newly launched *Nova* magazine represents the changing face of British fashion media, perhaps the first true stylist who would be responsible for picturing a street style now so resonant a part of our fashion identity. Her outfit reveals an eclectic and individual style; she wears 'a brown dyed vest, Civil war belt and scarf from Kensington Market, beige shorts by her dressmaker' (Keenan 1969: 59). The face-to-camera, head-to-toe shot, framed against the backdrop of a city street and captioned with the details of the subject's look signals the straight-up reportage popularized by the style magazines of the 1980s, for which Baker would provide a key influence.

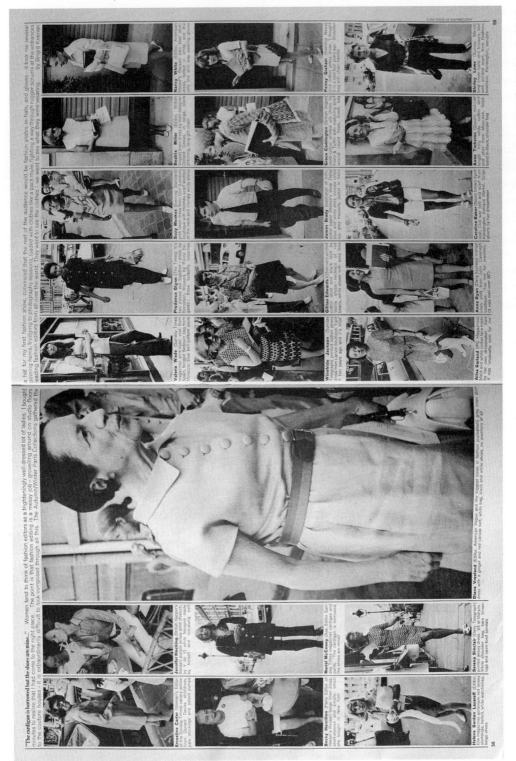

2.1. 'The Cardigan Is Borrowed but the Shoes Are Mine…', editorial by Brigid Keenan, photographs by Steve Hiett, *Nova*, September 1967. © IPC Media 2013

Caroline Baker is an important figure in the history of British fashion media and has enjoyed a career as a fashion editor and stylist spanning over forty years, yet few outside of the industry would be familiar with her name. Our contemporary understanding of the profession of a fashion stylist is a relatively recent one, and the origin of the role as we now understand it can be traced back to the sort of work Baker was performing in the 1970s, in this sense Baker is perhaps one of the first true stylists (Godfrey 1990: 208). After learning her craft on *Nova* magazine in the late 1960s and 1970s Baker went on to style for Vivienne Westwood and Benetton and create innovative fashion pages for *Deluxe, i-D, Cosmopolitan* and *Vogue*.

Whilst critical attention has been given to the medium of fashion photography and the creative practises of the photographer, less has been said about the fashion editors or the stylists, who dress the models, narrate the story and fashion the pictures on the page.[1] Also generally less discussed are the production networks at the core of fashion media; however, a growing interest in the processes of fashion image-making is seeking to redress this, and this is evident on a number of different platforms, notably the online broadcasting company SHOWstudio (Shinkle 2008). Fashion image-making extends beyond and behind the photographer and is a collaborative project that depends on the interplay between photographer, model, fashion editor, stylist, art director and designer, to name a few. To better understand fashion media, its histories and future, it is time that these individuals, working practices and creative networks are both acknowledged and critically evaluated.

Information and ideas gleaned from a series of oral history interviews with Caroline Baker, set against an examination of the editorial text and images from Baker's fashion spreads for *Nova*, reveal that her styling operated as an intrinsic part of both achieving a particular look and as a signifier of the new young fashionable consumer who read the magazine.[2] Caroline Baker's pages for *Nova* demonstrate that fashion editing is more than simply dressing a model on a page. Distancing itself from traditional and mainstream fashion publications, *Nova,* the revolutionary magazine published in Britain from 1965 to 1975, aimed to be, as stated on its cover, 'a new kind of magazine for the new kind of woman', and this in part involved a new take on fashion, beauty and the body. Under the direction of Caroline Baker, fashion in *Nova* became less about what was worn and more about how it was worn. Baker's task of styling a model through clothing, accessories, hair and makeup was critical—her pages were presented to magazine readers as a means to achieve both a complete look and as a way of adding that important mark of individuality. Importantly, Baker was not simply reporting fashion; she was creating it. Collaborating with art director David Hillman and photographers such as Harri Peccinotti, Helmut Newton, Sarah Moon and Hans Feurer, Baker produced fashion pages which were, according to Peccinotti 'almost an insult to fashion' at times, and the result of this was often what appeared to be an 'anti-fashion' statement (Williams 1998: 106).

DIY DRESSING: A NEW APPROACH

Baker made the leap from home assistant to fashion editor in October 1967 by way of a brief stint helping out her predecessor, the maverick Molly Parkin. She was employed by her editor, Denis Hackett, because she looked like she was into fashion, and from her initial appointment Baker's instruction was to do something different:

> At that time it was very early days for ... fashion editors. The word 'stylist' hadn't been
> coined ... and most fashion editors were society women because fashion was very

society-driven. My editor said to me 'I don't want you to do what is in *Vogue* or *Queen* magazine or *The Times* ... I just want different fashion.' I was always interested in fashion media, a compulsion to follow fashions mixed with the fact that there wasn't the money to buy designer clothing, meant me having to resort to DIY interpretations—this led me into finding a new way to dress myself and using clothing which I then introduced to my fashion pages ... I think, in retrospect, that *Nova* was very, 'street'. Street style came about because I started using elements of what people on the streets were actually wearing and dressing models appearing on my fashion pages in clothing inspired by what I had seen. (Baker 2007, 2010b)

With a radically open remit from her editor and working on a limited budget, Caroline Baker clothed and styled her models as she chose to dress herself, sourcing menswear, ethnic jewellery, uniforms and second-hand clothing from Portobello and Kensington Market and the Kings Road. Army surplus stores such as Lawrence Corner and Badges and Equipment were filled with US uniforms from Vietnam, and these provided the raw materials for spreads such as 'Dressed to Kill: The Army Surplus War Game', photographed by Harri Peccinotti (see Plate 4).

Baker took her inspiration from contemporary music, film and television, and what young people were wearing on the street. This was alternative fashion—not versions of the surplus look produced by designers such as Katherine Hamnett and Kenzo some years later but authentic drill uniforms which were pre-worn and cheap to buy and then customized by Baker, who cut up and dyed the garments for the shoot (Baker 1971a). For Baker, this choice of a way of dressing was articulated an act of rebellion:

> I was going against fashion at the end of the Sixties and early Seventies, because by then we were all a bit feminist really. So I began to fight this thing of always having to be groomed and wear lipstick and have your hair set, and to look like this woman—a really girly look ... I was breaking this down. The 'Ban the Bomb' protests were going on and people were beginning to wear army surplus jackets, and I was picking up a lot of references and looking at alternative fashion as well ... I really got into shopping from places where maybe waiters bought their clothes, or second-hand shops, and putting women into menswear. Nova was a really interesting magazine in that you were quite free to do all these things. (Baker 2007)

One of Baker's aims was to challenge established notions of ideal femininity, in particular the sort of conformist, dolled up, girlish look that she saw as dominating the pages of other women's magazines (Baker 2007). In 'Dressed to Kill', the styling of clothing on the body, the hair, make-up and accessories all contribute towards the construction of a more natural look; the models wear their hair loose and their skin bare, suntanned and freckled. The colour palette is carefully considered; a dull wash of khaki greens interrupted with splashes of bright red, and make-up is used here minimally to accessorize key details of the clothing; lips painted red and varnished nails are perfectly colour matched with a star-shaped enamel brooch and fine coral bead bracelet. The use of men's wear operates to both conceal and reveal the models' bodies; the garments are soft, creased, worn and frayed, and the fit is loose and large, but by folding up sleeves, cutting off trousers into short shorts and tying the oversized shirts tightly on the model's body, this masculine attire serves to emphasize feminine attributes rather than disguise them. In adopting both men's clothing and a cool stance, with the elegant yet casual gesture of the model smoking a cigarette gripped between her finger and thumb, these women convey a challenging and very modern image of femininity. The detail of styling transforms the look from a soldier's old uniform into a cool new chic; it presents an image of contemporary, cutting-edge fashion and a portrait of *Nova*'s new kind of woman.

ANTI-FASHION: A FASHION STATEMENT

Caroline Baker's editorial for *Nova* was consciously set against mainstream fashion, and her motivation was both political and aesthetic, as she describes:

> Fashion had got so terribly grown-up then, so bourgeois. How we dressed was totally in the hands of the designer and society women like Jackie Kennedy ... the beginning of my being a fashion editor was the beginning of breaking down that role, and their power over the people began to diminish ... you began to have more of a mass movement of women who were thinking for themselves when they dressed ... I was going against the status quo and against perceived ways of dressing and how one should present oneself. The magazine was my theatre ... every month I would try and bring in a relevant, up to the moment story that would be as creative and groundbreaking and original as I could make it ... Once you have an audience and a theatre to perform in, you are inspired to encourage readers to try out new ways of dressing. I suppose I became more and more rebellious as it all seemed to work. (Baker 2007, 2010b)

Notably, Baker demonstrated an irreverent attitude towards the fur industry; in 'Every Hobo Should Have One', photographed by Saul Leiter in 1973, Baker removed fur coats from their context of glamour, wealth and couture and used them as props to dress her model as a tramp, posing her on a litter-strewn city street (see Plate 5).

The graffiti-scarred walls act as a signifier for a gritty urban realism that would become a defining element of the style magazines of the 1980s (Rocamora and O'Neill 2008). Baker styles the model with dog at heel, pushing a pram containing all her worldly belongings. Across these pages she is pictured slumped on the pavement, bundled up in newspapers and sleeping rough in a park. The fur coat in each shot performs the essential task of keeping the woman warm—whether it is wrapped around her loosely or spread out over her sleeping body on the grass like a blanket. Her costume constructs a bulky figure, with Baker's characteristic look of 'thigh-high socks and socks rolled down' (Baker 1971c: 67) layered over woolly tights and thickly laced, crepe-soled boots. The furs remain luxuriant in texture, colour and cut, but the proximity of the model's companion dog draws attention more to the coat's function as a warm hide than an ostentatious status symbol. Baker recounts the initial concept behind the story:

> I had become aware of people who were living on the streets. There was this woman in particular, who was a down and outer, and I began to see her out there with her pram and all her stuff, and her dog ... The model was Leiter's girlfriend, and I did her as if she was a tramp. I had her tied up in strings and I had socks and flat shoes on. But the fur industry were absolutely furious ... 'Sleeping in the park with the pram!' ... But it was encouraged, you see. [*Nova*] really liked that ... You were pushed always to find something controversial to do. (Baker 2007, 2010a)

It would not be the first or last time that Baker and the *Nova* team would court controversy, but Baker was not interested in creating shock for shock's sake; her motivation lay in a desire to innovate and challenge the medium of fashion editorial, as she explains: 'Clothes are not necessarily one of the strongest visual leads ideas wise for fashion stories—and it's easy to fall into a cliché situation, so you have to think deeply into how best to portray a certain style so that it is visually arresting and extraordinary' (Baker 2010b).

ADDING UP THE LOOK

Fashion in the 1970s can be defined by the choice of styles and looks on offer. Valerie Steele has argued that during this decade 'fashion was not in fashion' but became 'optional' (Steele 1997: 280). Certainly Caroline Baker encouraged a fashionability that was defined by individuality and freedom, and her fashion pages demonstrated that style was less a matter of what to wear and more how to wear it. As she explains, 'This notion highlighted the way clothes were worn by the individual as being the most important aspect of getting dressed, as opposed to doing what was the done thing and wearing clothes to be accepted in society' (Baker 2010b). In an editorial for *Nova,* Baker writes, 'Fashion depends more upon the way an outfit is put together than upon the clothes themselves. The bits and pieces added make the look' (Baker 1973: 88). In Baker's styling, this could be perfectly illustrated by the idea of 'letting a safety pin do the work of a button or a zip' (Baker 1972a: 66) (Plate 6) or 'wearing a shirt un-tucked, and leg warmers over trousers, showing off your underwear or putting on more than one brooch' (Baker 2010b). To encourage readers to experiment with customizing a look, she suggested 'putting the veiling on first and then the hat, or vice versa ... dressing up figure hugging suits with no blouses ... bow ties, large and floppy ... worn with men's shirts ... tying pieces of veiling around your neck ... mixing jade with clear and plastic bangles ... in large quantities of course, sometimes on both arms' (Baker 1973: 88).

As well as providing visual and textual ideas on what to look like, Baker offered advice on how to achieve these looks and encouraged an active participation in self-styling through a constructive do-it-yourself approach that promoted bricolage and experimentation in making, customizing and sourcing clothing and accessories. This process was demonstrated explicitly in the feature 'Head for the Haberdashery'; the title of the shoot revealed for readers the source of her materials. Her editorial mapped out the context, acknowledging that 'fashions will go on changing endlessly ... Today it is the accessory that gives you away ... that indicates fashionability, individuality. You need that very much as clothes become more mass-produced. The way you wear your clothes ... has become the most important part of today's look' (Baker 1970a: 41). The model's body, dressed only in ropes, tassels and fringing, was photographed as three frames by Hans Feurer, and the images were positioned lengthways, back to back across three consecutive double-page spreads. By buying two copies of the magazine and pulling out and pining up the images together, a five-foot poster could be made. Caroline Baker's looks were designed to inspire—to be copied or created, deconstructed and reassembled on both the body and the wall.[3] Baker recalls her inspiration:

> I love rope and string, and strips of leather ... I didn't have those rules and restrictions around me telling me it was ridiculous ... I have a more 'out there' streak in me ... to have

a go at this or that and inspire people to do it … I got famous for tying things around the waist to make it fit … I always used to have fun with … pins and rope. (Baker 2007)

ALL DRESSED UP: NARRATING FASHION

At its most literal level, the fashion photograph functions to advertise clothing, accessories and make-up which can then be consumed by the reader, but rather than promoting specific garments, Baker's fashion editorial expressed the fun to be had in playing with fashion and encouraged the creative activity of constructing different fashionable personas through the process of dressing up (Baker 1970b: 64). In 'All Dressed and Made Up', photographed by Harri Peccinotti, a young girl is pictured in her bedroom playing with a life-sized doll (see Plate 7).

Baker's styling offers a tone and mood; the pastel colours, soft textures and fuzzy, gauzy fabrics construct a hazy dreamworld emphasized by low lighting, a grainy filter and soft-focus camera work. Paul Jobling suggests that such imagery 'beckons us into a world of unbridled fantasies by placing fashion and the body in any number of discursive contexts' (Jobling 1999: 2). Paradoxically, whilst Baker's fashion pages can be seen to encourage experimentation and promote creativity in the active production of a look, the model here is seemingly rendered passive by the work of the designers, photographers and stylists, who create the products and the image. Baker's editorial text makes explicit reference to this process of transformation, proposing for those readers 'who would rather be dressed than dress themselves—to save themselves thinking, searching, confusion and headaches, there are two girls, designers extraordinaire, who do it all for them … Mary Quant and Biba' (Baker 1972b: 62). It is as if the gesture of submitting to a total ready-made look has pacified the model; she is posed stiffly and doll-like but is at the same time soft and compliant in the routine of being 'all dressed and made up'. The act of creativity here lies in the hands of the little girl (and the reader who is addressed), who dresses and styles the model by building up layers from underwear to outerwear; she is pictured pulling up tights, folding down the collar of a coat and carefully adjusting a net veil. Baker's own craft of styling lies in creating and communicating the detail of the look as it would appear on the magazine page. She explains her working processes in constructing a fashion image:

> I'm seeing what I'm doing, I know what the camera is going to capture … As a fashion editor, as a stylist, you are completely responsible for the look of all the people in front of the camera. So you work very closely, and you stand right next to the photographer and you're watching every picture … You have to make it perfect … As I dress somebody I'm looking at it and thinking: 'Hmm, how can I make this more interesting, or make it more fitted, or do something with it?' So I'm getting the clothes and doing some work as a designer … and maybe showing them a different way of wearing it. (Baker 2007)

Jennifer Craik has observed that 'fashion images are consumed both compliantly and defiantly by readers who lust for the pleasures of the image as much as the clothes they depict' (Craik 1994: 114). Desire for the fashion image and the fashion product is shaped through the relationship between the words and pictures on a page, and it is often these descriptions that render the image 'intelligible' (Barthes 1984: xii). As Laird Borrelli points out, 'Both image and word function to articulate fashion and to create its narratives' (Borrelli 1997: 248). The interlinking roles of title, text, photograph and graphic design are crucial in introducing the theme of the photo story and in establishing tone and pace. Within the narrative sequence of this spread and framed by its wide expanse of white border, each image resembles a page in a children's picture book. The progressive element of clothes accumulating on the model's body as the little girl dresses her suggests the chronological passing of time and drives the narrative forward (Scott 1999). In a fashion spread, images are tied together by the thematic sequence of an unfolding picture story or by common formal concerns and motifs, such as layout, design or colour, and so on. Therefore, the creation of every fashion image relies on a series of interdependent and often very personal working relationships, as Baker explains:

> When you're going to produce a photographic story, you have to communicate with your photographer, explain what you want to do. Then they would have an idea, and so you'd go ahead. The clothes, the hair, the make-up, and the model, and make it happen. You'd create this story ... Quite often you'd find that a photographer and a stylist would fall in love with each other. You worked very well with each other and then you were just constantly getting ideas ... The photographer needs the fashion editor because you are giving them their photograph ... you are creating a scenario and making a story. So they are re-creating their fantasies through fashion editors. (Baker 2007, 2010a)

DRESSED OVERALL: FASHION, FUNCTION AND REFORM

In the 1970s, Caroline Baker conceptualized a new way of dressing and an approach to styling that went beyond mere decoration and ornament. An interest in the relationship between fashion and function, articulated through both word and image, characterized her fashion editorial for *Nova*. From the 1960s, developments in the technology of photography had allowed for 'outside' fashion (Harrison 1991), and this shift in fashion photography away from the location of the studio helped construct a new feminine ideal—the woman who was 'on the move' (Radner 2000). During its decade of publication, *Nova* magazine offered a 'running portrait' of this new kind of woman (Williams 1998: 105), and Caroline Baker's models were often defiantly active; an eye on clothes that were fit for this purpose led Baker to the continued use of sportswear on her fashion pages.

In 'High as a Kite and Twice as Flighty', girls jump about on a trampoline, caught in mid air by Hans Feurer's camera (see Plate 8). Baker's accompanying editorial responded to what she acknowledged was an almost overwhelming sense of freedom and choice in fashion. For those women who were 'confused as to mood, style and trend', Baker refused simple didactic instruction; instead she conferred the creative responsibility onto each reader by explaining, 'It's now entirely up to you to decide what you are going to wear, and how' (Baker 1971b: 64). The task for this shoot was not simply to select clothing that would look good in the air and on the page; Baker also had to work out which garments moved, stretched and allowed for the most impressive acrobatics. Her process of styling was responsive to both the photographer's wishes and the demands of the location, and as this was a story that was conceptually led, it was Baker's responsibility to visualize and materialize the photographer's ideas, as she explains:

> The photographer came to me with the idea; he had found these trampolines on a beach near Brighton and he wanted to do pictures of girls in the air captured when they were

jumping. I knew I had to think what clothes would work best in movement—and the sportswear theme was beginning as a source of inspiration for designers, but at that time there were quite a few shops selling second hand American sportswear which I then mixed with shorts and skinny trousers and tights and leg warmers—using ideas from sports and dance and layering clothes up in a colourful way adding fluffy bolero-like jackets for richer texture. I collected suitcases full of gear that could work and then in the back of the location bus I tried outfits on the models, layering them up to make it look as interesting as I could—then once the girl started jumping you could see if the clothes were working visually for the lens or not and change things if necessary. I would stand right next to the photographer, just behind so I could see exactly what the camera was capturing. (Baker 2010b)

Baker's interest in the aesthetic and practical qualities of functional dress would also develop in to her 'Layered on Thick' approach (Baker 1974c: 79). It was a look inspired by at least two very different sources: ballerina warm-up clothing and traditional Peruvian knitwear; she put together layers of legwarmers worn over tights and thick, loose cardigans worn over chunky jumpers. Baker's styling transformed the bulky into the sublime; she turned the jumpers and gloves inside out to reveal the abstract patterns of their knits and snipped and sewed together football socks to create extra-long legwarmers, which she showed worn over jeans and pulled right up to the inseam.

It could be argued that Baker has been involved in an innovative project of dress-reform her whole career; tackling hands on the fashion system's hierarchical structure, conventions and restrictions. Work wear and uniforms offered the ultimate antidote to fashion's relentless cycle and provided a response to the deepening economic recession faced by Britain in the 1970s. In 'Dressed Overall', photographed by Terence Donovan, Baker announced that 'fashion as we know it, with its bi-annual change of mood and style, will have to come to an end. A new approach to dressing will be needed ... That universal, uniform look must be a practical one ... The changes will have to be rung by each individual' (Baker 1974a: 39) (Figure 2.2).

The black-and-white photographs reveal a bleak urban landscape in which a solitary woman cuts a striking figure. The setting for the shoot may be dystopian, but the clothing is beautiful in its simplicity: 'classic classics in lovely shadowy camouflage colours, muted and un-extravagant, but very chic' (Baker 1974a: 39). The garments construct the narrative: fatigue jacket, blue-black velour sweatshirt, green gabardine Oxford bags, cobalt-blue cotton skirt and a striped cotton, sheered waist blouse; accessories add key details: a gentlemen's diver's watch, a tiny antique pearl choker, an ebony bangle, gold identity tags. Baker's styling transforms the wearer from standardized and uniformed factory worker into an original modern chic. Baker's commitment to core functionality of dress and a revision of fashion's conventions kept her questioning the limitations of women's clothing:

I was looking at menswear, and thinking 'why don't we wear what men wear? We don't need handbags ... we can put our hands in our pockets. We don't need lipstick, we don't need hairdos ... I don't have to wear heels to get myself a guy, or to keep my husband. I want to wash my clothes—I don't want to have to have them all dry-cleaned. I don't want stiff clothing, I want loose things—I have to run for the bus!' ... All these kind of feelings surfaced into my styling work. (Baker 2007)

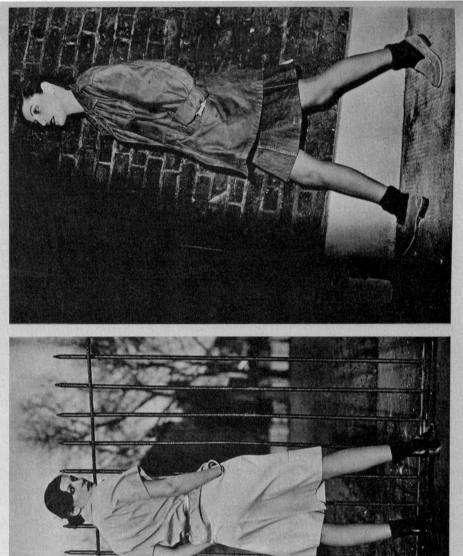

BELOW LEFT Gold khaki shirt by Mic Mac for Petits Chour, £9.50; khaki shorts by Katherine Hamnett for Tuttabankem, £12.50; gold tizard belt by Mulberry Co., £3.75; gold bangle at Butler & Wilson, £15; navy socks by Bonnie Doon, £1.20; navy sandals by Chelsea Cobbler, £9.99. BELOW RIGHT Army green paratrooper jacket at The Bargain Shop, £2.50; blue denim skirt by Emperor of Wyoming, £8; navy and white V-neck vest by Dorothy Perkins, £2.75; navy clasp at Butler & Wilson, £3.50; blue suede moccasins by Zapata, £30; white socks by Littlewoods, 24p. OPPOSITE Muddy khaki corduroy coat dress and trousers by Katherine Hamnett for Tuttabankem, £33.60, £17; navy cotton shirt at Laurence Corner, £2.19; brown leather boots by Olof Daughters—Sweden, £15.95

44

2.2. 'Dressed Overall', editorial and styling by Caroline Baker; photographs by Terence Donovan, *Nova*, March 1974. © IPC Media 2013

Baker's continuing interest in developing her concept of the natural woman would result in styling that embraced practical clothing, looser cut designs and unisex fashions. In 'Lady on the Loose', photographed by Hans Feurer, Baker abandoned the hair and make-up artist all together and created a story set around the idea of 'a shared wardrobe for all the family' (Baker 1974b: 60–1). As her text describes, the look was 'big and baggy, borrowed from the male—which means more to spend on the holiday and less on the clothes … no problem with the fit, the bigger the better' (Baker 1974b: 60–1). The oversize look would continue to inspire Baker well into the 1980s and is notable in the styling she contributed to Vivienne Westwood's 'Nostalgia of Mud' collection (1982/3). In 1975, the final year of *Nova*'s publication run, Baker dedicated a number of features to the philosophical premise and aesthetic qualities of the 'smock-shape', which represented 'the end of fashion and the start of something new' (Baker 1974b: 60–1). As she explained to her readers, 'The smock-shaped shirt-dress fits fat and thin, young and old and goes with everything. If we women don't want to be judged on sex appeal, why don't we adopt enthusiastically the one practical uniform we've been offered?' (Baker 1975b: 67). By her final issues on *Nova*, Baker appeared to dismiss the fashion system altogether; her article on denim entitled 'You Can Take a Blue Jean Anywhere' revealed a firm anti-fashion sentiment as she argued that 'couturiers and fashion magazines report po-faced on this and that look, and we waver between what we think we should like and what we know we do like … The only thing that changes year to year is the gimmickry, and even that is of no great importance' (Baker 1975a: 29). A double-page spread of a close-up of a woman's bottom tightly clad in a pair of worn Lee jeans celebrated denim as a sartorial solution, a default way of dressing which stood outside of fashion's waxing and waning. The following pages profiled Baker's favourite denim looks and offered a taste of the images she would construct for *Deluxe* and *i-D* magazines a few years later. For Baker, denim offered the ultimate solution: it was all at once uniform, practical, comfortable, affordable, versatile, unisex and sexy, and importantly it allowed the individual wearer to dress and stage her own identity.

CONCLUSION

Caroline Baker's fashion pages for *Nova* reveal that styling is integral to the achievement of an overall look, but equally significant, it encourages a way of dressing as a means to a way of being. In effectively defining the activity of styling and approaching this as both ideologically and aesthetically driven, Baker was able to communicate a series of fashion statements; the words and pictures of her fashion editorial play a crucial role in articulating the narratives of new and desirable feminine identities. Baker's fashion editorial for *Nova* changed the way fashion appeared on the magazine page and inspired a generation of young women to dress as they pleased. For Baker, the privilege that came with her role as a fashion editor lay in her ability to show by example, as she explains:

> Somehow or other it's quite brave to make that decision by yourself–to say 'I'm just going to go out wearing my pyjamas and my sneakers!' But if you see it somewhere, you think 'yes, I could wear my clothes like that' and I think that that is the power of the fashion editor … I always used to think I did a service to people … you actually were saying to women like yourself: 'Yes, this is what I feel like wearing now'. (Baker 2007)

ACKNOWLEDGEMENTS

The author would like to thank Pascal Bergamin for taking photographs of the images from the vintage copies of the magazine *Nova* which accompany her article.

NOTES

1. A welcome addition to the field of study is Penny Martin's exhibition and accompanying catalogue *When You're A Boy: Men's Fashion Styled by Simon Foxton,* The Photographers' Gallery, London, 16 July–4 October 2009.
2. This research draws on two oral history interviews (2007, 2010a) and written communication (2010b) with Caroline Baker.
3. *Nova*'s treatment of fashion and beauty editorial and its focus on design and layout marked out its specific appeal and difference to other women's magazines. As I have argued previously, *Nova*'s fashion pages encouraged an activity beyond buying the clothing or accessories featured; these images were actively consumed, torn out of the magazine, cut up and pinned to walls (Beard 2002).

BIBLIOGRAPHY

Baker, C. (1970a), 'Head for the Haberdashery', *Nova,* February: 42–7.
Baker, C. (1970b), 'Fancy Dressing', *Nova,* December: 64–73.
Baker, C. (1971a), 'Dressed to Kill: The Army Surplus War Game', *Nova,* September: 48–53.
Baker, C. (1971b), 'High as a Kite and Twice as Flighty', *Nova,* October: 64–73.
Baker, C. (1971c), Every Hobo Should Have One', *Nova,* December: 60–7.
Baker, C. (1972a), 'Safety Last', *Nova,* March: 66–7.
Baker, C. (1972b), 'All Dressed and Made Up', *Nova,* November: 62–71.
Baker, C. (1973), 'Adding up to Something Good', *Nova,* March: 88–91.
Baker, C. (1974a), 'Dressed Overall', *Nova,* March: 39–44.
Baker, C. (1974b), 'Lady on the Loose', *Nova,* July: 60–9.
Baker, C. (1974c), 'Layered on Thick', *Nova,* November: 78–85.
Baker, C. (1975a), 'You Can Take a Blue Jean Anywhere', *Nova,* July: 28–35.
Baker, C. (1975b), 'Is This the End of Fashion and the Start of Something New?' *Nova,* September: 66–73.
Baker, C. (2007), Personal communication with Alice Beard, 23 February.
Baker, C. (2010a), Personal communication with Alice Beard, 19 September.
Baker, C. (2010b), Personal communication with Alice Beard, 27 September.
Barthes, R. (1984), *The Fashion System,* London: Jonathan Cape.
Beard, A. (2002), 'Put in Just for Pictures: Fashion Editorial and the Composite Image in *Nova* 1965–1975', *Fashion Theory: The Journal of Dress Body and Culture,* 6/1: 25–44.
Borrelli, L. (1997). 'Dressing Up and Talking about It: Fashion Writing in *Vogue* from 1968–1993', *Fashion Theory: The Journal of Dress Body and Culture,* 1/3: 247–60.
Craik, J. (1994), *The Face of Fashion: Cultural Studies in Fashion,* London: Routledge.
Godfrey, J. (1990), *A Decade of i-Deas: The Encyclopaedia of the '80s,* London: Penguin.
Harrison, M. (1991), *Appearances: Fashion Photography since 1945,* London: Jonathan Cape.
Jobling, P. (1999), *Fashion Spreads: Word and Image in Fashion Photography since 1980,* Oxford: Berg.
Keenan, B. (1969) 'The Cardigan Is Borrowed but the Shoes Are Mine . . . ', *Nova,* September: 58–9.
Martin, P. (2009), *When You're A Boy: Men's Fashion Styled by Simon Foxton,* London: Photographers' Gallery.

Radner, H. (2000), 'On the Move: Fashion Photography and the Single Girl in the 1960s', in S. Bruzzi and P. Church Gibson (eds), *Fashion Cultures: Theories, Explorations and Analysis,* London: Routledge, 128–42.

Rocamora, A and A. O'Neill (2008), 'Fashioning the Street: Images of the Street in the Fashion Media', in E. Shinkle (ed.), *Fashion as Photograph: Viewing and Reviewing Images of Fashion,* London: I.B. Tauris, 185–99.

Scott, C. (1999), *The Spoken Image: Photography and Language,* London: Reaktion.

Shinkle, E. (2008), 'Interview with Penny Martin', in E. Shinkle (ed.), *Fashion as Photograph: Viewing and Reviewing Images of Fashion,* London: I.B. Tauris, 113–26.

Steele, V. (1997), 'Anti-fashion: The 1970s', *Fashion Theory: The Journal of Dress, Body & Culture,* 1/3, 279–96.

Williams, V., ed. (1998), *Look at Me: Fashion Photography in Britain 1960 to the Present,* London: British Council.

Plate 1. 'Tangier or the charms of exile', afternoon dress and cape by Paul Poiret, *Gazette du bon ton*, February 1920, N 1; Museum and Study Collection, Central Saint Martin's College of Art and Design

Croquis N° VI

Gazette du Bon Ton N° 1.

.15

Plate 2. Fashion drawing by Raoul Dufy, *Gazette du bon ton*, February 1920, N 1; Museum and Study Collection, Central Saint Martin's College of Art and Design

IL PLEUT ENCORE...

Tailleurs de Paquin, Lanvin, Dœuillet, Manteau de Paquin

Plate 3. 'It Is Still Raining', Tailleurs by Paquin, Lanvin, Doeuillet; Coat by Paquin; Fashion drawing by Valentine Gross, *Gazette du bon ton*, Summer 1915, nos. 8–9; Museum and Study Collection, Central Saint Martin's College of Art and Design

Khaki hat 99p, cotton drill shorts 83p, both at Lawrence Corner; khaki cotton safari jacket £2.90, Dylon dyed cotton vest 29p, both at Badges & Equipment

'Are all thy conquests, glories, triumphs, spoils, shrunk to this little measure?' *Shakespeare; Julius Caesar*

Khaki cotton zip-fronted flying suit £1.37 and long grey woollen scarf 33½p, both at Victor Lawrence; star brooch at Escalade 74p. Stockists on page 96.

'C'est magnifique, mais ce n'est pas la guerre' *Maréchal Bosquet*

Plate 4. 'Dressed to Kill: The Army Surplus War Game', editorial and styling by Caroline Baker, photographs by Harri Peccinotti, *Nova*, September 1971. © IPC Media 2013

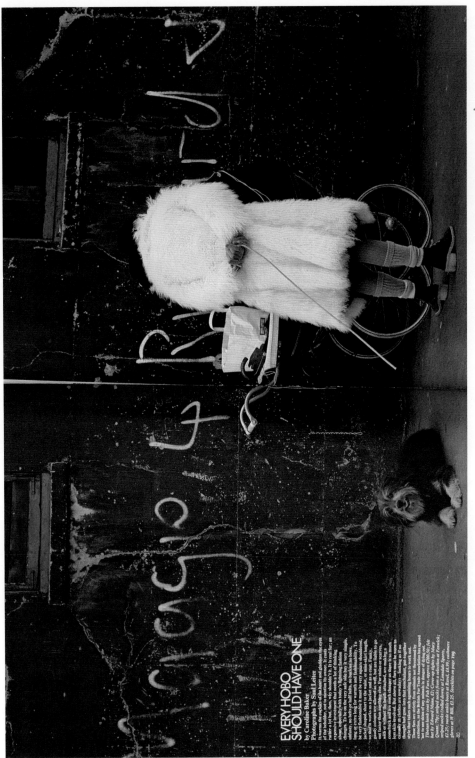

Plate 5. 'Every Hobo Should Have One', editorial and styling by Caroline Baker, photographs by Saul Leiter, *Nova*, December 1971.
© IPC Media 2013

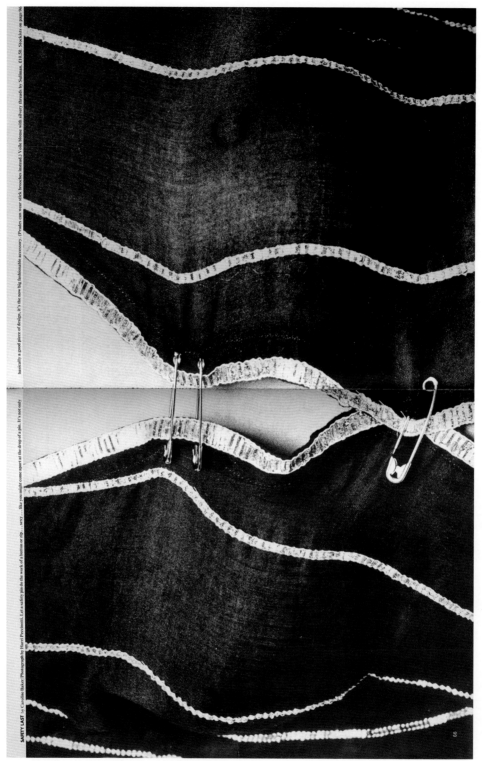

Plate 6. 'Safety Last', editorial and styling by Caroline Baker, photographs by Harri Peccinotti, *Nova*, March 1972. © IPC Media 2013

. . . matching nylon bra, 79p the set; angora tights, £1.50
Wool mixture angora skirt (matching sweater overleaf), £11.25 the set; two-tone pastel shoes, £6.50
68
69

Plate 7. 'All Dressed and Made Up', editorial and styling by Caroline Baker, photographs by Harri Peccinotti, *Nova*, November 1972. © IPC Media 2013

Plate 8. 'High as a Kite and Twice as Flighty', editorial and styling by Caroline Baker, photographs by Hans Feurer, *Nova*, October 1971. © IPC Media 2013

"Deep in the rainforest, our model Iekeliene listens to the mating call of a bird of paradise. New Guinea is home to 38 species of the bird; there are only 431 known in the world. The fauna of New Guinea is some of the richest in the world, and the country is a biological frontier, so it's worth recording any unusual animal you may see. Only a year ago I read about scientists discovering hundreds of new species in this lost world. A King of Saxony bird woke me every day on the stroke of 5.32am."

LOSE YOURSELF IN MOSSY-HUED GARGANTUAN CABLE-KNITS
Handknitted wool cardigan, £1,900. Handknitted wool scarf, £1,100. Both Giles, at Harvey Nichols. Silk socks, £55, Prada. Leather boots, £465, Balenciaga by Nicolas Ghesquière, at Harvey Nichols, Matches and Selfridges

TIM WALKER

137

Plate 9. 'To the Ends of the Earth', photography by Tim Walker, London *Vogue*, August 2007. © Tim Walker

MESMERISE IN CHLOE'S SACK
DRESS, BEDECKED IN
COLOURFUL PLASTIC CHARMS
Embroidered silk top, from £1,800.
Cotton skirt, from £600. Both Chloé,
at Chloé, A La Mode, Joseph and
Net-a-Porter.com. Wool and linen
waistcoat, £555, Noir, at Harvey
Nichols. Leather boots, from £600,
Chloé at Iris and Matches

TIM WALKER

Plate 10. 'To the Ends of the Earth', photography by Tim Walker, London *Vogue*, August 2007.
© Tim Walker

"*Papua New Guinea is home to one-sixth of the world's languages. The country's population of about 5.2 million speak some 820 very different languages, making it one of the most linguistically diverse countries in the world*"

Plate 11. 'To the Ends of the Earth', photography by Tim Walker, London *Vogue*, August 2007. © Tim Walker

Plate 12. *This Is Fashion* cover, n. 5, 1964

KOSTIUM CHANEL

Ogólną charakterystykę stylu Chanel przeczytaj w felietonie Lucynki i Paulinki. A oto cechy klasycznego kostiumu Chanel:

ŻAKIET prosty, rękawy normalnie wszyte, zawsze przykrótkie. Bez zapięcia, albo małe guziczki (ale i tak zawsze żakiet nosi się odpięty). Przecinane kieszonki, czasem 2 pary. Bez kołnierza, z kamizelkowym wycięciem.

Są też żakiety Chanel z malutką stójką pod szyją, albo z prostym kołnierzem, albo z prostymi klapami; klapy i kołnierz często nałożone tym samym materiałem z którego jest podszewka żakietu i bluzka. Często żakiet jest lamowany, lamówki w ogóle teraz modne: na przykład przy grubej wełnie lamówka z króciutkich frędzelków. Lamówka często czarna lub biała, albo z tego samego materiału co bluzka, albo gdy kołnierz z tego co bluzka, lamówka z tego co kostium.

SPÓDNICA wąska, w tym roku bardzo krótka.

BLUZKA gładka albo wzorzysta (Chanel lubi tureckie wzory), często lekko podrzucona. Z przodu albo gładka z okrągłym wycięciem na za dużej szyi, albo z prostym kołnierzykiem, tworzącym dekolcik (odsłania dołek między obojczykami), pod kołnierzykiem miękkie wiązanie z dwóch wąskich ogonów, jak by krawat. Rękawy koszulowe, krótkie lub długie. Znamienne dla stylu Chanel są też bluzki podrzucone i przewiązane w pasie, z boku kokarda i długie ogony.

DODATKI — kwiat, często sznur korali kilkakrotnie omotany na szyi, albo kilka sznurów pereł albo łańcuszek z wisiorkiem. Często na ręku bransoletka z korali albo z łańcuszka, Chanel w ogóle lubi łańcuszki, nawet w pasie (patrz kostium z tweedu po prawej).

WSZYSTKIE ZDJĘCIA tu zamieszczone przedstawiają oryginalne modele Chanela, z wyjątkiem kostiumu na zdjęciu młodej pary, który jest tylko w stylu Chanel.

Tweedowy kostium z ciemną lamówką i złotymi guzikami, bluzka z krawatowym wiązaniem, pod szyją perly, w pasie łańcuszek

MODA

Kostium na wielki dzwon z brokatu oblamowany materiałem bluzki, bluzka podrzucona i w pasie przewiązana, z boku kokarda

Kołnierz i wyłogi żakietu naszyte materiałem w turecki wzór, z którego jest też bluzka (zwróćcie uwagę na dekolcik bluzki znamienny dla stylu Chanel). Łańcuszek na szyi i łańcuszek na ręku

— Co mi zrobić osoba, która chce ubierać się modnie i wytwornie, a nie lubi poddawać się sezonowym bombom i efemerycznym liniom na różne litery, ani mieć wędrującej talii? — spytała Paulinka Lucynkę.

— Ubierać się w stylu Chanel — odpowiedziała Lucynka.

— Tak jest, szkoda że u nas styl ten jest mało popularny, bo naprawdę wdzięczny i życiowy. Pani Coco (naprawdę: Gabriela) Chanel zadebiutowała jako modystka jeszcze przed I wojną światową, a w okresie międzywojennym stała się wybitną osobistością paryskiego świata sztuki, przyjaźniła się ze Strawińskim, z Picassem, z Cocteau, z Diagilewem. Sprawiła szereg rewolucji o trwałych skutkach. Jej to zawdzięczamy wąską spódniczkę z pulowerem, który w początkach swej kariery nazywał się dżemperem (przed Chanelem trykoty były noszone tylko jako ciepła bielizna). Jej zawdzięczamy białe kołnierzyki i mankiety („mundur pokojówki", przeniesiony do salonów", jak pisał ówczesny dziennikarz). Ona to wprowadziła do szanującej się mody styl apaszowski który znamy z filmów z lat dwudziestych. Pani Chanel, dziś po siedemdziesiątce, ale daj nam Boże takiego zrywu, wciąż jest jednym z dyktatorów mody. Przy czym od lat 40 nie zmieniła na jotę zasadniczej koncepcji swoich kreacji, które mimo to są wciąż awangardowe. Przewalały się wokół pani Chanel newlooki, mody włoskie, linie A i Y, worki i trapezy, a pani Chanel niestrudzenie wypuszcza na świat swoje

kostiumiki z prostym żakietem. Mody przychodzą i mody odchodzą, Chanel zostaje. Oto cechy stylu Chanel:

● proste skromne plaszczyki, proste skromne sukienki na ogół z lekko podrzucona górą i wąskim dołem. Ale największą karierę zrobiły KOSTIUMIKI a raczej kompletiki (bo miękkie, bez kołnierza), wciąż te same od lat, a dotrzymujące kroku każdej modzie, wiecznie młode;

● styl Chanel jest przy całej swej prostocie subtelnie wyrafinowany; niby pojedynczy, ale nie surowy, praktyczny ale bardzo kobiecy, skromny ale z użyciem kobiecych ozdób;

● nadaje się dla każdego wieku, na każdą okazję (patrz kostiumiki wieczorowe) oraz prawie na każdą figurę z wyjątkiem może figury ze szczególnie wydatnym biustem;

● przez cały okres swego trwania styl Chanel wywierał silny wpływ na pozostałą modę, obecnie zaznacza się w popularnych kostiumach z równym żakietem, a skoro już chcesz uszyć sobie taki kostium, zrób go w klasycznym wy-

Plate 13. 'Chanel Suit', *Przekrój*, 1959, n. 723 (15 February), p. 20

Na firmamencie paryskiej „haute couture" Mademoiselle Chanel zajmuje tak wyjątkową pozycję, że ucieszyłam się bardzo, mając okazję właśnie o niej napisać reportaż dla polskich czytelników. Gabrielle Chanel przez fakt, że dała początek modzie dwudziestego wieku i ukształtowała jej niezmienne do dziś, zasadnicze cechy, jest w pełnym tego słowa znaczeniu współtwórcą współczesnej cywilizacji. „Chanel" — to nie moda, to elegancja, elegancja nie mająca nic wspólnego z sezonowymi „krzykami mody", wiążąca wszystkie jej wyznawczynie w rodzaj klanu tak, że każda z nich rozpozna drugą w najodleglejszym punkcie świata. Jak wyraziła się jej wierna klientka i admiratorka, aktorka filmowa Romy Schneider, w świecie elegancji istnieje „porządek Chanel", tak jak w architekturze mamy do czynienia z porządkiem korync-kim czy doryckim; jest to charakter kobiety prawdziwie dobrze ubranej, utrzymującej pewien określony typ sylwetki, lubującej się w określonych rodzajach tkanin i kolorystyce. Styl Chanel pozwala utrzymać także, bez anachronizmu, ciągłość i więź z młodą kobietą lat 50-tych, 30-tych i przede wszystkim 20-tych.

Ona, od 1918 roku, kiedy założyła w Paryżu dom przy ulicy Cambon, w pobliżu Place de la Concorde, dyktowała krótkie włosy i krótkie plisowane spódniczki z długimi prostymi bluzkami, styl młodzieńczy i sportowy, tak różny od wszystkiego, co było dotychczas. Stworzony przez nią typ dziewczyny — gar-

çonne — był wówczas wyrazem kultu naturalności i funkcjonalności ubioru, postawy sportowej, świadomej siebie kobiecości, wytworem epoki automobilów, kina, jazzu, tenisa i kobiet pracujących. Ona z czasem w wieczorowej sukni obcięła rękawy i wycięła głęboki dekolt na plecach, wylansowała głęboki kapelusz na oczy, miękki płaszczyk z otulającym szyję kołnierzem z długiego futra, dała początek blezerom, spopularyzowała jersey jako materiał na drapowaną su-kienkę popołudniową. Od Chanel biorą się szmizjerki, wszelkie cięcia i plisy, które pozwalają nie poszerzać dołem spódnicy, młodzieńcze białe kołnierzyki i mankiety, ona zarzuciła manierę ciasnego biustu i talii. Wreszcie, założyła firmę perfumeryjną, z której wyszły słynne „Chanel 5".

Na każdej prawie wystawie sklepowej przy eleganckiej ulicy Faubourg Saint Honoré oraz w popularnych magazynach, zobaczyć można „chanelowski" kostium zapięty pod szyję, niezbyt wcięty, jasny, obłamowany pasmanterią. Ten kostium, ubiór najbardziej prosty i zarazem szykowny uważany jest za najbardziej „portable" — do noszenia. Służy on kobietom jako przedmiot elegancji najautentyczniejszej i najbardziej demokratycznej: tym, które są bardzo dobrze sytuowane pozwala zachować pożądaną dyskrecję, a mniej zamożnym — być ubraną nowocześnie bez konieczności szycia stale czegoś nowego. Z programu Chanel wynika, aby stworzona

Plate 14. 'Mademoiselle Chanel', *You and I*, 1964, n. 3, p. 10

„Chanel"
kabátka

Készítéséhez kb. 50 dk zefir fonal hatos szála és 5-ös kötőtű szükséges. A kabát egyes részeit szabásminta szerint a munka színén sima, visszáján fordított sorokkal kötjük. A kezdő szemszámot úgy számítjuk ki, hogy a felhasználandó fonalból kötünk egy darabot, s azon megmérjük, hogy 10 szem hány centi. Ha a kötésmintán 10 szem 5 cm, akkor egy 50 cm-es darabot 100 szemmel kezdünk. Szabásminta szerint fogyasztjuk a karkivágást és a nyakkivágást is. Az elkészült részeket a visszáján nedves ruhán át kivasaljuk és összevarrjuk, majd a szélekre 2 sor kispálcát horgolunk saját szálával. A díszítést Mátra selyemfonal kettős szálával ugyancsak horgolással készítjük. A fehér kabáthoz olyan színű szegélyt készítünk, mely a szoknyánkkal egyezik. A selyemszegély első során a 2. kispálcasorba leöltve ugyancsak kispálcákkal horgoljuk. A kispálcák között 1—1 láncszemet horgolunk. A következő két sorban is 1 láncszem és 1 kispálca váltakozásával dolgozunk. Az ujjak és a zsebek szélén lévő díszesebb szegély 5 kispálca sorból áll. A középső sorba egy vastag, elütő színű gyapjú fonalat húzunk. A szegély szélére bogyókat horgolunk. A bogyót minden 2. kispálca után 5—6 egy lőbe öltött pálca képezi.

Plate 15. 'Hand-craft: "Chanel" Jacket', *This Is Fashion*, 1965, n. 3, p. 17

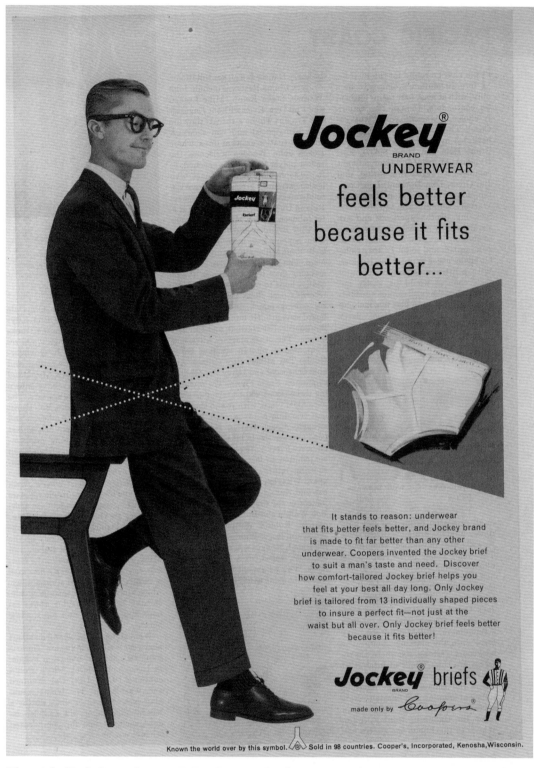

Plate 16. 'Feels Better Because It Fits Better...', advertisement for Jockey in *Sports Illustrated*, 1958. © Jockey International, Inc. Used with permission

3

'TO THE ENDS OF THE EARTH'
FASHION AND ETHNICITY IN THE *VOGUE* FASHION SHOOT
sarah cheang

INTRODUCTION

The August 2007 issue of British *Vogue* contains a twenty-page fashion story with the heroic, romantic and evocative title 'To the Ends of the Earth'. Photographed by Tim Walker in Papua New Guinea, a set of sixteen entrancing and startling pictures dramatize fashion through portraits of the model in physical and editorial juxtaposition with landscapes, forests and local tribesmen. These arresting images are deliberately set in place. They are given an explicit and expanded sense of location by writing and captions that tell the story of the shoot, adding layer upon layer of knowledge about the highlands of Papua New Guinea. There are details of flora and fauna on every page, as well as information on the Huli tribesmen and a story in the form of diary entries that gives a first-hand sense of the trials, tribulations and wonders of the *Vogue* team's journey. This is a place where, as the text itself underlines, 'cultures collided'.

Ethnic dress—fashion's Other and self-defining conceptual opposite—is regularly shown in magazines such as *Vogue,* where fashion shoots in non-Western spaces replace pristine studio sets with dusty Palestine, rural India or mountainous Peru. A formulaic parade of landscapes and cityscapes is served up as a scenic, unusual or edgy backdrop to Western fashion. These momentary vignettes of East/West contact bring models and local people together in narratives that can be explored for some important conceptual relationships between ethnicity, ethnic difference and fashion. The ephemerality of fashion and the format of a monthly fashion magazine lend themselves beautifully to a constant repetition of imagery; all too often, this is a continual reiteration that individual, modern and fashionable states of being are the preserve of Western society, even while they incorporate aspects of non-Western cultures.

Body adornment plays a crucial role in the signalling and maintenance of social categories—it is a primary means by which we announce our belonging to particular ethnic groupings and also experience that belonging. The discursive cultural practices that give shape to ethnic identities are based around notions of a common past, so that ethnic dress is a strong signifier of tradition and cultural heritage (Eicher 1995). Contrasts are therefore readily drawn between the modish sense that continuous style change is central to the concept of fashion, and the emphasis on tradition and heritage that characterizes notions of ethnic dress. The influential writings of early and mid-twentieth-century scholars of European fashion (Simmel 1904; Flugel 1930) reflected late-nineteenth century anthropological theories of dress as an extension of man's evolutionary progress through the use of tools, where the 'sophistication' of dress systems within Western society was equated with 'superior' civilization and the advancement of mankind (Baizerman, Eicher and Cerny 2008: 123–5). 'Fashion' became understood as the product of Western, capitalist, commodity-driven societies, the equivalent of which could not be seen in non-Western cultures.

It was during the 1990s that a series of challenges to the Western credentials of 'fashion' emerged, becoming a new key issue for fashion scholarship in the twenty-first century. Sustained attention to non-Western contexts for fashion production, dissemination and consumption within anthropology, sociology, dress history and cultural studies has given prominence to the dynamics of racism and cultural imperialism in the study of dress (Craik 1993; Eicher 1995; Rabine 2002; Neissen 2003; Baizerman, Eicher and Cerny 2008). Doubt has been cast on the drawing of simple oppositions between Western fashion and non-Western dress, and the existence of non-Western fashion systems has been given credence. Scholarship on fashion and diasporic black identities has established black style past and present as a distinct and entirely valid area within Western fashion studies (Mercer 1994; White and White 1998; Tulloch 2004). Increasingly, textbooks define fashion as a prevailing dress custom with 'a shared and internalized sense of the modish style of the time' that can occur in many cultures (Craik 2009: 2). Fashion is argued to be a product of social systems but not specifically of Western mercantile capitalism (Loschek 2009: 21–8).

'Ethnic' simply means 'cultural' and refers to any kind of cultural grouping, East or West, minority or majority, Caucasian or of colour. Fashion magazines tend towards the very common and rather reductive use of 'ethnic' to mean something or somebody non-Western and often non-Caucasian. In such fashion contexts, the 'ethnic' is foreign, exotic and different—the home of novel ingredients with which to spice up a dull Western existence, but this is a distortion or second meaning for the term. To say that somebody or something is 'ethnic', is to imply that 'ethnicity' is an inherent quality of marginality and Otherness, and this includes a person's relationship to fashion. The very positive public response to the first all-black edition of Italian *Vogue* in July 2008 has shown that for both consumers and industry professionals, ethnicity can be a powerful and motivational issue. But, does this mean that white, Eurocentric definitions of fashion have been decentred within high-end fashion media? Is it possible to discern any engagement with recent academic fashion debates in the editorial content of a magazine such as *Vogue*? This chapter focuses on early twenty-first-century depictions of fashion *out of place* that secure particular meanings for both 'fashion' and 'ethnicity'. A detailed investigation of nonstudio location shooting by photographers Tim Walker, Patrick Demarchelier and Mario Testino explores the ways in which ethnic identities are played out in the pages of British *Vogue,* opens up the tensions between aesthetic and semantic considerations, and reflects on the opportunities that may exist for fashion photography to challenge or interrogate racial and ethnic stereotypes as well as exploit them.

FASHION ENCOUNTERS ETHNICITY

As a genre of fashion representation, it is a fairly common experience for readers of *Vogue* to be presented with the staging of fashion in nonmetropolitan or foreign settings. For example in British *Vogue* between January 2009 and December 2011, there were twenty-four substantial editorial fashion shoots that made significant use of nonstudio locations outside of London; ten of these were in North American settings and four were shot in Britain while the rest featured locations in Europe, India, Africa, east central Asia, the Caribbean and the Middle East.

Diana Vreeland, editor of American *Vogue* between 1963 and 1971, has been credited with introducing unexpectedly exotic location shoots to the *Vogue* title during the 1960s as part of her pursuit of perfect fashion fantasies (Angeletti and Oliva 2006: 190–3). With the advent of commercial jet planes, distant locations were more accessible, while a new interest in 'ethnic' clothing was making unusual non-Western locations more relevant, from Indian palaces to Peruvian temples. Non-Western locations had been used prior to the 1960s, perhaps most famously in the India shoot photographed by Norman Parkinson and published in British *Vogue* in November 1956; however, a process of transformation was taking place from colonial relationships to postcolonial *and* neocolonial engagements between the Euro-American culture industry and notions of global citizenship. Where fashion photo stories before the 1960s communicate emphatically colonial scenes in which models stalk imperiously through foreign territories with native servants, later shoots increasingly communicate a kind of submersion through moments of sympathetic resonance in dress. 'Going native' at the level of fashion styling (as opposed to fashion back drop) has become part of the logic and raison d'être of most exotic shoots ever since.

The concept of fashion that the *Vogue* title encapsulates is predicated on a series of interrelated ideas about modernity, cosmopolitanism and individual identity construction in an aspirational consumer culture. Comprising a Western capitalist system of designers, retailers and consumers and a trickle down modus operandi, it is in many ways one of the narrowest definitions of fashion we could make. Here, fashion creates distinct social groupings that revolve around the innovation and imitation of style leaders and new individual ways of dressing, while any local and traditional matters of ethnicity appear to be transcended by a set of cosmopolitan cultural dynamics linked to globalization. Fashion is shown to be a globetrotting overlay in endless juxtapositions of designer-clad models, who are citizens of the world, with indigenous people, who belong root and branch to one particular place. The products of the *Vogue* fashion world, although centred on the capitals of Paris, London, Milan and New York, are projected as a free-floating, universal phenomenon in opposition to an explicitly geographically grounded ethnicity. Fashionable identities and ethnic identities emerge as conceptual opposites, encouraging majority/minority, centre/margin binary oppositions in the creative moment of fashion imaging—modernity versus tradition, the occident versus the orient, the pale versus the colourful, the everyday versus the rarely seen. In many instances, visual differences between some elements of the models' bodies and the bodies of the locals, normally termed 'racial' difference, produces a further mode of separation between fashion and 'the ethnic'.

In Patrick Demarchelier's shoot entitled 'Indian Summer' (September 2007), model Gemma Ward poses in a variety of North Indian scenes. Details such as bags, suitcases, rucksacks and aluminium drinks bottles strung on D-rings establish Ward as a traveller, a tourist or a bohemian adventurer on the hippy trail. Her hair is styled so that it tends towards dreadlocks, becoming a 'modern gipsy' according to the accompanying text. Within the British context, the notion of a white European travelling on a shoestring and experiencing local colour is a successful formula for locating fashion in a quasisympathetic relationship with ethnic dress but at the same time retaining the necessary conceptual distance between fashion and the ethnic through framing, storytelling and choice of model. Indeed, this template was repeated in March 2008 by the same fashion editor, Lucinda Chambers, in 'Trail Blazers', shot by Mario Testino, with an almost frame-by-frame substitution of Peru for India in an identical traveller narrative.

In the 'Indian Summer' story, Demarchelier's photographs document an imaginary journey in which the model moves through a rural landscape by camel train, by boat or on foot, eschewing taxis and other motorized luxury products of the industrialized world in favour of a hands-on, authentic Indian experience. Local people, in what is presented as their everyday clothing, make up a significant proportion of the content of these images, along with animals such as camels and cows. Across the twelve images published here, there are a total of sixty-three anonymous people, pictured in lively interactions with each other and with the model as she hangs out at street stalls and pauses on stone steps. Vermillion turban cloths, vibrant saris, colourful embroideries and an abundance of gold and silver jewellery worn by the men and women around Ward are pictured with such clarity and detail that they vie for our attention. She is shown sharing a joke at the water pump with Indian women who are, we are led to presume, simply going about their daily business of drawing water from a well. The styling is superbly done—layered head gear (a vintage beanie on top of a Muhlbauer cap) and a dazzling Emanuel Ungaro sequinned coat worn over a Diesel padded gilet effortlessly echo the sari-wrapped colour and metallic glitter of the local dress. And yet there can be no confusion for the reader. In an image containing six women sharing a single task of drawing water, it is clear who wears fashion and who wears ethnic dress. We have been following the model's journey so we know her to be the central figure of this drama, but even if we had not, physical difference and racial categories also play a central role in identifying the tall, white-skinned, blonde-haired goddess—the lone Caucasian—as the embodiment of fashion in a sea of ethnic others.

In an industry whose physical norms are tall and lean, models are selected in part for a height that is above average.[1] However, one striking aspect of the 'Indian Summer' story is the way in which Demarchelier's images work to greatly exaggerate Ward's height. Through the use of perspectival distance and the selection and positioning of men, women and children bending, crouching or seated, Ward towers over all. Such strategies ensure that the model is never decentred and will always draw the eye, and this is clearly one of the main aims of a fashion photograph. In the process, a blonde giantess is produced who both physically and symbolically dominates the scene. The notions of fashion and ethnicity that sustain the meaning of this scene are inescapably rooted in Eurocentric constructions of selfhood, themselves a product of colonial histories, unequal societies and racist cultural attitudes. In these photographs, location is everything, and the corporeal focus of fashion—that is the body as the focal point of fashion and beauty—makes the primary visual indicators of race difficult to elude in these lavish photo stories of fashion meets ethnicity.

The ethnic and racial ecology of the location fashion shoot has been known to create public debate but only in the most overt instances. For example the 'Out of Africa' shoot of June 2007 in American *Vogue* was accused by bloggers and their cyber commentators of glorifying colonial racism because of the depiction of actress Keira Knightley in dominant positions over groups of anonymous Maasai people or nostalgically posed in the African landscape in clothing that recalls the colonial era (Van Kerckhove 2007). Criticism was aimed at the editors and at *Vogue* in general as a vessel of unprogressive, racist or lazy thought but also at the African people who took part in the shoot for failing to be the right kinds of ambassadors for Africa and the African diaspora. In August 2008, the Indian edition of *Vogue* caused a minor furore when a shoot that used ordinary Indian people as models was picked up on in the *New York Times*. People apparently living in poverty were pictured joyfully sporting items by Fendi, Hermès and Burberry. This was seen as distasteful, vulgar and showing a scandalous indifference to the terrible reality of economic inequality in India (Peterkin 2008; Timmons 2008). In her defence of the images, *Vogue* India's editor, Pirya Tanna, reportedly argued that fashion should not be taken so seriously—it is about fantasy and aspiration. For her critics, located outside of India, it seems that fashion had been placed in the hands of people who are normally only ethnic background, who are usually just fashion's foil rather than its bearers, and the images lost their semantic coherence and tipped over into carnivalesque grotesquery.

The need for clear conceptual and visual divisions between models and background local 'colour' suggests that Caucasian models and styles would be favoured for non-Western settings. Mario Testino's fashion editorial 'Ocean Colour Scene', shot in Zanzibar for the March 2011 edition of British *Vogue,* at first appears to break this rule. The models walk along a white sand beach with open weave palm leaf baskets on their hips, wearing plain cotton maxi skirts and loose-fitting shirts described as 'simple peasant tops'. Their clothing is reminiscent of Caribbean and Creole dress in a fusion of African and European styles, an effect that is cemented by the use of headscarves that echo the headtie (Tulloch 1999). A positive investment in black style and black beauty can also be detected here in the use of black British model Jourdan Dunn alongside Caucasian Estonian Karmen Pedaru. Positive attention is paid to the visual qualities of Dunn's skin in statements such as 'a beautiful pea green silk dress needs no embellishment except glowing skin and sparkling eyes' or 'nothing illuminates the skin like a potent serum'. At the same time, the pointed valorization of Dunn's body as a site of beauty begins to fetishize her dark skin and eyes within a cultural arena that, in spite of a noticeable increase in the use of black models within the advertising and catwalk imagery of *Vogue* in 2011, is still dominated in its editorial content by Caucasian models.[2] Yet this does not imply some form of ethno-blindness, for later in the same fashion story, contrasts between fashion and the ethnic come strongly into play.

For the first five images, Pedaru and Dunn appear to be alone together in a tropical, palm-fringed paradise. Then, in a distinct change of direction and atmosphere, a double-page spread shows Pedaru at the centre of a group of six Maasai men, recognizable by traditional Maasai dress, jewellery and hairstyling. While still retaining the headtie/headscarf, the model's styling also shifts to a more contemporary fashion register. Her yellow canvas tunic dress creates contrast between block colour trends of 2011 and the wrapped and draped plaid and striped patterns of the Maasai men's clothing. Similarities become apparent between the posing of Gemma Ward in Demarchelier's 'Indian Summer' shoot and the arrangement here of the six Maasai men around the model. This is underscored by the words 'Bask in the golden light of Michael Kors' cotton tunic dress', as the Maasai men orbit the golden sun of Pedaru wrapped in Kors's outfit, like planetary bodies in a Western fashion solar system.

The ethnically diverse population of the island of Zanzibar is not typified by the Maasai, who are an important group within the representation of East African culture but who might here be regarded as a touristic importation. However, as the location of Zanzibar is in fact suppressed within the story—no specific country or even continent is mentioned in the editorial framing of the piece—the Maasai become even more important in securing a generalized location of 'Africa' as a setting that functions as exotic to both Caucasian and black ciphers of Western fashion. There is still no blurring between fashion and its ethnic others, which makes the work of Tim Walker all the more extraordinary and worthy of attention in the Papuan adventure 'To the Ends of the Earth', which turned the *Vogue* team into naturalists and ethnographers.

TIM WALKER AND THE NATURE OF FASHION

Tim Walker's interests often lie in unreality—in the fantasy spaces that fashion photography enables—so that the photograph's environment appears as a major motivating force in his work. His location shoots are sometimes placed at one remove from the usual contrasts between modern fashion and ethnic others, in a deliberate play of time and make-believe. For example in 'White Mischief' (May 2011), shot in a deserted and sand-engulfed mining village in Namibia, the model Agyness Deyn is not a fashion traveller in search of ethnic experiences but has the look of a character in a book or film set in the 1940s and 1950s. Like the mining village itself, Deyn also appears to have been abandoned since 1945, and her Ralph Lauren, Rochas, Chloe and Fendi dresses are crumpled, dirtied and look burnt at the edges. Deyn is pictured traversing the desert landscape with Simmon, a San Bushman guide, in scenes that powerfully bring to mind the film *Walkabout* (1971) with its undercurrent of ritualistic and transformative separations from society. The story plays on historical colonial relationships between Europeans and Africans and subverts them through the model's desolation and one-to-one encounter with a named (rather than anonymous) Bushman.

In 'To the Ends of the Earth', Papua New Guinea is, at first glance, a paradoxically real fantasy environment, complete with its own local actors. In some respects, therefore, this fashion story remains within that established mode of narrative framing, wherein model Ikeliene Stange is styled as a bohemian traveller in a non-Western land. But, as Stange shelters under an umbrella of giant leaves, she is dwarfed by the scale of rainforest vegetation and strangely shrunk like an Alice in Wonderland. She crouches among the undergrowth and is captured wearing leaf-feather-tulle-satin-insect ensembles. She embraces a tree, wearing a scarf and cardigan created from an outsize gauge of yarn and needles to make cable knits of enormous proportions; the earthy greens and browns of Stange's clothing and the careful positioning of the scarf to follow the lines of the tree trunk blend in with the mossy bark from which her face emerges as if she had truly become one with the tree (Plate 9). Closer examination of this shoot begins to reveal still other ways in which the model, fashion and *Vogue* itself have been transformed by their travels.

In this fashion story, the model and her clothing have been decentred, both visually and through a range of supporting texts. Small editorial comments stressing the tribal, the elemental and the bizarre begin the details of the fashion worn but are significantly outweighed by the inclusion in larger print of a commentary by Walker that gives details of tribal customs, the wonder and remoteness of the location, and the exotic wildlife. We learn, for example, that Papua New Guinea is a place where volcanic activity can cause the sea to boil, and the people are likened to birds of paradise. Additional text by fashion assistant Michelle Duguid provides the day-to-day experiences of the *Vogue* team in the form of a diary, revealing sleepless nights and jungle treks. This wealth of geographical and autobiographical detail vies with images that are by turns fashion photography and ethnographic photography. Of the sixteen images chosen to appear in the magazine, only five are portraits of the model. Five show just the tribesmen and four contain the model interacting with the tribesmen, while two feature only landscape and no people. In terms of visual expression alone, equivalence is being displayed between the model and the Huli as the subjects/objects of fashion, and in total, Papua New Guinea and its people have been allowed to eclipse the presence of *Vogue*, rather than the other way around, in a mesmerizing assertion that the ethnic dress of the Huli tribesmen, produced for traditional dance spectacles, is no different from fashion (Plate 10).

Walker's choice of Papua New Guinea as a location is pregnant with meaning for fashion historians and theorists. In the early twentieth century, Austrian architect Adolf Loos placed Papuans alongside fashionable Western women in his attack on decorated surfaces as 'backward' and 'uncivilised' (Loos 1998). Loos was attempting to demonstrate the inferiority of both women and 'savages' in the appreciation and development of 'good' design principles but reflects a propensity for cultural commentators to perceive body adornment as common ground between Papuan men (seen as primitive in evolutionary terms) and Western women (seen as intellectually inferior and culturally deviant).

Since the mid-twentieth century, anthropologists have moved towards positions of cultural relativity and away from social Darwinism. Jennifer Craik, working within the discipline of cultural studies but drawing extensively from anthropology, has also identified Huli male dancers as a key example in the consideration of fashion outside of Western contexts (Craik 1993: 18–26). Craik argues that many aspects of Huli body adornment robustly satisfy a definition of *fashion*—individuality through aesthetic management of appearance, and style change attached to a sense of contemporaneity—that can be meaningfully distinguished from *dress* but that does not rely on and is not derived from Western capitalist frameworks (Craik 2009: 54–8). This approach does not simply identify differences and similarities between Huli dancers and Western fashion but explores a parallel fashion system. Comparisons can be drawn between these notions of communality between European and Papuan dress systems, and *Vogue*'s 'To the Ends of the Earth'—where a photograph of four Papuans in elaborate wigs, make up and headdresses that included the use of plastic toy bats and a Coca Cola packaging box—is accompanied by these remarks: 'The hair, make-up and dandified displays of male vanity I witnessed here outdo anything the Paris, Milan or London shows have to offer'.

Walker claims no direct familiarity with the work of Craik or with recent scholarly debates on fashion and Eurocentricism (Walker 2011). He has, however, arrived at the same place through the practice of photography and has inserted that discussion into the pages of *Vogue*. One particular image from the Papuan shoot stands out: a full-page portrait of a Huli man whose necklaces, bracelets and headdress combine manmade textiles, plastic, shells and feathers and speak of invention and visual sensation (Plate 11). His face is painted a vivid yellow, and he has stopped in the act of applying a new layer of red decoration that outlines and accentuates his mouth and eyes and then begins to extend across his cheeks. He regards the camera steadily, posing, and holds up a small mirror beside his head in which a second image of his face appears. But, there is another mirror in the picture. In the bottom left-hand corner, an unknown hand holds an irregular piece of broken glass that is angled directly towards the reader. In a moment of visual incoherence and subject/object doubling, the reader could expect to see his or her own face reflected in the mirror, at the same time realizing the impossibility of this idea. Instead, the face of another Huli man looks back at us. In this complex moment of looks and regards, Walker has seen and captured an instance of utter equilibrium between the body adornment systems of the Huli and the preoccupations of a fashion photographer, a fashion editor and a potential fashion magazine reader. Where decorative tribal costume in other location shoots forms a sympathetic or contrasting background to Western fashion but is entirely separated from it, Walker's Huli mirror Western fashion.

A further way in which this imagery goes beyond the bounds of *Vogue* photography is through an overt ethnographic and zoological interest. Indeed, Walker's desire to shoot in Papua New Guinea was first kindled by birds of paradise in a nature documentary (Walker 2011). In these pictures, there is a desire to make sense of the Western fashion system by believing in fashion as an aspect of nature and common to all humans. The lacy wings of insects are nature's tulle, and conversely, French tulle is mankind's coxcomb, mating colours or status display. Walker invests deeply here in the notion of a 'thin veil between the animal and the human' which photographic moments like these can reveal (Walker 2011). In this way, Walker proposes a new way of approaching fashion and beauty which is uncannily appropriate to twenty-first-century academic fashion discourse: the Huli men are seen as people in possession of a cultural arena for the universal 'need' for gorgeous display and self-expression, the same as that which Western male fashion designers project onto the bodies of the women that they design for.

CONCLUSION: *VOGUE GEOGRAPHIC*

A highly internalized understanding of fashion as evolutionary—and the use of tribal cultures to comprehend Western society—explains the closeness between Walker's visual repertoire and popular ethnographic forms of photography typified by the journal *National Geographic*. In common with social anthropology's curiosity in human diversity and quest to understand culture through the communalities between human societies, Walker asks questions about how fashion separates one human group from another and yet unites them. It is interesting to note another precedent for this crossover between fashion and anthropology. The book *National Geographic Fashion* (2001) uses images from the *National Geographic* archive in juxtaposition with quotations on haute couture fashion, presenting, for example, an image of a Maori woman beside a statement on Western fashion by the couturier Mainbocher; unsurprisingly, the Huli feature prominently. While the book's flyleaf promises 'vivid visual proof of our universal fascination with fashion', an introduction by anthropologist Joanne B. Eicher strikes a more ambivalent and cautious note. She directs the reader to be wary of misleading photographic representations of everyday non-Western 'realities'; she lays out the key argument for the Eurocentric, aggressive, imperializing tendencies of concepts of Western fashion, and she questions the meaningfulness of the book's structure (Eicher 2001). However, Eicher also suggests that such a book could help to achieve a more open-minded approach to the type of style changes that fashion connotes and broaden interpretations of the fashionable in ways that have merit.[3]

Critiques of both ethnographic and touristic photography have pointed out the way that documentary realism has been exploited to naturalize and fix constructions of ethnicity and Western modernity (Urry 1990; Pinney 1992; Lutz and Collins 1994). It is striking how many of the images published in 'To the Ends of the Earth' work to dismantle the reality of the fashion fantasy by foregrounding the mechanisms by which the shoot was achieved, such as scenes of bus transport to a hilltop location. Margaret Maynard has described fashion photography as unstable but densely anchored. It may produce images that play with definitions of gender, sexuality or ethnicity, but it inevitably reconfirms consumer desire on an unconscious level as natural (Maynard 2008). Thus, different registers of ethnicity—race, narratives of global and local, nostalgia, the familiar and the unusual—can ultimately all be used to cement a certain understanding of fashion as desirable, and Walker's vision can still be admitted into the spaces that sell high fashion. His 'An Awfully Big Adventure' shoot in Mongolia (December 2011), which has a similarly ethnographic direction, shows how *Vogue* has a positive appetite for this kind of occasional disruption, which can be celebrated as elite romantic escapism.

Magazines are primarily spaces of consumption. In addition to the cover price, their pages paid for several times over through advertisements, advertising features and editorial advice on which objects and experiences to buy. Here, in the depiction of non-Western cultures, the visual language of Western fashion photography, travel photography and anthropological photography overlaps in a reiteration of exotic, attractive and/or unusual places that are used to tantalize or fascinate Western consumers. In the majority of *Vogue* non-Western fashion shoots, appealing fashion images are created through the juxtaposition of Western fashion and ethnic dress, in which the idea of Western fashion produced is simultaneously European, international and 'beyond' ethnic categorization. Non-Western cultures are correspondingly reinforced as static and beyond the realms of fashion. The inclusion of non-Western cultures within high-end photographic fashion stories seems to imply that 'ethnic' styles are part of fashion's cosmopolitan mix, celebrating cultural diversity within Western style innovation. However, in most instances, the lines between Western fashion identities and ethnic otherness continue to be drawn, maintaining coherent meanings for high fashion. Where these rules are challenged, the result has sometimes been judged in bad taste—nevertheless, haute couture fashion culture's strong investment in artistic fantasy and the edgy occasionally provides a space for the successful inclusion of more complex approaches.

ACKNOWLEDGEMENTS

The author wishes to thank Joanne Entwistle, Reina Lewis, Djurdja Bartlett, Jenna Rossi-Camus and the postgraduate communities of the London College of Fashion and the Royal College of Art for their thoughts and comments in the development of this work.

NOTES

1. The average height for women in the United Kingdom is 5 feet 4 inches (162 cm) (Carvel 2002). The British Association of Model Agents advises that to go into modelling, a woman should be at least 5 feet

8 inches (173 cm), although based on a sample of portfolios on the websites of Storm, Premier and Models 1, in 2011 the majority of women on the books of UK modelling agencies were 5 feet 9.5 inches (181 cm) and above.

2. During 2011, black models appeared in British *Vogue* thirty-eight times, compared to nineteen times in 2010 and twenty-four times in 2009. Fashion that could be interpreted as black style was featured seven times in 2011, four times in 2010 and twice in 2009.

3. A second introductory essay by fashion historian Valerie D. Mendes pushes forward the discussion on the meaning of *fashion* in relation to concepts of East and West (Mendes 2001).

BIBLIOGRAPHY

Angeletti, N. and A. Oliva (2006), *In Vogue: The Illustrated History of the World's Most Famous Fashion Magazine,* New York: Rizzoli.

Baizerman, S., J. B. Eicher and C. Cerny (2008), 'Eurocentrism in the Study of Ethnic Dress', in J. B. Eicher, S. L. Evenson and H. A. Lutz (eds), *The Visible Self: Global Perspectives on Dress, Culture and Society,* 3rd ed., New York: Fairchild, 123–32.

Carvel, J. (2002), 'Britons Stand Tall, if Slightly Heavy, in Europe', *The Guardian,* 28 August, http://www.guardian.co.uk/ul/2002/aug/28/science.research, accessed 30 November 2011.

Craik, J. (1993), *The Face of Fashion: Cultural Studies in Fashion,* London: Routledge.

Craik, J. (2009), *Fashion: The Key Concepts,* Oxford: Berg.

Davis, F. (1992), *Fashion, Culture, and Identity,* Chicago: University of Chicago Press.

Eicher, J. B., ed. (1995), *Dress and Ethnicity,* Oxford: Berg.

Eicher, J. B. (2001), 'Introduction: The Fashion of Dress', in C. Newman, *National Geographic Fashion,* Washington, DC: National Geographic, 17–23.

Flugel, J. C. (1930), *The Psychology of Clothes,* London: Hogarth.

Loos, A. (1998), 'Ornament and Crime', in *Ornament and Crime: Selected Essays,* Riverside, CA: Ariadne Press, 167–76.

Loschek, I. (2009), *When Clothes Become Fashion: Design and Innovation Systems,* Oxford: Berg.

Lutz, C. and J. Collins (1994), 'The Photograph as an Intersection of Gazes: The Example of National Geographic', in L. Taylor (ed.), *Visualising Theory: Selected Essays from V. A. R., 1990–1994,* London: Routledge, 365–84.

Maynard, M. (2008), 'The Fashion Photograph: An "Ecology"', in E. Shinkle (ed.), *Fashion as Photograph: Viewing and Reviewing Images of Fashion,* London: I.B. Tauris, 54–69.

Mendes, V. (2001), 'Introduction: The Fashion of Fashion', in C. Newman, *National Geographic Fashion,* Washington, DC: National Geographic, 29–35.

Mercer, K. (1994), 'Black Hair/Style Politics', in *Welcome to the Jungle: New Positions in Black Cultural Studies,* New York: Routledge, 97–128.

Neissen, S. (2003), 'Afterword: Re-orienting Fashion Theory', in S. Niessen, A. M. Leshkowich and C. Jones (eds), *Re-orienting Fashion: The Globalization of Asian Dress,* Oxford: Berg, 243–66.

Peterkin, T. (2008). 'Anger at Indian Vogue Photoshoot', *Telegraph,* 3 September, http://www.telegraph.co.uk/news/worldnews/asia/india/2673306/Anger-at-Indian-Vogue-photoshoot.html, accessed 9 October 2010.

Pinney, C. (1992), 'The Parallel Histories of Anthropology and Photography', in E. Edwards (ed.), *Anthropology and Photography 1860–1920,* New Haven, CT: Yale University Press, 74–98.

Rabine, L. (2002), *The Global Circulation of African Fashion,* Oxford: Berg.

Simmel, G. (1904), 'Fashion', *International Quarterly,* 10: 130–55.

Timmons, H. (2008), 'Vogue's Fashion Photos Spark Debate in India', *New York Times,* 1 September, http://www.nytimes.com/2008/09/01/business/worldbusiness/01vogue.html?_r=0, accessed 9 October 2010.

Tulloch, C. (1999), 'That Little Magic Touch: The Headtie', in A. de la Haye and E. Wilson (eds), *Defining Dress: Dress as Object, Meaning and Identity*, Manchester: Manchester University Press, 63–78.

Tulloch, C. (2004), *Black Style*, London: V&A.

Urry, J. (1990), *The Tourist Gaze: Leisure and Travel in Contemporary Societies*, London: Sage.

Van Kerckhove, C. (2007), 'Vogue's Glorification of Colonial Racism', *Racialicious—The Intersection of Race and Pop Culture*, 8 August, http://www.racialicious.com/2007/08/18/vogues-glorification-of-colonial-racism/, accessed 9 October 2010.

Walker, T. (2011), Interview by S. Cheang, 9 December.

White, S. and G. White (1998), *Stylin': African-American Expressive Culture from Its Beginnings to the Zoot Suit*, Ithaca, NY: Cornell University Press.

4

COCO CHANEL AND SOCIALIST FASHION MAGAZINES
djurdja bartlett

INTRODUCTION

The encounter between Coco Chanel and the world's first socialist country—the Bolshevik Russia—did not happen in the early 1920s when both Chanel and socialism were still modernist projects. Following the 1917 October revolution, the Bolsheviks embraced the speed of the new era, worshiped the machine and acknowledged a crisis in the representation of the female gender. Moreover, the main Bolshevik artistic supporters—the constructivists—chose geometric abstraction as their visual language. In that sense, 1924 dress drawings by Varvara Stepanova and Coco Chanel's drawing of a little black dress published in the American *Vogue* in the same year share the same modernist aesthetics, characterized by flatness and overall economy of style. While both Stepanova and Chanel proposed functionality and simplicity in dress, their similarities were only aesthetic. Operating within the postrevolutionary utopian fervour, the Bolsheviks completely rejected fashion, as it, for them, belonged to a decadent and frivolous bourgeois lifestyle. Consequently, Coco Chanel could not have been accepted as a sartorial comrade. She will only become one three decades later, when both the socialist regimes and Coco Chanel herself were not revolutionaries any longer. This chapter interrogates the socialist fascination with a Chanel suit in a specific historical period, starting in the late 1950s and lasting throughout the 1960s and 1970s in six former socialist countries: the Soviet Union, Czechoslovakia, East Germany, Hungary, Poland and the former Yugoslavia. At that point, both socialism and Coco Chanel left their revolutionary ideals behind and, consequently, embraced sartorial convention.

SOCIALIST FASHION MAGAZINES

In socialism, all the fashion and women's magazines were state-owned, and the regimes channelled the official policies on dress aesthetic and the changes in the concept of gender through them.[1] In this context, these magazines were informed by the conventions of both fashion journals and more or less sophisticated political bulletins. Following the 1917 Revolution in Russia and the 1948 Communist coups in Eastern Europe, the ideal was an austere and unadorned woman. In their fashion sections, socialist magazines published hundreds of examples of work uniforms for nurses, tram conductors, women factory workers, female laboratory scientists, traffic wardens and police women. A woman in a working uniform was supposed to show that the concept of a sartorial seasonal change, by which the fashion system operates, was irrelevant in the socialist societies. The denunciation of fashion also gave rise to a crisis in the representation of the female gender. Two distinctive choices emerged within the new visual economy of a woman's body. She could enter the new world by physically resembling a man or be excluded from it as a creature of the past clinging to a redundant display of femininity and fashionability. In order to be accepted into the body politic, women were expected to change both their dress and their looks. Besides the importance of robustness and strength in the shaping of the ideal female socialist body, modesty and asexuality played significant roles in its final look.

The initial approach against fashion eventually softened both in the Soviet Union and in Eastern Europe, as the utopian ideals struggled to survive in the everyday. In the 1930s, Stalinist media channelled a new conservative cultural policy which abandoned the early Bolshevik ideals and established a concept of Soviet style luxury. The Bolshevik austere woman was exchanged with a mythical superwoman who was an exemplary worker, good mother and political activist but nevertheless well groomed and smartly dressed. Existing under the Soviet political influence, the Eastern European socialist regimes soon left behind their utopian ideals and accepted the Stalinist traditionalist approach to gender from the mid-1950s on. The woman in a masculine-style uniform disappeared from the fashion magazines to be replaced with a woman in a conventionally smart dress. The official approval of the traditional female ideal reflected the failure to engineer a new socialist woman. Apart from regular paper patterns for home dressmakers, women's mass media also published numerous columns on appropriate dress and proper behaviour. Women were strongly encouraged to be pretty but simple, and equally strongly dissuaded from being extravagant and sexy.

In each country, the concepts of modesty and luxury were promoted through different women's magazines, which were meant for different audiences and also served the differing needs of each regime.[2] One group of magazines published smart one-of-a-kind dresses—designed and produced within the centralized fashion institutions—and presented them as success stories of the domestic clothing industry. Their style was luxurious but conventional and timeless. The other group of magazines, meant for the mass public, recognized the shortages and poor quality of clothes in everyday life. These magazines offered practical advice on making and repairing your own clothes. Moreover, unlike the first group, mass magazines promoted a conventional but modest style, which conformed to socialist values of modesty and moderation and showed discomfort with individuality and unpredictability. In the end, both representational luxury and everyday modesty opposed and blocked contemporary Western fashion trends and the concept of change that they might have introduced. Coco Chanel's timeless suit was present in the imagery of both luxury magazines and those meant for the mass audiences. The mass magazines offered women advice on producing their own versions of the Chanel suit. On the other hand, the magazines at the high-end published many images of that famous suit, covering Chanel's originals from her contemporary collections, as well as the smart copies, designed and executed within their respective centralized fashion systems.[3]

SOCIALIST SLOW MASTER NARRATIVE AND THE CHANEL SUIT

The new political and social circumstances only helped the Chanel suit to become an official vestimentary favourite. Following Stalin's death in 1953, the Soviet Union had a new political leader, Nikita Khrushchev, who wanted to break with the Stalinist isolationist policies and open the country towards the West. This ideological turn brought about a change in official attitudes towards fashion in the Soviet Union and the Eastern European socialist countries. Against the backdrop of the Cold War, the encounter between socialist fashion and Western fashion brought a huge clash between the two systems of representations. Forced into the competition in everyday life cultures in which they lagged far behind the West,[4] the socialist regimes suddenly had to try to produce their own version of socialist fashion. The earlier utopian attempts to design and produce a genuinely new socialist dress were abandoned both in the Soviet Union and the Eastern European socialist countries under its control, along with the early utopian urge for an immediate change and a total novelty in the everyday. The socialist countries were not ruled by the idealistic revolutionaries any longer but by the powerful yet ossified bureaucracies. At that point, socialism could not sartorially compete with the Western fashion and certainly did not want to. It desperately needed ready-made models, which would be smart but would not challenge its slow concept of time.

Thus, the political relaxation towards fashion did not mean that the regimes wanted, or could possibly risk, changes in existing practices, as those changes might bring their rule into question. The field of fashion production could not be organized on different principles to those on which the whole system was organized. The ever-changing phenomenon of fashion was made to exist within the five-year plans, which disciplined every aspect of fashion through the lengthy and complicated decision-making within the hierarchically organized textile and clothing boards. In fact, this economic model, and its centralized systems of clothes production and distribution, enabled the socialist regimes to control and tame fashion changes. Central fashion institutions started to design their own versions of Chanel suits, which, produced only as prototypes, were either paraded at the socialist fashion congresses or published in fashion magazines. The annual collections designed within the socialist central fashion institutions condensed real time into an ever-repeating, controlled cycle. The socialist predilection towards stability implied the design and production of conventional, repetitive clothes. The Chanel suit—classical, elegant and timeless—corresponded to this slow flow of time.

Socially, a new dress was needed to dress up the new socialist middle classes in civilian clothes. Socialism was reconciled to fashion through the emergence of a new socialist middle class which owed its appearance in the public arena to its tacit deals with the regimes. The new socialist middle

4.1. Chanel suit designed by German Fashion Institute, *Sibylle,* 1962, n. 2, p. 69

classes played two important roles. First, the regimes needed a loyal middle class to support the system once the revolution settled into quiet societal patterns. Second, the regimes required a large and relatively mobile social group which they could trust with public performances of middle-class rituals in order to compete more convincingly with the West. In contrast to the privileged highest strata of Nomenklatura, whose members clandestinely enjoyed expensive status symbols, the new middle classes were publicly encouraged to move into the socialist sartorial version of prettiness and cosiness. The regimes bought the loyalty of their middle classes with material rewards and imposed a culture of propriety on them, drawn from the previously despised bourgeois culture. The state therefore had a crucial role in the creation and dissemination of the new socialist middle-class culture, its imagery and its etiquette. From the late 1950s on, abundant educational texts and images of hats and gloves, cocktail dresses and hairstyles promoted new rules for the female members of the new socialist middle classes. A Chanel suit, a reliable classic, perfectly suited the requirements on socialist middle-class women to look chic but not overtly fashionable.

It could be said that a fear of change brought together Chanel and socialist fashion. Socialist magazines emphasized that Coco herself did not want, or indeed need, any changes to her already perfect suit. The Hungarian journal *This Is Fashion (Ez a divat)* claimed that 'Mademoiselle Chanel' had fought 'corsets and starched skirts' in her youth while 'her today's enemies are short skirts and extravagant fashions' (Kovásc 1968). Yet, *This Is Fashion* continued, 'she created a collection that is youthful, practical, comfortable and super feminine even in the smallest details. Her cuts are timeless and every woman, regardless of her age, could wear her clothes' (Kovásc 1968). A reporter from the Yugoslav illustrated magazine *Globus* described Coco Chanel as 'a promoter of functional and comfortable fashion that emphasizes female beauty and is totally feminine, in opposition to her competitors Dior, Givenchy or Balmain, who insist on bizarre and spectacular effects' (R.V. 1959). The magazine stated that Coco Chanel had already caused several fashion revolutions in the past but stressed that she rejected the role of fashion revolutionary in the latest phase of her career. According to *Globus,* Chanel understood that there was no need for a new revolution, as contemporary fashion already fulfilled all women's needs and 'allowed a woman to dress aesthetically and practically, but still look beautiful, be free in her movements, elegant, and even to attract attention' (R. V. 1959).

MATCHING AESTHETICS

In an article published in the French *Marie Claire* in 1967, Roland Barthes stated that Chanel chic could not stand 'the look of newness' and that a change in a 'discreet detail' was the only distinction in dress it allowed for (Barthes 2006). Contrasting Chanel with a revolutionary newcomer, Andre Courrèges, Barthes emphasized: 'So, it is the notion of time, which is a style for one and a fashion for the other, that separates Chanel from Courrèges' (Barthes 2006: 107). Socialist fashion shared this predilection for an eternal chic, which, in its case, was embedded in the socialist realist concept of time. Socialist realism was the official aesthetics under socialism once the modernist utopian experiments were abandoned. Quite contrary to its name, socialist realism's aesthetics had nothing to do with the reality of everyday life. The official brief to the artists was to aestheticize the existing reality 'according to the laws of beauty and harmony'.[5] Consequently, socialist realism created a new parallel, mythical reality, which was disseminated through mass media, from films to fashion and women's magazines.

The historian Donald J. Wilcox stated that there are three main chronotypes—or temporal manifestations—in narrative structures: absolute time, objective time and subjective time (Wilcox 1989). Delineating the life of the hero, subjective time is in constant flux and interaction with objective time which relates to the world around him. In contrast, absolute time is the unchangeable time of absolute truths. Following from here, it could be said that socialist realism preferred the absolute temporal sphere.[6] Eternal and unchanging attributes of absolute time explain both the search for classic forms in socialist fashion and reveal its relation to the aesthetics of socialist realism and its fascination with the heritage of classical aesthetics. As a historian of socialist realism, Leonid Heller observed, 'The very idea of a classic depends on classification, on judgments of normativity, on categorization—thus was the doctrine of socialist realism formulated through debates about norms and categories' (Heller 1997: 55). That is why the style of socialist fashion designers matched that of the classicist Chanel and her eternal chic. Socialist fashion magazines, such as the East German *Sibylle*, Czechoslovak *Woman and Fashion (Žena a móda)* and Hungarian *This Is Fashion* published many versions of a Chanel classic suit during that period, which were created either by the designers within the central fashion institutions, such as Deutsche Modeinstitut, the Hungarian central fashion institute and the Soviet All-Union House of Prototypes, or produced by the magazines themselves as unique, one-off outfits for their fashion editorials. In 1964, *Sibylle* dedicated nineteen pages to Chanel suits, many of which were designed and executed only for that specific fashion story (M. P. 1964).

Sibylle's editor during the 1960s, the modernist Dorothea Melis, was not alone in her opinion of the Chanel suit as modern classic. The Polish fashion designer Barbara Hoff, who would eventually become the main promoter of quirky, youthful fashions during the socialist period, started her career by praising simplicity and elegance of Chanel suit (Hoff 1959). In their struggle against the ossified style of socialist fashion, these two fashion practitioners in fact related to Coco Chanel's initial modernist call on geometrical cut, functionality and comfort in woman's dress. At the very beginning of the 1960s, such efforts corresponded with a modernist streak of the Soviet and Eastern European cultural policies. In the Soviet Union, the constructivists were again praised in the media, while the representatives of the Western abstract art, such as Pablo Picasso, were promoted in the Eastern European art and illustrated journals.

However, modernism, whether in the arts or fashion, had no serious chance within the restrained and closed off socialist systems. Socialism was not really interested in the initial radicality of Chanel suit. Instead, it related to its later petrified chic. More conventional in her style, Žuži Jelinek, owner of the private fashion salon located in Zagreb's main square, was pronounced 'our Coco Chanel' in the Yugoslav media. In her 1960 interview with the magazine *Globus* she said, 'I hate overdressed women. Therefore, I suggest simple fashion to our women. Simple fashion is always elegant, and thus a woman that dresses simply but tastefully is always elegant' (S. K. 1960).

The Chanel suit perfectly fitted into prevailing aesthetics of socialist fashion, which I call socialist good taste. Introduced in the late 1950s, both as an official aesthetics and style guide for the emerging middle classes, socialist good taste incorporated the concepts of elegance and prettiness but insisted that only simplicity is elegant and beautiful. As the new aesthetics of middle-class dress had to be decided quickly, promoted through the media and applied in everyday life, socialism was forced to borrow its new official dress style from the reservoir of bourgeois culture. A new official taste

4.2. 'A Beautiful Day Just for You', *Sibylle*, 1964, n. 3, p. 37

combined the socialist values of modesty and moderation with the previously despised bourgeois values of prettiness and conventional elegance. Those borrowed values were needed to dilute the asceticism of proletarian style, which socialism never officially renounced. Socialist good taste gained political approval because it was simple, conventional and moderate.[7] There were clear boundaries between the categories of appropriateness and inappropriateness, within which socialist fashion operated, and the socialist women's magazines relentlessly preached against any transgression.

The timeless style of socialist good taste conveniently matched a socialist slow concept of time. Just as a Chanel suit itself, socialist good taste allowed for a change in detail while avoiding any radical changes in cut or silhouette. Thus the text, accompanying the Hungarian-executed collection of Chanel suits in the magazine *This Is Fashion* in 1966, focuses on various details of these otherwise conventional outfits: contrasting ribbons sewn on the edges of the jackets, discreet collars, delicate silk blouses and feminine waistcoats lurking under them. The article states that this collection was especially designed by the Hungarian central Prototype Clothing Design Company (Ruházati Mintatervezö Vállalat) and the prestigious Special Dresses Salon for Women (Különlegességi Nöi Ruhaszalon)[8] in Budapest in order to be presented by the export company Hungarotex at the catwalks and exhibitions in Toronto and Montreal later that year ('Photo Report' 1966). The West might have been interested in these socialist fakes of the Chanel suit. They were undoubtedly cheaper than their Western counterparts and certainly well-executed, as the socialist fashion institutions offered much better quality in their export collections than to their respective domestic markets. Anyway, nobody expected originality by Coco Chanel any longer, and the socialist copies belonged to the same world of safe, conventional taste.[9] Similarly to socialist magazines, the references to Chanel in French fashion media were strictly atemporal. French *Vogue* declared Chanel's fall 1958 collection a 'manifesto of elegance in simplicity' and claimed that 'five outfits on these pages show that a formula can evolve, renew and strengthen itself, while staying strictly faithful to its unchangeable style' ('Le Manifeste Chanel' 1958).

Apart from offering an escape from fashionability and the dangers of temporality, fashion media's attention to detail had also economic reasons. As observed by Roland Barthes, 'One detail is enough to transform what is outside meaning into meaning, what is unfashionable into Fashion, and yet a "detail" is not expensive…the detail consecrates a democracy of budgets while respecting an aristocracy of tastes' (Barthes 1990: 243). While Barthes in his *Fashion System* interrogates the 1950s French fashion media, the semantic value of the so-called 'little nothing that changes everything' was even much stronger in the socialist fashion magazines' efforts to fulfil the dreams of their female readership while being limited by the repressed socialist market which was unable to deal with changing and desirable images of femininity.[10]

GENDER ISSUES

The Chanel suit did not fit into the socialist sartorial narrative only because of its timelessness. By the late 1950s, it happened to be an updated version of the early socialist dream that envisioned women wearing clothes that would be as equally uncomplicated, practical and sexually neutral as those worn by men. Speaking of herself in third person, Chanel apparently told Salvador Dali, 'Chanel always dressed like the strong independent male she had dreamed of being.' Socialism started with a utopian desire to abolish gender difference. New man and new woman were supposed to be equal. For the early Bolsheviks, the role model for both sexes was the Nietzschean *Übermensch*.[11] But, after initial postrevolutionary experiments with a unisex vision of gender, socialism returned to the most traditional patterns of womanhood, leaving behind the image of a masculinized woman on a tractor. Moreover, in the Khrushchev's Soviet Union women were actively discouraged to wear trousers. Instead, prettiness and elegance were officially promoted, both in the Soviet Union and the Soviet bloc countries.

Yet, the fact that Coco Chanel was inspired by male dress codes in her design contributed to her appeal within the field of socialist fashion. Socialism always borrowed selectively from Western fashion, and recoded those borrowings to suit its ideological needs (Bartlett 2010). In that context, socialism was not interested in Chanel's dandy or English aristocratic references, but the link between Chanel jacket and workers' and soldiers' clothes was an appropriate reference.[12] A smart suit that could be related to a uniform of the preferred social class was an ideal option. Moreover, a functional yet conventionally elegant Chanel suit appeared to be an efficient shortcut to Western smoothness and femininity. But, for socialism in general, there was a dignity in a dress code that could be traced to a working-class origin. In this dress code, proletarian austerity was not abandoned; it was just embellished with the categories of prettiness and elegance.

The Chanel suit never lost its status of an elegant yet practical and functional dress. Its eternal allure was only supported with the romanticized stories on Coco Chanel and her life published in the socialist fashion media. Her social background of having been an illegitimate child brought up in an orphanage, and her determination to succeed against all the odds, was much emphasized.[13]

Her appreciation of fake jewellery was also praised. The Czech *Woman and Fashion* reassured its readers that 'women can be beautiful even without diamonds and sapphires' (Solarová 1971). In those stories, Coco Chanel was presented as a role model, almost a friend who could give you a few tips on how to achieve the perfect style. Such articles were carefully orchestrated in the socialist fashion media. *Sibylle*'s fashion editorial 'A Beautiful Day Just for You' presents models, dressed exclusively in Chanel-style suits, in a series of leisure activities: drinking coffee with a friend, strolling in the park, eating at the smart restaurant and visiting a museum. The text accompanying the visuals nevertheless recognizes a reality of a socialist woman, whose life is overburdened with work and family. The images of quietly elegant and discreetly feminine Chanel suits offer a dreamy promise that such a beautiful day, which she would be able to dedicate just to herself, might happen sometime in the future (M. P. 1964). Women were encouraged to be feminine but were unable to perform femininity as a commoditized activity within a system burdened by permanent shortages and poor-quality clothes. The images of socialist Chanel suits were embedded in the world of socialist realism, meaning that they were executed only as perfectly crafted representational samples. Socialist factories could not produce such clothes on a mass scale. As expert on socialist realism, Evgeny Dobrenko observed, 'The problem of the Soviet economy was always one of representation. Ideology filled the gaps in the system by supplying the feeling of happiness that was lacking…of course in the realm of imaginary' (Dobrenko 2007: 6). While the high-end fashion magazines had an important role within this realm, the regular advice columns in the more mass-oriented publications resolved the strange encounter between the fantasy world of high fashion and socialist dysfunctional consumerist reality. Those columns communicated to their readership that the fantasy could be achieved by self-provision. As the ideological pressures transformed into softer versions, socialist women could wear a Chanel style suit but had to knit or crochet it themselves. In 1971, the Czechoslovak magazine *Woman and Fashion* published two Chanel-inspired suits. Those suits were published in the magazine's do-it-yourself pages and were not made of Chanel signature soft tweed but crocheted and were accompanied by drawings and patterns ('Háčkovaný dvojbarevný kostým' 1971).[14]

In fact, the Chanel suit was not only ideologically imposed. Socialist women were pleased with dresses which emphasized their femininity, in preference to the latest fashions. They lived in an ideological and economic limbo, and their ideas of what they longed to wear and how they dreamt of looking were informed both by the scarcity of information about Western fashion trends and by official socialist concepts of gender and taste. Thus, the appropriation of Western fashion was informed both by the cultural isolation to which women were exposed and by their limited material resources. The timeless chic of Coco Chanel was ideologically approved by the regimes and embraced by many women who favoured her effortless elegance over the new trends. Whether a woman internalized the official concepts of gender and taste or simply could not afford a new suit each season, a Chanel-style suit seemed to be an ideal option. It did not clash with the socialist ideals that permitted smartness but banned any excess.

The Chanel suit was standardized but nevertheless polished uniform. While in the early utopian phase of the socialist projects, both in the Bolshevik Russia and Eastern Europe, women did not like the austere and masculinized uniform that the regimes wanted to impose on them, a Chanel-style uniform was welcomed by socialist women. In his essay 'Chanel's Cosmos', Richard Klein describes Jackie Kennedy in her pink Chanel suit following the assassination of President John F. Kennedy in Dallas in 1963 as 'a soldier in politics': 'Seeing Jacqueline in that photo we realized, perhaps for the first time, that this woman of such elegance, such informed intelligence and taste, was also a soldier in politics, wearing Chanel's uniform on this occasion in which she was compelled to be First Widow ... Her Chanel suit said she was dressed to do her duty' (Klein 1998: 251). Under the different ideological circumstances, wearing their versions of the Chanel uniform, socialist women also tacitly agreed to be 'soldiers in politics'.

CONCLUSION

Paul Poiret's definition of Chanel's style as 'misérabilisme de luxe' encompasses what socialism needed and indeed borrowed from Coco Chanel: smartness polished to a highest degree that nevertheless managed to look modest and simple. Socialism embraced the Chanel suit at a specific historical moment, starting in the late 1950s and lasting throughout the 1970s. This encounter took place when both socialism and Chanel left their revolutionary ideals behind and, consequently, embraced sartorial convention. Although Coco Chanel might have seemed an unlikely comrade for her socialist counterparts, she was a natural choice as she was merely perfecting, season after season, the same smart woman's work suit. On the other hand, while the modernist impulses had been calmed down, their traces were still visible. Both Chanel and socialism wanted to dress woman in a suit that—concerning comfort and a neutral, standardized shape—would make woman equal with man. For socialist women, equality came with a price. The Chanel suit allowed them only a controlled amount of smartness and femininity, and they had to crochet it themselves. Ultimately, it turned them into disciplined soldiers of socialist fashion.

NOTES

1. The research was partially funded by the British Academy Small Research Grant, 2009–10.
2. Divisions among women's magazines started to develop very soon following the end of the war based on differences in the symbolic production of fashion. For example Hungary had the popular weekly *Woman's Journal (Nők lapja)* and the elitist monthly *This Is Fashion (Ez a divat)*, while Czechoslovakia had the popular weekly *Vlasta* and the elitist *Woman and Fashion (Žena a móda)*. In the Soviet Union, the weekly *Working Woman (Rabotnitsa)* was accompanied by a smarter monthly *Fashion Journal (Zhurnal mod)* and the even more elitist *Fashions of the Seasons (Modeli sezona)*, which was published four times per year.
3. The Soviet Union established its central fashion institution Dom modelei (House of Prototypes) in 1935. Following the end of the Second World War, the newly founded socialist countries under the Soviet political influence followed the same route. Czechoslovakia was the first to inaugurate its central fashion institution in 1949, and by the mid-1950s Hungary, East Germany and Poland accepted the same model. One of the main activities of these central fashion institutions was the organization and participation in the annual socialist fashion contests, which each year were held in a different socialist capital. The first of these events took place in East Germany in 1950, and only Czechoslovakia and the host country took part in it. Soon they were joined by the Soviet Union, Hungary, East Germany, Poland, Bulgaria and Romania, each of them showing their own new collection. These gatherings were initially modestly called 'Contest in Dress Culture' but eventually acquired the pompous title 'Socialist Fashion Congress' at the Moscow event in 1959. This activity lasted to the very end of socialism, with the last socialist fashion congress taking place in 1990.
4. For example, during the *American National Exhibition* held in Moscow in 1959, American fashion was presented by four 35-minute fashion shows that took place each day, each of them attended by 3,000 to 5,000 Russians. The clothes, consisting of youthful clothes, leisure wear, daily ensembles and formal long evening dresses, were selected from a regular offer on the shelves in the American department stores. As the Soviet citizens could not buy such clothes in their stores, fashion contributed the huge propaganda effect that the *American National Exhibition* provoked in Moscow.
5. For an overview of socialist realism, see Heller 1997 and Dobrenko 2007.
6. For the application of Wilcox's concepts to the socialist realist literature, see Balina 2000.
7. Fashion historian René König recognized the petit bourgeois essence of socialist good taste: 'The union of the beautiful and useful, which was sometimes called functionality, is in no way humanistic, but, in the best of ways, 'petit-bourgeois', as it can embellish everyday life without a trace of transgression, at the same time damaging any impulse towards real creativity' (1988: 272).
8. Klára Rothschild was a prewar Hungarian fashion designer, who was allowed by the communist regime to reopen her salon after the war, but her salon did not carry her name anymore. It was called Különlegességi Női Ruhaszalon (Special Dresses Salon for Women) and renamed Clara Salon in 1976.
9. Observing similarities to her styles from the 1920s and 1930s, the Western media pronounced Chanel's 1950s collections conservative and old-fashioned (de la Haye and Tobin 1994). Valerie Steele (1993) claimed that, contrary to the French and English, only the American magazines, which themselves feared fashion changes, praised Chanel after her comeback in 1954.
10. In the West, the postwar woman and notion of femininity were socially articulated in the context of advanced consumer economies. For an overview, see Nolan 2003, Carter 1997 and Ross 1996.
11. For an overview of visual representations of early Bolshevik woman, see Waters 1991; on the concept of the Nietzschean Superman within the Bolshevik culture, see Glatzer 2002.
12. For an overview of the mixture of various social class elements in Chanel's suits, see Garelick 2001 and Rose 1969.
13. For example see Czartoryska 1964. The Croatian women's journal *World* also published a couple of stories on Chanel, depicting her life and her fashion (1971: N 2; 1974: N 20).

14. The Hungarian *This Is Fashion* published advice on knitting your own Chanel suit in its column 'Kézimunka' (no. 3 [1965]: 17). A hand-made Chanel suit was also presented on the cover of *This Is Fashion* (no. 5 [1964]), while the advice on the DIY version accompanied Barbara Hoff's article on Chanel suit in her fashion column in *Przekrój* (Hoff 1959: 20–1).

BIBLIOGRAPHY

Balina, M. (2000), 'Playing Absolute Time', in M. Balina, N. Condee and E. Dobrenko (eds), *Endquote: Sots-art Literature and Soviet Grand Style,* Evanston, IL: Northwestern University Press, 58–74.

Barthes, R. (1990), *Fashion System,* Berkeley: University of California Press.

Barthes, R. (2006), 'The Contest between Chanel and Courrèges. Referred by a Philosopher', in *Roland Barthes: Language of Fashion,* Oxford: Berg, 105–9.

Bartlett, D. (2010), *FashionEast: The Spectre That Haunted Socialism,* Cambridge, MA: MIT Press.

Carter, E. (1997), *How German Is She,* Ann Arbor: University of Michigan Press.

Czartoryska, C. (1964), 'Mademoiselle Chanel', *You and I,* 3 (March): 10–13.

de la Haye, A. and S. Tobin (1994), *Chanel: The Couturiere at Work,* London: Victoria and Albert Museum.

Dobrenko, E. (2007), *Political Economy of Socialist Realism,* New Haven, CT: Yale University Press.

Garelick, R. K. (2001), 'The Layered Look: Coco Chanel and Contagious Celebrity', in S. Fillin-Yeh (ed.), *Dandies: Fashion and Finesse in Art and Culture,* New York: New York University Press, 35–58.

Glatzer Rosenthal, B. (2002), *New Myth, New World: From Nietzsche to Stalin,* University Park: Pennsylvania State University Press.

'Háčkovaný dvojbarevný kostým' (1971), *Woman and Fashion,* 8: 18–19.

Heller, L. (1997), 'A World of Prettiness', in T. Lahusen and E. Dobrenko (eds), *Socialist Realism without Shores,* Durham, NC: Duke University Press, 51–75.

Hoff, B. (1959), 'Kostium Chanel', *Przekrój,* 15 February: 20–1.

Klein, R. (1998), 'Chanel's Cosmos', *Sites: The Journal of Twentieth-century Contemporary French Studies,* 1/1: 251–62.

König, R. (1988), *Umanità in passerella,* Milano: Longanesi.

Kovásc, M. (1968), 'Chanel Chanel', *This Is Fashion,* 5: 12–13.

'Le Manifeste Chanel' (1958), *Vogue (Paris),* September: 120–3.

M. P. (1964), 'Ein Schöner Tag für Sie Allein', *Sibylle,* 3: 36–49.

Nolan, M. (2003), 'Consuming America, Producing Gender', in R. L. Moore and M. Vaudagna (eds), *The American Century in Europe,* Ithaca, NY: Cornell University Press, 243–61.

'Photo Report on the Hungarotex Export Fashion Show' (1966), *This Is Fashion,* 8: 4–5.

Rose, F. (1969), 'Chanel Always Now', *Vogue,* December: 116–22.

Ross, K. (1996), *Fast Cars, Clean Bodies: Decolonization and the Reordering of French Culture,* Cambridge, MA: MIT Press.

R. V. (1959), 'Chanel 1959. Pariz: Jesenja moda za normalne žene', *Globus,* 22 August.

S. K. (1960), 'Ambasador mode', *Globus,* 6 June, 28–9.

Solarová, H. (1971), 'Ženy mohou být krásné i bez briliantů a safírů', *Woman and Fashion,* 8: 8–9.

Steele, V. (1993), 'Chanel in Context', in J. Ash and E. Wilson (eds), *Chic Thrills,* Berkeley: University of California Press, 118–26.

Waters, E. (1991), 'The Female Form in Soviet Political Iconography, 1917–32', in B. Evans Clements, B. Alpern Engel and C. D. Worobec (eds), *Russia's Women: Accommodation, Resistance, Transformation,* Berkeley: University of California Press, 225–42.

Wilcox, D. J. (1989), *The Measure of Times Past: Pre-newtonian Chronologies and the Rhetoric of Relative Time,* Chicago: University of Chicago Press.

5
ADVERTISING MEN'S UNDERWEAR
shaun cole

Pity the poor underwear manufacturer. His product is usually small. The variety of shapes in which his ware is sold is extremely limited, and respectable society is at best reluctant to see the product too explicitly shown ... About the best the maker can hope for is to seek a way for the person modeling his latest creation to do it in some eye-catching manner— without exceeding the limits of current convention.

(Goodrum and Dalrymple 1990: 201)

This statement seems at first to underline that there is not a great deal to the advertising of men's underwear; that as the garments are small and hardly vary in form, there is little that could be done in terms of advertising such goods, and so by association such advertising is not worth investigating. However, the reality belies this assumption. In the 130 years that underwear manufacturers have been producing advertisements to sell their wares, there has been a multitude of approaches to the way in which these garments have been promoted. Certainly since the 1980s, with the changes in approach to the representation of the male body in mass media, the garments have become secondary to the body upon which they are portrayed, and the place of such representation has been afforded an important role in discussions of fashion, masculinity and contemporary culture. But there is a full and interesting history of men's underwear advertising that existed prior to Calvin Klein's groundbreaking 1982 presentation of his branded designer garments. The mid-twentieth century saw a huge boom in underwear as a 'designed' item in which form and function were closely linked, offering a rich area for investigation in relation to the media in which it was promoted.

In addressing men's underwear advertising, a number of problems are posed, associated particularly with the fact that its visual representation falls into the interstice between the fully clothed man and the male nude. Fashion historian and curator Richard Martin noted these problems were specifically centred around 'masculine cultural identity, definitions of male discretion, and the engineering principles of the underwear garments vis-à-vis the human body' (1992: 19). Social insecurities about displaying the semiclothed male and notions of cultural modesty led to a series of techniques which underplayed the body upon which these garments would be worn. Alongside such approaches was a focus, in the written text, upon how fit, comfort and ease of care were key to selling male underwear to both men and women in the mid-twentieth century. As in advertising more broadly, it was the combination of forthright or ambiguous images and extensive descriptive and explanatory text in mid-century men's underwear adverts that offer a rich source for investigation.

Adverts for men's underwear appeared in popular weekly magazines such as *Punch, Picture Post* and the *Radio Times* in Britain and *Life* and *The Saturday Evening Post* in the United States, which had both male and female readership. Men's underwear advertisements also appeared in men's specialist interest or hobby magazines, such as *Flight*. Whilst there were no fashion-specific magazines aimed at the general male consumer in the mid-twentieth century, trade press magazines such as *Menswear,* published by Emap, provided a rich source of advertisements for men's undergarments. The adverts featured in this journal were a mixture of those that also appeared in more general press and those specifically created to promote the benefits of the garments to retailers and encourage them to promote and sell those specific brands to their male and female customers.

William O'Barr (1994) identifies two types or motivations in advertising, the primary being the messages that are openly portrayed about the qualities of the goods or services advertised, and the secondary being ideas that are conveyed about society and culture: so, for example, in many mid-century men's underwear advertisements, the fact that women were primarily responsible for laundering such garments is implicit, although there were also adverts in which this message was made explicit. Helga Dittmar (2008) develops on this notion explaining how psychological rather than functional motives for purchasing advertised goods are linked to underlying value systems that place a strong emphasis on financial wealth and material possessions as a means to achieving important life goals. Thus underwear advertisements that present happy father/son or broader familial relationships underpinned mid-century notions that heteronormative family life arrangements were synonymous with success and happiness. While underwear may seem to be a frivolous means of achieving such goals, the adverts that emphasize comfort and fit and particularly those which juxtapose the comfortably underwear-clad male with a dressed and successful working man or sporting figure are promoting messages that if comfortable and well-fitting, underwear sets up the wearer to concentrate on achieving quotidian tasks or life goals. The notion of jealousy or comparative success and pleasure (as further elaborated by Dittmar [2008] and Rachel Bowlby [1993]) is also apparent in men's underwear advertisements, particularly those such as Musingwear's photo-strip series, which appeared in *Life* magazine in the late 1930s and early 1940s, in which one man is comparing his new and better undergarments to those of his friend, colleague or teammate, which are old-fashioned, less well-fitting and uncomfortable.

ILLUSTRATION OR PHOTOGRAPH

Although printing techniques such as the half-tone process made the use of photographs possible in newspapers and periodicals from the late 1880s, it was not until the late 1940s that photography began to challenge illustration as the favoured type of image in men's underwear advertising. In 1936, British trade journal *Advertisers Weekly* had stated that hand-drawn illustrations were preferable to the realism of photography, as depicting an undergarment on 'the masculine form is to reveal it in its most undignified and ridiculous garb' and 'to show the garments themselves is not only dull, but useless, for one brand looks much the same as another' (Jobling 2005: 124). This form

5.1. 'He's a Big Boy Now', advertisement for Jockey in *Life* magazine, 1937. © Jockey International, Inc. Used with permission

of illustrated advertisement remained the primary image type in Britain until the late 1960s, in contrast to the United States where photography took prominence over other image forms.

When Coopers introduced its Jockey brief in 1935, the window display at Marshall Field department store in Chicago was comprised of full-sized underwear-clad mannequins and posters and a life-size photograph of model Hugh Millen wearing Y-fronts and the new sleeveless athletic undershirt. In the photograph, Millen stands with his legs akimbo, hands on hips: a pose that drew on images in physique photography. Despite his not being as muscle-bound as the physique models, he is still suitably athletic and therefore modern. In the late 1930s, Coopers began to include photographic images similar to that of Millen alongside other photographic images, illustrations and line drawings in its American and British ads (see Figure 5.1). A double-page advertisement in British trade journal *Menswear* in 1939 juxtaposed two small illustrations of silhouetted figures wearing 'spring styles' against a photographic image of a man, who, while posed similarly, is tucking his vest top into his Y-fronts. The same figure reappeared in 1942 when the text emphasized ease of wear and the country's national interests and in a 1952 *Menswear* advertisement alongside the Olympic torch under the banner 'Ease in Action'. Variations of this pose also featured in American advertisements in 1952, such as in *The Saturday Evening Post* ('How much does comfort cost?'); additionally, there were adverts that appeared in *The Saturday Evening Post* and *Life* magazines in 1954 and 1955, where the strapline 'It's in style to be comfortable' was further emphasized by images of fully dressed men. It was not only Coopers who used this confident masculine pose in its advertisements: in Britain in *Punch* magazine, Meridian used it to declare 'my word for underwear is Meridian', while Harvester used a figure cut off at the neck to state that its underwear was 'a head above the rest!', with design, detail and fabric that gave 'greater comfort and longer wear', and in the United States, Hansley was unbeatable 'for comfort…for ease' in a 1951 advert in *Collier's Magazine*.

ACTIVE MEN

The modern athletic male body had pervaded underwear advertising in the 1930s in adverts such as Meridian's 1939 'Support for Sport' (which appeared in *Menswear*) and continued after the war. Bonnie English has noted that in mid-century advertising, 'salesmanship in print' was often backed up by ostensibly scientific data and testimonials from prominent social figures, including sportsmen (2007: 26). Using named sportsmen to advertise underwear was common in the United States from the 1930s, with each manufacturer and brand having a star sportsman to endorse its garments through the use of its name and image. These sports stars were never shown in underwear; instead they were pictured in sports kit or as a portrait alongside a garment and testimonial, such as in the 1959 Munsigwear advert with baseball star Ed Matthews that appeared in *Life*. Thus the athletic male and the named sportsman were presented as a masculine archetype that 'ordinary' men could emulate by wearing the same underwear. Both professional and amateur cricketers were targeted in the text of a 1952 advert for Lentonia (manufactured by Thomas Reddish) that appeared in *Menswear*. The main image is a batting cricketer demonstrating the 'freedom of action' that is afforded by Lentonia's garments, which are illustrated on a smaller, formally posed figure (that nods to Millen) in the bottom right. The importance of the mesh fabric is emphasized by forming the background of the 'box' in which the smaller figure is placed. Three years earlier, the Cellular Clothing Company had used cricket to sell its Aertex brand 'underwear, shirts and pyjamas for the Active Man' in an advert that combined photographic and drawn images. A small, sketchy drawing of a cricket pavilion sits behind two 'active men' photographed in active sporting poses: one dressed in cricket whites with a bat, and the second striking the same pose in a light-weight athletic union suit.

During the Second World War, men were presented in advertisements (for a whole range of products, as diverse as towels, cigarettes, boot polish and dairy products as well as underwear) as heroes, fighting the good fight, during times of national crisis and economic hardship. Just two months after the outbreak of the war, in November 1939, Chilprufe ran an advertisement in *Punch* that declared its underwear was 'Best for National Service' (see Figure 5.2). Alongside a drawing of an underwear-clad man that had been used the previous year in an advertisement for the same garments ran the lines, 'To keep really fit for long hours of duty in trying conditions you must be *warm and comfortable.*' This use of slightly altered text and an identical image reflected a quick response to the needs of men who were signing up for an active role in the war. A 1940 advertisement in *Flight* magazine hinted at warfare through an airplane and a uniformed, seated man, as well as declared that Y-front underwear was 'scientifically designed underwear ideal for the man in uniform'. American adverts, such as Coopers' 'What's a "Skivvy" to a "Civvy"?' for *Life* from 1945, also used uniformed men to highlight the war effort and shortages to civilians. Nottingham-based company Cooper and Roe promoted the shrink-resistant qualities of its Shepherd Wool garments in 1942 with an image of sheep (rather than the wearer) to emphasize quality of materials. Its wartime-specific 'Stella utility' ranges (in cotton mixtures and rayon) emphasized 'durability, comfort and shape-retention' in 1943 with a line drawing of a man sitting on a stool in a bathroom getting dressed, a form of image that had been popular in prewar years. Both these advertisements included the CC41 utility mark to stress the 'coupon value' of the garments in times of hardship, and the appearance in the trade journal *Menswear* emphasized this point to both retailers and consumers.[1] Banner's immediate post-war advert also brought together similar notions, stating that the brand stood for 'complete comfort plus hard wear', which had been 'appreciated...during the war years'.

NEXT BEST THING TO NAKED

After the end of the Second World War, underwear manufacturers began to make up for the shortages of the war and encourage a renewed vigour in consumer spending, advertising innovative new fabrics, new colours and patterns, and developments which increased comfort. It was specifically through the advertisements' text that comfort was emphasized as a key selling feature. Coopers' Jockey Y-front briefs had, from their launch, emphasized the masculine support in the styling of the front pouch, and other brands similarly described the benefits of the cut and construction of their garments. In 1947, Expanso shorts were promoted for their newly patented 'balanced-bias cut' which 'prevents Creeping, Crawling, Chafing, Binding'. Two years later, Hanes used a similar selling point for its new bias-cut Givvies shorts, which would not give the wearer the 'creeps'. 'New Comfort—Plus Support' stated the banner headline of a 1943 Reiss Scandals advert in *Life,* while in British *Menswear,* Conbrief more methodically promoted its 'scientifically constructed garment featuring a new method of crotch formation and assembly' alongside a photograph that

November 1 1939   PUNCH or The London Charivari

ROLLS-ROYCE

Rolls-Royce Limited wish to state that, at the request of the Government, they have TEMPORARILY ceased to manufacture motor car chassis.

This has enabled the whole of their manufacturing resources to be devoted to Government work.

The Company are in a position to supply Rolls-Royce cars from stocks of cars completed and in process of completion at coachbuilders.

All enquiries should be addressed to:
ROLLS-ROYCE LIMITED
129a Preston Hill, Kingsbury, near Harrow, Middlesex. Telephone: Arnold 2131
or 14-15 Conduit Street, London W1. Telephone: Mayfair 6201-6

5.2. Page from *Punch*, November 1939, showing 'Best for National Service' advertisement for Chilprufe alongside advertisements for Rolls-Royce and Mitre Bond stationery

followed the format of physique photographs (much like Coopers' Millen image) and was similar to advertisements promoting physique photographers' studios and those advertising male posing pouches that appeared in British physique magazines such as *Health and Strength*.

One of the developments that also aided comfort was the use of nonshrink fabrics. British company Courtaulds advertised its new 'Viscana' viscose rayon short—which was 'comfortable to wear, lasts long' and 'doesn't shrink'—in *Illustrated* magazine in June 1953 (see Figure 5.3). An element of humour was built into some of these adverts as a counterpoint to the sometimes-problematic representation of the male body. Promoting its new 'Duo-Shrunk' process, Wolsey compared the discomfort of traditional nonpreshrunk garments to the instance of the 'modern' 'Duo-Shrunk man', wearing beautifully fitting shorts and vest in a 1949 advert in *Menswear*. A similar theme was used four years later in *Punch* when the modern 'Wolsey type' who 'shows his form in lightest wool, Well-tailored and athletic' was compared to the old-fashioned 'Earnest sweater' in his 'rustic underclothes that cause his brow to drip'. In a long-running series of adverts for its Jockey brand which appeared in a variety of weekly magazines including *Life*, Coopers used humour to portray the embarrassment in social situations of wearing uncomfortable underwear, assuring the wearer that 'Jockey's patented Y-front construction gives mild, restful support, eliminates squirming, assures convenient no-gap opening' (see Figure 5.1). American company Duofold played with a similar notion in *The Saturday Evening Post* in 1946 for its 'Du-Ons' one-piece underwear, using a cartoon illustration of the fidgeting man 'aping' a pretzel by tying himself up in knots with discomfort when not wearing Duofold's comfortable undergarments. According to Richard Martin (1995), such advertisements offered a new way of thinking about men's underwear that was less serious than many of the previous, earnest advertisements that focussed on the processes of buying and selling; the new advertisements allowed questions about the intimate relationship the wearer had with his undergarments to be asked.

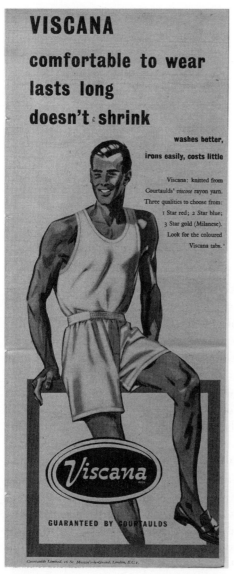

5.3. 'VISCANA Comfortable to Wear Lasts Long Doesn't Shrink', advertisement for Viscana in *Illustrated* magazine, June 1953

THE UNDERWEAR-CLAD BODY

Some adverts juxtaposed a clothed body with images of the flat garments or an underwear-clad body in a similar pose. Each of the adverts in Coopers' late 1950s 'Feels Better Because It Fits Better' campaign featured a photographic image of a suited man with graphic device that leads the eye to the underpants it is implied he is wearing (see Plate 16). A British advertisement for Coopers' Y-front from 1953 also uses the comparative dressed/undressed image with the text 'FOR EASE…AND COMFORT' running at a diagonal between a small drawing of a suited man on the telephone and a larger image of the same man in his Y-fronts and matching vest in the centre of the image. In an advert that was intended for trade use appearing in *Menswear,* Sunspel (1948) featured a close-up of the detail of its cellular fabric with line drawings of shorts/trunks and vest into which the fabric was made and two fully dressed men over the top of the fabric detail (see Figure 5.5). Nine years later, Harvester announced in the same journal that it was 'leading the field for FREEDOM and COMFORT' by juxtaposing a photograph of its flattened briefs and vest against an illustration of a running figure wearing the same garments, thus allowing the consumer to see how they provided 'firm, gentle, positive support' on the body. In the mid-1940s, Munsingwear ran two campaigns in *Life* magazine in America that juxtaposed a fully clothed figure against that of an underwear-clad man. One featured sportsmen, stating that to play the sport like a professional you needed to 'dress like this'. The other for its 'Stretchy-seat' underwear showed two rear views of men bending over, both fully dressed and only in underwear, to emphasize this comfort detail of the garments.[2]

A number of brands used the idea of cropping the male form at the neck and thighs to show the underwear-covered male form but to emphasize an idea of anonymity and the 'everyman'. These adverts appeared both in the trade and popular press, such as *Punch.* Pegasus' 1952 ad used this image to promote the postwar reintroduction of its 'Center-front' briefs, which had a Y-front opening similar to Coopers but with an additional seam in 'the obvious place for an opening' as well as a 'longer waist rise for comfort'. An advert for 'Underwear in "Celanese" Fabric' from 1952 used this cropped male form posed in a semblance of movement and activity alongside a block of text that opened 'FOR COMFORT' and reinforced the idea of comfort, the lightness and hard-wearing qualities of this manmade fibre fabric. Two years later (in an advert in *Illustrated* magazine) Luvisca (made from Courtaulds 'Viscana' knitted fabric) placed garments in a similar pose but rather than cropping the body at neck and thighs in its illustration, it removed the body completely. The trunks and vest are drawn as if on a body in motion, and the sense of the body that should be inhabiting these garments is represented by the text, which reads, 'sound value long-lasting really comfortable' and is placed as part of the image to represent the head and arms of the wearer (see Figure 5.5). The previous year, Courtaulds itself had promoted the benefits of identical garments but sold under the Viscana label. In this instance, again in *Illustrated* magazine, they are presented on a suave, athletic-looking male figure, who is sitting casually on a graphic element box that emphasizes the brand logo. The way in which the man's leg is raised to allow him to perch on the box means that the garments are portrayed in an almost identical pose to both the Luvisca and Celanese adverts of the preceding two years (see Figure 5.3).

Other advertisements presented the garments without actually depicting a semiclothed (or semi-naked) body. Such techniques fell in with the point made in *Advertisers Weekly* on 5 November

1936 that to 'show them on the masculine forms to reveal it in its most undignified and ridiculous garb' (cited in Jobling 2005: 124). 'Morley Winter Underwear' in 'shrink resistant Theta' advertised in *Menswear* in 1952 had photographs of two styles of underwear laid out flat, and in 1954 Celanese used a drawing of its 'Wool acetate staple blend' trunks and short-sleeved vest, which were depicted crumpled as if just removed from the body, in *Menswear*. Guardian's 'Step Out' advert of 1959 implied the male figures wearing sets of both long and short underwear by using an illustration that had the garments walking across the page as if populated by a living body. Whilst these adverts completely removed the body from the undergarments or the advert image, others hinted at the bodies under the garments. In this postwar period, the male body had not yet been confronted as it eventually would in men's underwear advertising. As the technology of garments changed and they became closer fitting, the idea of the body was addressed. A 1943 advertisement for Du-ons by Duofold, which appeared in American weekly *Saturday Evening Post*, claimed that wearing these garment was 'like wearing a shadow'. An illustration of a silhouetted, naked male body, with its modesty masked by a towel, cast the shadow wearing the 'one smooth garment' that 'can't "bunch-up" on you!' British company Tenbra used a similar technique in 1959 with clear drawings of singlet vest and trunks over a silhouetted male figure standing arms akimbo.

In order to avoid showing a realistic male human form, some advertisements—such as a mid-1950s series for Hanes in *Life* magazine, which featured photographs of its garments laid flat over cartoon line drawing illustrations of men and boys engaging in activities such as hunting, fishing and gardening—combined two representational techniques. By 1956, Hanes was depicting the garments on anthropomorphized animals in a series of 'chalk' drawing advertisements. This technique further reduced the possibility of needing to show men's bodies and especially what was inside the briefs and was used in adverts in both trade journals such as *Menswear* and other popular press such as *Punch* and *Life*. Celanese used a drawing of a vest on a half-mannequin in an advert, for 1951, replicating how the garment might be displayed in men's clothes shops to hint at the corporal form that would wear the garment without needing to use a real body. The following year, a similar image was used but with close-up details of 'mesh' and 'interlock' fabrics to advertise 'New Textures'. In 1944, Pegasus used a similar technique with a photograph of a three-quarter male shop mannequin, and in the late 1960s Jockey photographed its garments on a full shop mannequin.

IN THE PRIVACY OF HIS OWN HOME

Interior locations such as locker rooms and bedrooms have often been used in adverts to justify why men may be together in their underwear. In some instances, the whole room is not shown, but single items are used to signify a domestic situation. A mirror serves a double purpose, as it both signifies the bedroom or bathroom and allows the advertiser to show both the front and back views of the garments. A 1950 advert series for Jockey used a mirror not to reflect the figure but as a cartouche to frame the text and illustrations explaining the benefits of Jockey underwear. In Montfort's postwar ad of 1946, a line drawing of a man shaving in a bathroom (a scenario frequently used both before the war and right up into the late twentieth century) accompanies the specifically end-of-the-war text that contrasts the age of utility, deprivation and rationing with a

5.4. 'Sunspel the XXth Century Man's Underwear', advertisement for Sunspel in *Men's Wear*, 17 January 1948

new vision for the future: 'After years of restrictions and uniformity, underwear designed primarily for comfort and style is once again becoming available.' Meridian's adverts from the same year, which appeared in both *Menswear* trade journal and *Punch* magazine, used the strapline, 'Every smart man knows dressing up begins with MERIDIAN' but with different pictures. Smaller body text aimed at retailers in the *Menswear* version acknowledges the postwar restrictions on 'dressing up' but, like Montfort, notes the improvements to come by stating, 'Things are getting better', as the garments now once again have buttons and elastic waistbands, which had been sacrificed to war efforts in the preceding five years.

Chilprufe for Men's 1955 advert for woollen underwear that appeared in *Punch* also uses a domestic interior environment (possibly a bedroom) as the setting for its illustration, which places

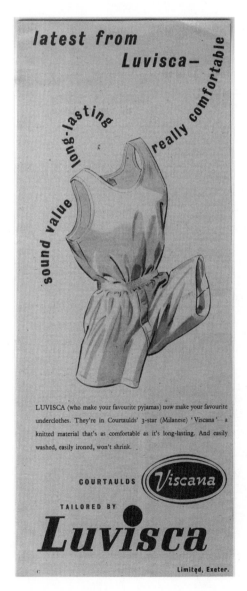

5.5. 'Latest from Luvisca', advertisement for Luvisca in *Illustrated* magazine, 1952

two men together. The older sits in a director's chair while the other perches on what may be a bed to light his cigarette. The text immediately to the left of the image—'active service underwear'—implies that this could be a military scenario in which these men are enlisted in military service or undertaking their National Service duties. The main text of the advert highlights the qualities of the brand's underwear, concluding that 'there is lasting comfort, fit, and immaculate appearance'. The scenario is similar to those common in men's underwear advertising before the Second World War and has, as both Paul Jobling (2005) and Bruce Joffe (2007) have identified, an ambiguity about the relationship between the two men. The act of lighting a cigarette in an intimate location could perhaps be indicative of a burgeoning sexual relationship between these two underwear-clad men. Or, given the age gap, they could just be father and son.

APPROVED BY WIVES AND MOTHERS

During the 1950s, an increasing number of underwear advertisements promoted both men's and boys' garments and tied into notions of postwar domesticity. Elaine Tyler May (1999) contends that family life was configured as a vision of reassuring certainty in an unpredictable and threatening world. Suburban domesticity in the 1950s ascribed complementary gender roles within the family: men were breadwinning fathers and husbands but also had to fit ideals of 'masculine domesticity' (Osgerby 2001: 68). Magazines such as *Picture Post* and *Illustrated* in Britain and *McCall's* and *Life* in the United States carried advertisements which promoted both men's and boys' underwear in the same advert through portrayals of fathers and sons engaging in a range of sporting and domestic activities. In 1946, Banner declared, 'Their Protection is Yours' alongside an image of a man sitting on a bed and an image of a boy in similar underwear. Between them in a separate drawing lie a variety of flattened undergarments, implying both the protection of the body through Banner underwear and of British children by fathers who had fought in the war. Meridian used a father-and-son bonding moment of a pretend boxing match in a bedroom in an advert in *Illustrated* magazine in 1954 (see Figure 5.6). The fact that underwear was so similar to boxing outfits, and indeed gave its name to a particular garment, perhaps justifies the semiclothed condition of men and boys in adverts in such poses. The popularity of Meridian underwear that is 'made of he-man stuff' is attributed to the combination of 'softness and flexibility' and 'tough resistance to wash and wear'.

These familial scenes were designed to appeal not just to the male wearers of the garments but also, and perhaps more importantly, to their wives and mothers. The language emphasized elements that would to appeal to the female buyer, particularly as the majority of men had their underwear purchased for them by women: by the early 1950s in Britain, women were buying 85 per cent of underclothing, a survey by Smith & Co. discovered (Jobling 2005: 129). Harvester's 1946 ad, versions of which ran in both *Picture Post* and *Menswear*, declared, 'made only for men and boys' but 'thoroughly approved by wives and mothers'; the main drawing shows a father and son, and there is a smaller drawing of the head of the approving mother and wife. The small print text highlights why the underwear appeals to both male and female members of the family, noting the construction and wear for males and women who wash and mend the garments can 'appreciate the coupons it saves'. After asking, 'What do women know about men's underwear?', a 1954 Meridian ad points out that 'women know which materials wash best and wear longer' and with their 'shopping sense' know how to 'get the best value for money'. The language in Durene's 1952

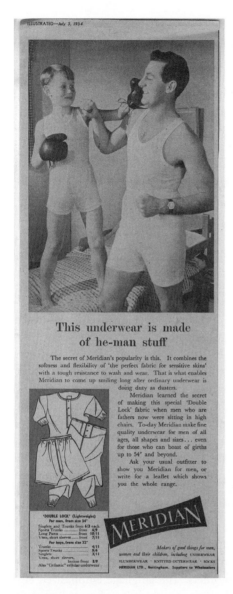

This underwear is made
of he-man stuff

The secret of Meridian's popularity is this. It combines the
softness and flexibility of 'the perfect fabric for sensitive skins'
with a tough resistance to wash and wear. That is what enables
Meridian to come up smiling long after ordinary underwear is
doing duty as dusters.

Meridian learned the secret
of making this special 'Double
Lock' fabric when men who are
fathers now were sitting in high
chairs. To-day Meridian make fine
quality underwear for men of all
ages, all shapes and sizes... even
for those who can boast of girths
up to 54" and beyond.

Ask your usual outfitter to
show you Meridian for men, or
write for a leaflet which shows
you the whole range.

MERIDIAN

'DOUBLE LOCK' (Lightweight)
For men, from size 34"
Singlets and Trunks from 4/3 each
Sports Trunks _____ from 4/9
Long Pants _____ from 10/11
Vests, short sleeves ____ front 7/11

For boys, from size 22"
Trunks _____ 4/11
Sports Trunks _____ 3/6
Singlets _____ 3/11
Vests, short sleeves,
button front 3/9
Also "Cellastic" cellular underwear

Makers of good things for men,
women and their children, including UNDERWEAR
SLUMBERWEAR · KNITTED OUTERWEAR · SOCKS
MERIDIAN LTD., Nottingham. Suppliers to Wholesalers

5.6. 'This Underwear Is Made of He-man Stuff', advertisement for
Meridian in *Illustrated* magazine, 3 July 1954

advert is aimed entirely at the female readers of *Ladies Home Journal,* giving instructions on what
to look for when buying a husband's underwear. The imagery illustrates the garments but not the
men who would wear them.

'Made for men... Who think a lot of their wives' reads the headline on a 1946 advert for Harvester, which pairs this idea with an image of an underwear-clad man looking at a picture of his
wife on the mantelpiece. This heterosexual gazing is in contrast to the ambiguity of relationships
that occurred in a large number of prewar adverts where two men were portrayed together in a domestic environment that could be interpreted as indicative of a homosexual interaction and intention (Jobling 2005; Joffe 2007; Cole 2010). Like many other adverts advertising directly to both
the male wearer and the female carer of these garments, the text has two emphases: firstly, that

of the man's consideration for his 'little woman', who has to wash, mend and spend the clothing coupons and, secondly, that 'most men agree that HARVESTER is about the most comfortable and sensible' underwear. The emphasis on value for money that would appeal to 'thrifty' housewives in both these examples was common in British and American adverts throughout the 1940s and 1950s. Some adverts aimed at the female consumer featured images of women alongside the men wearing the garments. When launching its Viscana range of men's underwear in 1940, the adverts (featured in a promotion in the trade journal *Menswear*) featured cartoon-like images of both men and women in various domestic situations, including a husband and wife each reading an announcement about Viscana's new men's underwear in a newspaper. Each ad also had a small drawing in the bottom right in which a sales assistant is telling a female shopper, 'They wear wonderfully, Madam! And no special washing instructions are needed.' A large body of text that is also included in these adverts highlights the 'foolproof washing', 'real hard wear' and 'perfection and comfort' of Viscana, reinforcing the points made in the illustrations. The inclusion of women in men's underwear advertisements served to detract from a male-only intimacy and offered a more reassuring heterosexual view. So, in many instances the emphasis on the nuclear family was key, and the women were shown commenting on their menfolk, as in a 1948 Hanes advert in *Life* magazine in which a wife and mother discusses garments 'for my *two* boys . . . three and thirty!' and, for the same company, in a 1959 advert, where a photographic image of two women holding up 'one kind of underwear' is placed beneath line drawings of very different types of husbands.

CONCLUSION

The mid-twentieth century saw a huge boom in underwear as a designed item in which form and function were closely linked. This led to a diverse range of illustrative techniques to show the benefits and unique selling features of each brand to both male and female consumers, whilst also contending with questions of the appropriate form in which to show male bodies. In an age in which sexuality and gender roles were being increasingly questioned, the sexual and homoerotic ambiguities of earlier advertisements were increasingly replaced by images of the masculine sporting hero and concerned, respectable family man, but almost always there was a continued emphasis on masculine support, fit and comfort.

ACKNOWLEDGEMENT

I would like to thank Giselle La Pompe Moore for her assistance with picture research.

NOTES

1. In Britain, during the Second World War, clothing rationing was introduced in June 1941. Alongside rationing the British government introduced the Utility Clothing Scheme, through which manufacturers were encouraged to produce a limited range of garments in approved fabrics. All utility garments were labelled or stamped with the CC41 utility mark.
2. This pose raises a huge number of thoughts and questions about men, masculinity and male sexuality, the viewer and the gaze. It is explored in more detail in Cole 2010 and 2012.

BIBLIOGRAPHY

Bowlby, R. (1993), *Shopping with Freud,* London: Routledge.

Cole, S. (2010), *The Story of Men's Underwear,* New York: Parkstone International.

Cole, S. (2012), 'Considerations on a Gentleman's Posterior', *Fashion Theory,* 16/2: 211–34.

Dittmar, H. (2008), *Consumer Culture, Identity and Well-being: The Search for the 'Good Life' and the 'Body Perfect',* Hove: Psychology Press.

English, B. (2007), *A Cultural History of Fashion in the Twentieth Century: From the Catwalk to the Sidewalk,* Oxford: Berg.

Goodrum, C. and H. Dalrymple (1990), *Advertising in America: The First 200 Years,* New York: Harry N. Abrams.

Jobling, P. (2005), *Man Appeal: Advertising, Modernism and Menswear,* Oxford: Berg.

Joffe, B. (2007), *A Hint of Homosexuality: 'Gay' and Homoerotic Imagery in American Print Advertising,* Philadelphia: xlibris.

Martin, R. (1992), 'Fundamental Icon: J. C. Leyendecker's Male Underwear Imagery', *Textile and Text,* 15/1: 19–32.

Martin, R. (1995), '"Feel Like a Million!": The Propitious Epoch in Men's Underwear Imagery, 1939–1952', *Journal of American Culture,* 18/4: 51–8.

May, E. T. (1999), *Homeward Bound: American Families in the Cold War Era,* New York: Basic Books

O'Barr, W. (1994), *Culture and the Ad: Exploring Otherness in the World of Advertising,* Oxford: Westview Press.

Osgerby, B. (2001), *Playboys in Paradise: Masculinity, Youth and Leisure-style in Modern America,* Oxford: Berg.

Section 2

PAINTING, PHOTOGRAPHY AND FILM

6

FASHION AND THE LAW
THE MUSLIM HEADSCARF AND THE MODERN WOMAN
barbara vinken

If fashion has made headlines in the popular media during the last decade, it was mainly for two reasons: for anorexia and for the Islamic headscarf and the niqab, the covering of body and face, the 'visible Muslim' (Tarlo 2010). The concern with body weight, and with the ideal body promoted through fashion photography, publicity and fashion shows seems negligible, though, compared to the uproar a simple piece of cloth, the headscarf, has caused. This is no surprise in a global situation no longer determined by the clash of ideologies but by a 'clash of civilizations' due to the by now almost proverbial 'return of religion'. Courts and parliaments in France, Germany, Canada, Belgium, Spain and Italy have debated over the hijab, and public battles have raged. Laws have been passed: France banned the headscarf in public schools in 2003 and the niqab from public spaces in 2010, as did Belgium—in both countries, it is now forbidden to wear the niqab on the street. The European Court of Justice has intervened to determine whether these dress regulations violate human rights. Germany has negotiated in sixteen courts whether a teacher should be allowed to wear a headscarf in the classroom (Oestreich 2004; Bahners 2011). Rarely has a piece of cloth stirred such public debate and legal and media attention.

The political debate has been carried out on a different level in fashion, in both collections and the media. What is prohibited by the law has been thematized—and often embraced—in fashion collections, photography and advertisements.

One of the not-so-subtle ways of addressing the debate was Flavio Lucchini's vision of the veil in a series of fake *Vogue* photographs at the Venice Biennale in 2011 (Plate 17). There was not a hint of eroticism, and Lucchini was obviously not attracted by the ostentatious show of what was in hiding. Hide-and-seek was not his game. The images he presented did not fascinate; rather, they mourned the loss of what classical fashion magazines feature: irresistible femininity, elegance, chic and trendiness. Eyes are the only thing you see of these women; sometimes even the eyes are hidden behind a grid in order to heighten the effect of imprisonment and exclusion. They are never made up in spite of this irresistible oriental fashion, which promises everything under the veil. Any trace of eroticism was carefully erased by Lucchini. His cloaked women were much more reified than fashion dolls dressed up by designers. The spectres of the past will not vanish, Lucchini implies; enshrouded women will be the global future. These cloaked women are not tempting and do not want to tempt us. Lucchini sees in the burka what the Catholic Church sees in the veil of the nuns: a renunciation of beauty, carnal love and flirtation. It marks the end of the modern, emancipated woman and thus brings to an end an erotic, courtly relationship between the sexes (Plate 18).

In contrast *Vogue,* in its fashion shots of headscarves, went heavily oriental. To assure the viewer that truly everything, even a headscarf, can be terribly sexy, the magazine accessorized the models with all the erotic fetishes Western fashion had to offer. This seems less off the mark than the Lucchini campaign.

The headscarf can certainly be used in a revival of odalisque sensuality, as both a modest and a sexy item.[1] The headscarf is not necessarily a renunciation of all things worldly; it does not have to mark the rejection of worldly seduction, femininity and beauty. On the contrary, the headscarf has become—and may have always been—a fashion accessory. And what is true for every clothing item holds true for the headscarf as well: it does not matter what you wear, but how you wear it. The headscarf can do much more than just cover the hair as a *pars pro toto* of feminine charms; the way one covers the hair can be an attraction in its own right. YouTube videos explain which colours to choose, which material is the most becoming, and the most alluring ways to tie the scarf. No wonder that the Turkish turban and the headscarf have almost become mainstream. In its advertising campaign of spring 2011, Bloomingdale's urged New Yorkers to 'get scarfed'. The neologism 'scarfed', clearly alluding to the headscarf, is also a pun, since you hear in it both 'scar' and 'scarf'. The stigma that the headscarf is—and that should now be worn by everybody and thus destigmatized—carries in this ad the tribal moment. It alludes to the scars of African tribes that, together with tattoos, have become all the rage in the modern capitals of the West. In the West, this advertisement suggests, room should be given to the scars but also to the scarf—the Other of modernity.

In the discussion of the scarf and burka, parts of the fashion media, of the art world and also of the collections themselves, have offered a subtle self-reflection of the Western fashion industry. The French 'niqabitches' and the Parisian anonymous artist Princess Hijab are examples of such a self-reflective intention. A great reflection on the naked and the clothed via the burka and niqab was the point of the Hussein Chalayan collection of spring/summer 1998 with its naked, half-naked and veil- and burka-covered bodies. Such veiling and baring of the female body was already the theme of Alba D'Urbano (*Couture: Die Stücke der Kollektion 1995–97*) and adapted by Chalayan to the headscarf and burka.

The law, however, was less flexible than the self-reflection within fashion collections and the fashion media. Compared to this, the verdicts passed were astonishing. While laws on how to dress were common, as consumption laws, throughout the Middle Ages, they had disappeared from modern Europe. Louis XIV, the sun-king of France, abolished the last luxury restrictions in the seventeenth century. The last law passed in Europe prescribing what to wear was enacted by Napoleon: it denied women the right to wear trousers (Wolter 1994). It is thus at first sight not so much the burka or the hijab but rather the legal debates surrounding them that are 'medieval' (Nordmann and Vidal 2004: 6). For the first time in decades, the freedom of how to dress has been drastically limited. Only once before was there a curiously similar debate, interestingly also with an oriental link, about an allegedly offensive way of dressing: whether the naked belly, which was a rage some seasons ago, should be permitted in French public schools. However, there were no laws passed in the case of naked bellies. A study of the relationship of oriental modes of clothing to the fashion of the modern age would be a most fruitful project. Already, in the first modern female silhouette, there was oriental translation at work: Paul Poiret, who succeeded in doing away with the corset, attempted in vain to introduce another oriental feature instead, namely the North African male pants.

If there were consumptive prescriptions and laws up to modernity—on who was allowed to use what fur and in what length; how deep the décolleté could be cut; on what colours were allowed to whom; and similar rules—they disappeared with the triumph of the bourgeoisie. Dress codes, based on mutual consent—on customs of the country, so to speak—came into use. To dress properly became a question of breeding and know-how, but was of no legal concern; numerous books were written on how to dress for success, but no laws were written. Legally, everybody was entitled to dress as she or he pleased.[2] There are within the West still some law-like remnants, which are actually enforced, but these are relevant in private spaces outside of public jurisdiction where specific requests are in place. Churches in Italy and mosques in Istanbul are such places. Modesty is a norm in Catholic churches. Women have to cover shoulders, décolleté, arms and thighs; men must cover the upper body and thighs. Shoes must be removed in order to enter a mosque (though this seems to have nothing to do, originally, with modesty but with hygiene). In certain clubs in the United States and Britain, you may have to wear a tie, tailored trousers and formal shoes to be admitted. But there are no longer any restrictions, prescriptions or laws on how to dress in public. In most cities, you cannot simply go naked, but this is the only limitation when it comes to rules of dress. Generally speaking, the public is open to fashion in the West.

This is quite different outside of Europe and North America, where laws on how to dress have been passed in direct, pointed response to modernization. One could argue that the path to modernity for non-Western countries was paved by laws and governmental initiatives forcing the dress of modernity on their public appearance. In some countries, Western clothes had to be worn by law in public or at public functions. In early twentieth-century Japan, men employed in the service of the state, such as policemen, teachers and railway officials, were ordered by imperial decree to abandon the traditional kimono (which was a Chinese import and thus of foreign origin anyway). Japanese officials had to wear Western suits. Similarly, army and school uniforms followed Western fashion by decree. Women did the same, and like the men adopted Western fashion; they went West by choice. Thus in the 1930s the kimono had become, even for women, a folkloristic relic in Tokyo, like a Bavarian *dirndl* in Munich. Similarly, when Atatürk led Turkey into modernity, he followed emphatically, with aplomb, the French model of *laicité*. He banned the headscarf as a religious symbol from the Republican space of schools, universities and court rooms; the Turkish parliament, too, was until very recently free of headscarves. Accordingly the father of the last Persian Shah, Reza Pavlevi, also banned the chador.

Today, the modern world as embodied in Western fashion seems under pressure in its very own 'heartland', and European nations such as France feel compelled to act like Atatürk in the 1920s, defending modernity by confusing the public space of civil liberties with the Republican liberation from religious repression. Once again the stakes of modernity are played out on the female body (Göle 2005), as evident already in the historical prelude of the French colonial politics in Algeria (Shepard 2004). Modernity has to defend itself, it seems to many, with utterly antimodern measures (Balibar 2004: 24). How can this be explained? 'Are we so despicable and impure in your eyes that you refuse us any contact, any relationship, not even a polite smile?' was Élisabeth Badinter's argument against the burka in the French weekly *Le Nouvel observateur* in July 2009:[3] an argument in favour of decorum and politeness, of courtly behaviour, of the public space as a space of exchanging glances and smiles, of giving and receiving pleasure with our fellows. Fine, but should the discretion to apply such politeness be a matter of the law, and can it, will it, be the same if enforced by law? Will anybody feel like smiling if she is obliged to wear it, unscarved, on her lips?

What is at stake in the ideological fight around the headscarf and burka is women in public spaces. Those who oppose the headscarf and burka consider both as symbols of suppression, as the enforcement of female subjection to their Islamic husbands, brothers and fathers. If you allow it to be worn, women will be forced to wear it, seems the underlying certainty. Women who wear them are considered as being denied the right to self-determination (Schwarzer 2002). They deserve to be protected by an emancipated civil society against their backward male families and patriarchy in general (Delphi 2004). As Gayatri Spivak put it, fittingly in the language of children's books from colonial times: brown women are defended by white men against brown men (Spivak 1988); but we have to add, sad to say, this wisdom of children applies to white women as well, these days.

Worse, if girls and women are not forced to wear the veil but wear it of their own accord, they are said to underwrite their subordination and unwittingly endorse the alienation from their own sexuality. They must be freed by force for their own good (Nordmann 2004). According to this opinion, the niqab and also the headscarf become essential symbols of the negation of a founding value of modern societies—the equality of the sexes (Scott 2005). This strife, from the perspective of a French Republican, was always opposed by the very antagonist of the French Republic: religion—the Catholic Church—which is seen as the very counterpart to modernity, a patriarchal institution set on seducing or subjugating women (Vinken 2004; Borutta 2010; for the impact of this model on Algeria, see Fanon 1968). In parenthesis one might add that punishing women for not properly wearing the niqab, the stock argument of the protectionists, is also a rather modern phenomenon stemming from and enacting the open confrontation with the modern. In brief, to be modern means to fight the niqab, to fight the hijab and thereby defend the principles of secularized societies. It means to strengthen the self-determination of women, who are endangered by patriarchy and the obscure forces of religion. Thus, in the fight against the headscarf and the niqab, Republican traditionalists and feminists have become strange bedfellows, indeed (Fekete 2006; Farris 2012).

Two assumptions form the basis of these prohibitive tendencies in law and civic affairs: First, that the headscarf is a clearly determined religious symbol, and second, that women and men appear in the same way in public display of their sexuality. The Hebrew Bible and the New Testament are much more explicit on the subject of covering female hair than the Qur'an (Wielandt 2009). And let me remind you, that our great-grandmothers, and even our grandmothers, would not have dreamed of going to church without covering their hair. Similarly, the headscarf and niqab are not a religious must, but depend on varying interpretations of the Qur'an. Much more than a religious requirement, they symbolize the fight against modernity, whose battlefield is the female body. The Muslim veil is not a prescription but a custom that greatly varies according to time and place. It is clearly meant in the Qur'anic *suras* as a reminder to dress modestly in public and is linked to social status; thus, it distinguished a free wife from a slave (Nökel 2002; Wielandt 2009).

Today, there is not one but many headscarves and their meaning is situational. It depends on the diaspora and derives its meaning mainly from its relation to the West. The first headscarves I saw were the opposite of modest and were more of a political than a religious statement. It was in Aix-en-Provence in February 1979, just after Khomeini, who had been exiled in France, took power in Iran. Suddenly, Persian girls appeared in university classes with headscarves. The Shah, like Atatürk, had forbidden wearing the chador. Thus the wearing of the chador by these students was no act of modesty but a public demonstration of a triumphant Otherness in opposition to the Shah imposed by the West, and thus a political statement not only in some public space but in the heart of Western ideology, the French Republic.

Peacefully but unmistakably, the empire fought back. It is thus a crass misunderstanding to interpret the wearing of the scarf as a traditional gesture. If there is an Islamic tradition, it is for women to stay completely out of the public space, to stay at home (Rommelspacher 2002; Ghadban 2005). In contrast, a woman wearing a headscarf today makes a public statement—and the most public statement, at that. In the eye of the public, she goes public and is exposed more than a naked girl could be. It is no coincidence that 30 per cent of the women wearing a burka in France do not come from a traditional Muslim background, but are a most peculiar blend of modern converts. Something similar holds for the scarfed girls in Germany. Their mothers, coming from secularized Turkey, usually did not wear a headscarf. These girls wear it very much in public as a protest against the Kemalist, secularized elites in Turkey and the European secularization that did not keep its promise of equality of the sexes (Nordmann and Vidal 2004: 11; Oestreich 2004: 142, 146). They wear it in decidedly modern places, where they do not traditionally belong, such as in the workplace (Klinkhammer 2000a: 266, 2000b; Nökel 2002; Karakasoglu 2003). The headscarf is reclaimed, one is tempted to say, as something stigmatized by the West on its unstoppable trajectory towards 'progress'. This trajectory is said to move towards a greater equality of the sexes, including their public exposure.

To take a closer look at the relation between fashion, sexuality and public space, let us look into a relation taken for granted, between fashion and the modern, *la mode* and *modernité*, *Mode* and *Moderne.* Ever since the French Revolution, fashion has been linked to the free individual in democratic, capitalist societies. Fashion and bourgeois democracy became synonymous. In democracies, where nobody would prescribe what to wear, the lower classes could still imitate the upper classes. The dynamics of fashion described by sociologists embodied with its trickle-down effect the desire for democratic upward mobility (Simmel 1997). Nobody's place was fixed by birth; everything could change by one's own effort, starting with fashion.

And yet, the relation of fashion to modernity, far from being a simple support for upward mobility, is fraught with ambiguities, ambivalences and paradoxes. There is a blind spot in this relation between fashion and the modern that remains invisible from the vantage point of its ideology. It is this blind spot, I would like to argue, that is brought to light, betrayed by the veil, the *foulard,* the headscarf. A most telling witness to the ambivalence remaining between fashion and modernity is the fashion discourse which remained up to now strangely split. For there is fashion and fashion. While male fashion is not properly speaking fashion but rather a functional garment without superfluous adornment, classical and in universal success clearly modern, female fashion is a remnant of the old aristocracy, a frivolous frill, an all-in-all dysfunctional ornament, in constant need of impossible modernization. The 'new woman' is born in agonizing pain, and perpetual and perennial fall-backs have to be witnessed: Dior's New Look, which included the unhealthy corset, limiting every movement, is the classic example for such a fall back; a slap in the face of the modern aesthetic dogma that form follows function. Ornaments like frills on the dress reappear again and again in recent seasons. In a way, female fashion proves to be not fit for reform; it cannot become fully modern. Female fashion is bound to contradict modernity. This line of argument connects Adolf Loos with Le Corbusier; its latest version is Anne Hollander's *Sex and Suits* (1995), an argument with a twist, though, highlighting not function but beauty—that is, the sexiness of the male suit. It is only male fashion—thus not fashion in its true sense—that is modern. All modern innovations of cut have been made by male tailors of male suits, never by female milliners. Women should do everything to catch up with the fashion of the modern as fast as they can to conform to the beauty of modern aesthetics. Coco Chanel is seen as a trendsetter on this stony path of fashion and femininity towards the modern.

On an analytical level, one might say that fashion has never separated the sexes strictly before in modernity—that is, roughly speaking, before the French Revolution. As a consequence, it becomes feasible that the separation of the classes in the old regime was replaced by a probably even more rigid separation of the sexes (see Plate 19).

Not only did men and women never dress more differently than after the French Revolution, but also their relation to sexuality differed radically. Within the old aristocracy before the Revolution, both sexes highlighted the attraction of their bodies: emphasizing male legs and the buttocks, even exposing for a while (during the Renaissance) an oversized, seemingly erect member in a *braguette;* while women's décolletés could drop so deep that the bare nipples were on view (see Plate 20). After the Revolution, things changed drastically; it was now the female sex alone that marked its sexuality by a display of eroticized body parts, while the male sex went markedly unmarked (Flugel 1930). Gaultier's witty revival of the *braguette* in 1986 was bound, as he himself clearly foresaw, to be a complete failure, and his kilts for men met with the same calculated failure.

That the relation to sex was thus radically different for the sexes implied their relation to modernity: while men were dressed for work or sport—functionally, that is—women were to become, and expose themselves as, pure ornaments. Jil Sander's fall/winter 2010 advertising campaign shows the female body transformed into an arabesque (another oriental reminiscence). Like *mobilia,* Thorstein Veblen has put it most strikingly, women adorned their keepers. By exposing a body utterly unable to work, fashionable women showed that they had to be kept, and at a very high cost, at that. Their distinction was their inability to work. They illustrated the financial power of their husbands and lovers. A woman's function was to be functionless, a man's ornament. Women therefore could not be modern (Veblen 1924); this included their inability to implement a functional aesthetics (Bartlett 2010).

As the Other of modernity, fashion performs the return of the repressed. In fashion, the vanished aristocracy returns in the wives of the bourgeoisie, and the bourgeoisie exposes the castration of both, the aristocracy and women, putting the erotically charged female body on display and excluding at the same time women from power (Vinken 2006). Since it was the female body on which aristocracy entered the scene of modernity, this body was eroticized with such consequence. This heavy influence of the bygone aristocratic era on female fashion manifests itself in recharging the female body as an erotic body—citing how both male and female bodies looked in aristocratic display. This eroticization can happen through denudation, but there are many other ways; it might also be achieved by the upholstery and padding of erotic parts like breasts and hips. Yamamoto's lines did nothing but stage, in a playful, ironic way, a historical refashioning of the female body in the court masks of the sixteenth, seventeenth and eighteenth centuries.

However, the female fashion of modernity not only bared the breasts like earlier centuries, but also legs and bottom, the erotic domain of male fashion. It would be a mistake to understand so-called 'unisex' as a generalized adaptation of male fashion. There is an additional sexual kick in the female version of unisex, since female trousers, aside from being practical, expose what a woman had to hide before: legs and buttocks. One of the last steps in the total eroticization of the female body was to uncover or expose hair, an overtly sexual message; straight out of bed, one might say. Thus, everything that used to be covered—a lady would never leave the house without a hat and gloves, never show bare legs, of course, and, evidently, always do her hair—was laid bare in public. Far from a unifying effect, the systematical enhancement of her erotic qualities makes the female appearance into the radical opposite of modern manhood. Not so, though, rhetorically. Rhetorically these strategies were advertised as 'comme des garçons'. Under the banner of unisex and emancipation, women should become modern at long last. The systematic eroticization of the female body was performed in a strange disguise, in the guise of modernization, whose hallmark was and remains masculinization. It is thus a crucial misunderstanding to write the history of fashion as a history of emancipation or as the coming into being of the new, finally modern woman. The effect of cross-dressing, once upon a time Chanel's credo—'I took everything male and made it female'—had as its main effect a shifting of erotic zones (Steele 1991). Women appropriated the erotic male zone, which had been abandoned by modern men. The basic divide between female and male dress—marked versus unmarked sexuality—was never questioned; it remains unquestioned in the fashion of the West. Today it is marked as rigidly as it was after the French Revolution, at the beginning of the bourgeois era. Still, this divide runs between the functional male body and the erotic female body. A fashion like trousers might happen to be functional, but this was always a pretext, a rationalization.

The headscarf and hijab are more than a symptom in this process; they are a political response to the eroticizing subjection of the female body and have thus begun to reveal in an extraordinary fashion the modern dialectics of the gender divide. The strategies of eroticization are *ex negativo* addressed in the headscarf and hijab, but they are no less visible in the so-called Muslim fashion of modern times. This Muslim fashion is a reaction against the female fashion of the West by applying

Western fashion in a way that completely twists its purpose. It is thus no reactionary response but firmly situated within the modern dialectic of showing and veiling (König 2007). By wearing a loose dress or coat over loose trousers, Muslim fashion covers what is laid bare in Western fashion: the female silhouette, the bottom and the legs. In an appropriation in the negative, Turkish women wear trousers the same way a man would wear them, and reverse the process this piece of dress underwent in being adopted into female fashion of the West by reversing the means of its eroticization: these trousers are the opposite of sexy, tight-fitting jeans. In turn, Western fashion has begun to re-appropriate the Muslim silhouette over the last three or four years as a dress worn over trousers or leggings. This was a previously unthinkable and, in fact, senseless move in Western fashion, where you wore either trousers or a skirt but not one on top of the other. Going West, the Muslim silhouette, born out of the desire to hide what is shown, is erotically re-charged—and once more reversed. In the Western adaptation, the Muslim jeans become super-skinny, so that they show the legs, and the skirts, super-short, are made from a clinging, soft material that reveals the silhouette from feet to bottom.

By veiling what Western fashion bares, Muslim fashion points to the fact that the female fashion of the West keeps pretending to be modern but has in fact fastened women in a realm that once was the Other of modernity. Paradoxically fashion keeps things as they were by dressing women as modern. Women in the modern world are ornamental, and as an arabesque, they are indeed oriental. Today's Muslim fashion brings to the light of day that men and women in modernity are not what they are content to assume: equal. They cannot appear, as far as their sex is concerned, in the same way in public, because their unisex equality is everything but a settled achievement.

NOTES

1. While there is, of course, also the modernist rejection of the veil, such as in the Turkish *Vogue*, there are other journals like the Turkish journal *Âlâ*, which feature the odalisque 'oriental beauty'.
2. There were nevertheless some exceptions concerning gender appropriateness and sexual orientation. In the Netherlands and New York State there were laws in the first half of the twentieth century regarding gender-appropriate clothing. In New York, at least three items of gender-appropriate clothing had to be worn, and in the Netherlands, the trousers worn by women had to be unequivocally women's—with a side opening instead of the front fly.
3. 'Sommes-nous à ce point méprisables et impurs à vos yeux pour que vous nous refusiez tout contact, toute relation, et jusqu'à la connivance d'un sourire?'

BIBLIOGRAPHY

Badinter, E. (2009), 'Adresse à celles qui portent volontairement la burqa', *Le nouvel observateur,* 9 July (2331).
Badiou, A. (2004), 'Behind the Scarfed Law, There Is Fear', *IslamOnline.net,* 3 March, www.lacan.com/islbad.htm, accessed 1 August 2013.
Bahners, P. (2011), *Die Panikmacher: Die deutsche Angst vor dem Islam: Eine Streitschrift,* Munich: Beck.
Balibar, E. (2004), 'Dissonances dans la laïcité', in C. Nordmann (ed.), *Le foulard islamique en questions,* Paris: Editions Amsterdam, 5–27.

Bartlett, D. (2010), *FashionEast: The Spectre That Haunted Socialism,* Cambridge, MA: MIT Press.

Borutta, M. (2010), 'Genealogie der Säkularisierungstheorie: Zur Historisierung einer großen Erzählung der Moderne', *Geschichte und Gesellschaft,* 36: 347–76.

Delphi, C. (2004), 'Une affaire française', in C. Nordmann (ed.), *Le foulard islamique en questions,* Paris: Editions Amsterdam, 64–71.

Fanon, F. (1968), 'L'Algérie se dévoile', in *Sociologie d'une revolution: l'an V de la révolution algérienne,* Paris: Maspero, 16–47.

Farris, S. R. (2012), 'Femonationalism and the "Regular" Army of Labor Called Migrant Women', *History of the Present,* 2/2: 184–99.

Fekete, L. (2006), 'Enlightened Fundamentalism? Immigration, Feminism and the Right', *Race & Class,* 48/2: 1–22.

Flugel, J. C. (1930), *The Psychology of Clothes,* London: Woolf.

Ghadban, R. (2005), 'Das Kopftuch in Koran und Sunna: Das Frauenbild hinter dem Kopftuch', *Dossier: Konfliktstoff Kopftuch,* 28 June, http://www.bpb.de/themen/IYRYVB,0,0,Das_Kopftuch_in_Koran_und_Sunna.html, accessed 1 August 2013.

Göle, N. (2005), *Interpénétrations: L'Islam et l'Europe,* Paris: Galaade Éditions.

Hollander, A. (1995), *Sex and Suits,* New York: Kodansha.

Karakasoglu, Y. (2003), 'Islam und Moderne, Bildung und Integration: Einstellungen türkisch-muslimischer Studentinnen erziehungswissenschaftlicher Fächer', in M. Rumpf, U. Gerhard and M. M. Jansen (eds), *Facetten islamischer Welten: Geschlechterordnungen, Frauen- und Menschenrechte in der Diskussion,* Bielefeld: Transcript, 272–89.

Klinkhammer, G. M. (2000a), *Moderne Formen islamischer Lebensführung: eine qualitativ-empirische Untersuchung zur Religiosität sunnitisch geprägter Türkinnen der zweiten Generation in Deutschland,* Marburg: Diagonal.

Klinkhammer, G. M. (2000b), 'Zur Bedeutung des Kopftuchs für das Selbstverständnis von Musliminnen im innerislamischen Geschlechterverhältnis', in I. Lukatis, R. Sommer and C. Wolf (eds), *Religion und Geschlechterverhältnis,* Opladen: Leske + Budrich, 271–8.

König, A. (2007), *Kleider schaffen Ordnung: Regeln und Mythen jugendlicher Selbst-Präsentation,* Konstanz: UVK.

Nökel, S. (2002), *Die Töchter der Gastarbeiter und der Islam: Zur Soziologie alltagsweltlicher Anerkennungspolitiken: eine Fallstudie,* Bielefeld: Transcript.

Nordmann, C., ed. (2004), *Le foulard islamique en questions,* Paris: Editions Amsterdam.

Nordmann, C. and J. Vidal (2004), 'La Republique à l'épreuve des discriminations', in C. Nordmann (ed.), *Le foulard islamique en questions,* Paris: Editions Amsterdam, 5–14.

Oestreich, H. (2004), *Der Kopftuchstreit: Das Abendland und ein Quadratmeter Islam,* Frankfurt am Main: Brandes und Apsel.

Rommelspacher, B. (2002), *Anerkennung und Ausgrenzung: Deutschland als multikulturelle Gesellschaft,* Frankfurt am Main: Campus.

Schwarzer, A., ed. (2002), *Die Gotteskrieger und die falsche Toleranz,* Cologne: Kiepenheuer & Witsch.

Scott, J. W. (2005), 'Symptomatic Politics: The Banning of Islamic Head Scarves in French Public Schools', *French Politics, Culture & Society,* 23/3: 106–27.

Shepard, T. (2004), '"La bataille du voile" pendant la guerre d'Algérie', in C. Nordmann (ed.), *Le foulard islamique en questions,* Paris: Editions Amsterdam, 134–41.

Simmel, G. (1997), 'The Philosophy of Fashion', in M. Featherstone and D. Frisby (eds), *Simmel on Culture,* London: Sage, 187–206.

Spivak, G. (1988), 'Can the Subaltern Speak?', in C. Nelson and L. Grossberg (eds), *Marxism and the Interpretation of Culture,* Urbana: University of Illinois, 271–313.

Steele, V. (1991), *Women of Fashion: Twentieth-century Designers,* New York: Rizzoli International.

Tarlo, E. (2010), *Visibly Muslim: Fashion, Politics, Faith,* Oxford: Berg.

Veblen, T. (1924), *The Theory of the Leisure Class: An Economic Study of Institutions*, London: Allen & Unwin.

Vinken, B. (2004), 'Herz Jesu und Eisprung. Jules Michelets *devotio moderna*', in B. Menke and B. Vinken (eds), *Stigmata: Poetiken der Körperinschrift*, Munich: Wilhelm Fink, 295–318.

Vinken, B. (2006), *Fashion Zeitgeist: Trends and Cycles in the Fashion System*, Oxford: Berg.

Wielandt, R. (2009), 'Die Vorschrift des Kopftuchtragens für die muslimische Frau: Grundlagen und aktueller innerislamischer Diskussionsstand', http://www.deutsche-islam-konferenz.de/SharedDocs/Anlagen/DIK/DE/Downloads/Sonstiges/Wielandt_Kopftuch.pdf?__blob=publicationFile, accessed 24 September 2013.

Wolter, G. (1994), *Hosen, weiblich: Zur Kulturgeschichte der Frauenhose*, Marburg: Jonas.

7

FASHION, MEDIA AND GENDER IN CHRISTIAN SCHAD'S PORTRAITURE OF THE 1920s

änne söll

In her book *Seeing through Clothes,* Anne Hollander develops the idea that fashion only exists through visual media. For Hollander, fashion and media cannot be separated. We dress with images of fashion in mind: 'It is an essential fact that without the constant reference of its interpretation, fashion could not be perceived. Certain ways of looking could not be seen as more desirable than others, as acceptable or in need of subversion or further exaggeration, without the visual demonstration that pictures provide' (Hollander 1993: 350). Hollander extends her argument further to claim that clothes are designed and worn in order to work well in certain media and that the right kind of medium can 'elevate the current fashion to the level it aspired to' (Hollander 1993: 331). Thus, it comes as no surprise that, for Hollander, the shift to a creative kind of fashion photography in the 1920s is accompanied by a change in women's clothes which, together with photography and eventually film, produced a look that reflects spontaneity, simplicity and movement. 'Clothes,' claims Hollander, 'are designed for the flashbulb' (Hollander 1993: 329). Painting, she concludes, is at a loss: 'Ever since photography acquired its total graphic authority, it is the painted portraits of people in modern elegant clothing that have become frumpy-looking' (Hollander 1993: 328). Taking Hollander's claims as its point of departure, this chapter will deal with a pair of what Hollander calls 'frumpy-looking' portrait paintings produced at the moment when photography began to be the principal medium for the representation of fashion. The portraits in question, entitled *Count St. Genois d'Anneaucourt* (dated 1927) (Plate 21) and *Baroness Vera Wassilko* (dated 1926) (Plate 22), were painted by the German painter and photographer Christian Schad in the style of New Objectivity (*Neue Sachlichkeit*). In contrast to all of Schad's other portraits, the sitters for these pieces have never been clearly identified, despite the apparent exactness of information regarding their names provided in the titles. Though painted a year apart, Schad conceived the portraits as belonging together, and they should be seen as a couple.[1] Their repeated use as book covers and illustrations in art historical literature on the 1920s has made the pair emblematic of a decade characterized by social and economic upheaval, a decade dominated by a shift in gender relations and radical change in women's fashion, as well as a proliferation of mass entertainment and fashionable nightlife. I will argue here, in opposition to Hollander's view, that these portraits are far from 'frumpy'; that in his treatment of fashion and paint in relation to the gendered body, Schad manages to bring to portrait painting both fashionability and chic in a single stroke. Indeed, as I will argue, it is the very challenge of photography itself that makes these portrait paintings endure and attractive still today. Rather than photography superseding painting, if you will, it is, in fact, the productive tension between the two media, painting and photography, that gives rise to a visual space *in-between,* a space that allows for the gendered body to become visible and negotiable through the embodiment of fashion in paint.

FASHION, PHOTOGRAPHY, PAINTING

With few exceptions, German fashion magazines around the time of the First World War employed studio photographs in the tradition of nineteenth-century portrait photography, which, in the spirit of painted portraiture, showed women in artificial settings in a series of theatrical poses (Figure 7.1) owing much to the dramatized photographic portraits of nineteenth-century actresses (Holschbach 2004: 205–15). Photography was considered an indexical medium that provided the viewer a glimpse of 'reality'. It was mainly fashion illustrations, then, which expressed artistic, individual perspectives on fashion, incorporating references to new ideas on lifestyle, alluding to a narrative and/or referencing a particular avant-garde style, such as expressionism or art deco (Dogramaci 2006). Influenced by what in Germany was called *Neues Sehen* (New Vision), photography became a major player in German fashion media by the 1930s, on equal footing with—if not surpassing—fashion illustration. Laszlo Moholy-Nagy's 1927 book *Malerei, Fotografie, Film* illustrates what the new aesthetics meant for photography: extreme viewpoints, spontaneity, graphically designed images working with strong light and shadow contrasts. Through these techniques, photography was to become a means of artistic self-expression, experimentation and unique style. But for photography to be able to rise to the status of artistic medium, it had to emancipate itself from painting, still considered the superior and most noble medium of art and the one best suited for portraiture. The materiality of paint and its application by the painter was thought to better lend itself to artistic thought than the photographic lens. Light and paper were considered too immaterial to be able to convey what painting could show through the material and physical treatment of paint and canvas. Ernst Kallai's essay 'Painting and Photography', published in 1927 in the Dutch avant-garde magazine *i-10*, opened up a debate that would define the future of photography. Here, Kallai argued that photography lacks what in German is called *Faktur,* or

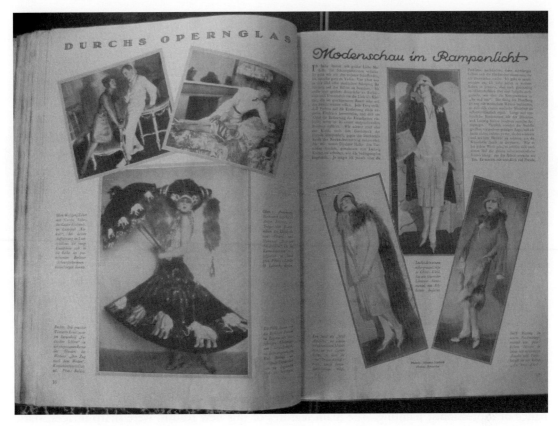

7.1. *Elegante Welt*, September 1926

the visible signs of the artist's application of paint on canvas. Without the physical trace of the artist, photography, in Kallai's mind, was neither able to express the mental state of the artist nor to reflect its own creative process through the treatment of its material. Moholy-Nagy, however, argued that light was, in fact, an artistic 'material' that produced something he called '*Licht-Faktur*', which enables artistic expression in photography as paint does in painting. For Kallai's opponents in the debate, the camera was not merely a technical instrument only able to document reality but the equivalent of the painter's brush and, therefore, a valid means of personal and artistic expression (Kallai 1927).[2] It is through the work of Moholy-Nagy and others that photography emancipated itself from the constraints of its putative indexicality—its status as a tool for recording what is—and began to be seen as a creative medium which would eventually dominate the public domain through its increased use in magazines and newspapers.[3]

In the aftermath of these debates of the 1920s and 1930s, the depiction of fashion in Germany became marked by an ongoing tension between painting and photography. In 1926 and 1927, when Christian Schad produced his couple in question, German fashion photography continued to be dominated by a type of theatrical studio photography in the spirit of Adolph de Meyer and the glamorous fashion portraits of Edward Steichen. Tobia Bezzola astutely discerns the latter's work as inspired and invigorated by and essentially rooted in the tradition of painted portraiture. He writes, 'Steichen's photographs for Condé Nast—as stylistically and methodologically diverse as they are—are united in their drive towards elevating the "lower" genre of portrait photography and fashion photography with the help of painting's traditional strengths, its repertoire of forms and ideas' (Bezzola 2008: 194, my translation). Consequently, Schad's portraits were produced at a time when the boundaries between fashion photography and fashionable portraiture were being re-negotiated. Painting and photography were not merely in competition with one another but rather became participants in a close and productive dialogue. For this discourse, Schad's portraits consti-tute a prime example because they relate both to fashion photography in the manner of Steichen *and* to realist painted portraiture. By painting in the New Objectivity style, he makes reference to photography's indexical qualities at the same time he shows us painting's power to deceive. Com-pared to the relatively stiff and old-fashioned-looking fashion photographs available in German fashion magazines of the mid-1920s, Schad's portraits are cool, subtle and seductive—in a word, modern—using fashion to lure us into an unstable but attractive visual constellation.

Christian Schad always considered himself a painter; he experimented with photography as an artistic medium and created *Schadographs*, cameraless images created by positioning objects on light-sensitive paper, producing uncanny, abstract black-and-white shapes, a technique also used by Man Ray and Moholy-Nagy. By the early 1920s, however, Schad had abandoned this and other practices inspired by Dada and surrealism for what is now known as *Neue Sachlichkeit*. Yet, as a painter, Schad's dialogue with and interest in photography did not end when he stopped his experi-ments in photography in the early 1920s. Painting and photography converge in his oeuvre and are taken up self-consciously, informing one another and played off against each other at the same time: in his paintings in the style of New Objectivity, he uses painting as if he were taking pictures, and he takes photographs in an almost painterly manner.

On the whole, New Objectivity is best described as a reaction against the continued predomi-nance of expressionist painting. The main features of this new realism were sharp images, static compositions and sober engagement with technology and daily life, producing paintings with a smooth, almost shiny surface. Though most artists working in the new mode were well aware of photography as an artistic medium,[4] New Objectivity painting did not necessarily resort to pho-tography to redevelop this new kind of realism. Instead, these paintings relate to a tradition in nineteenth-century realism, the contemporary Italian style of *Pittura Metafisica* as much as cer-tain types of Renaissance painting, especially in portraiture. Schad's travels in Italy allowed him to study Renaissance portraiture first-hand, and it is a well-documented fact that Schad used paint-ings such as Raffeal's *La Fornarina* as inspiration for his own images (Mirabile 1997). But Schad never stopped photographing. In fact, he used his own portrait photographs and pictures of Paris to help create his painted portraits (Lloyd 2003). Considering both Schad's experimental, almost painterly Schadographs and his photographic portrait paintings, it is evident that both techniques inform each other in his work.

Though photography would eventually become the primary medium for representing fashion, it was painting in the form of fashionable portraits that was featured on most covers of German fashion magazines in the 1920s and 1930s. Schads portraits of fashionable ladies and starlets were also used as covers for magazines such as *Die Dame, Jugend* and *Sport im Bild,* as the portrait of the actress Mulino von Gluck from 1930 shows (Plate 23). The employment of portrait paintings as covers is indicative of painting's status as the superior artistic medium. Yet, portrait painting was never considered a medium for fashion but rather the inverse. The portrayal of fashion was thought to be a by-product of portrait painting, since its main aim was to convey the personality and soul of the sitter, not the extravagance or banality of his or her attire. While dress, as Aileen Ribeiro (1999) has made the case for Ingres's portraits, has become an art form in its own right within the genre of traditional portraiture, generally, depictions of clothing and fashion were always considered subordinate to the latter's pre-eminent aims. Nevertheless, clothing and/or fashion in portraiture can develop a life of its own—as the German art historian Wolfgang Waetzold pointed out as early as 1908, writing, 'Independently from the sitter, clothing can develop in its very own interest, a material and structural quality, thereby showing the charms of its surface' (Waetzold 1908: 197). The hierarchy of the arts, separating high from low, or dividing applied arts from fine arts, ensured that in 1926, fashion was still seen to be in the service of portraiture. In his 1926 catalogue essay for one of the very first fashion exhibits in Berlin to combine portraiture and fashionable clothes, the curator Wolfgang Bruhn writes, 'The images of women by classicist painters, by the romantic school, the dynamic painters of representative women's portraiture of the 1850s and 1890s ... all know how to put colour, decoration and the tactile quality of surfaces in the service of portraiture without losing psychological depth' (Bruhn 1926: 4, my translation). So, to Bruhn, the depiction of fashionable clothes puts portraiture in danger of being superficial. Thus, for portraiture not to become a fashion in itself, it had to keep fashion in check. Portraiture, on the other hand, could lend to fashion what fashion did not seem to possess itself—namely, the status of art. In his paintings, Schad works with the tensions between the allure of fashion's surfaces and the noble aims of portraiture. By citing and then reinterpreting the staid-looking German fashion photography of the time with the means of realist painting, he is able to use fashion's potential to play with surface, appearance and depth to disturb ideas of gendered identity.

SEE-THROUGH DRESSES, TRANSPARENT GENDER?

Not being particularly popular at the time of their production, Schad's portraits have only become well-known since the 1960s, when a new wave of interest in New Objectivity began. Schad's self-portrait from 1927, in particular, is one of the most reproduced images of New Objectivity portraiture, owing its notoriety mainly to Schad's see-through outfit, which veils the torso as much as it exposes it (Plate 24).[5] The presentation of bodies in transparent clothes is a feature Schad also employs in the portraits the count and the baroness (Plates 21 and 22). The main contrast in both paintings stems from the difference created by the flimsy, see-through material of women's dresses and the dark opaque surface of men's evening clothing. Though transparent material is more commonly associated with 1920s women's fashion, we also see a male body adorned with translucent fabric in the portrait of the count. The transvestite to the count's right wears a rose-coloured sheath dress that reveals his naked buttocks. The dress leaves much of his back exposed, directing our gaze to a black spot near his upper right shoulder, which might be a mole, a beauty spot or perhaps even a sign of venereal disease.[6] The woman on the count's left and, in the companion piece, the Baroness Vera Wassilko herself, are also wearing transparent dresses, revealing the female bodies beneath. This voyeuristic effect is counterbalanced in the first instance by the diverted gaze of the woman toward the upper-right-hand corner, while the baroness's blank stare appears immune to the viewer's gaze, looking through and beyond its potentially objectifying effect. The bunch of violets, which hold the baroness's dress together, served in the 1920s as a symbol of lesbianism (Schader 2004: 170–5). This suggestion of the baroness's sexual orientation towards other women together with the count's association with the figure of the male transvestite undercut the assertion made by the portraits of the count and baroness as a noble, heterosexual couple. This ambiguity concerning their sexual orientation is likely the reason why the existence of count and baroness could never finally be verified: because of their sexual orientation, they probably were and had to be a product of fiction, and the realist style of New Objectivity helped to make this deception even more effective. Clearly, then, a photographic portrait was never an option.

Whereas the count and baroness themselves show no obvious signs of their sexual orientation, their bystanders do. Especially the body of the transvestite to the count's right is revealed as deviant. Like Schad's own body in his self-portrait, it is exposed as a painted surface, presented as an image to be looked at. The transvestite's dress fits so tightly that the ornamental flowers on the upper part of the garment look as if they are tattooed or painted directly onto his body, collapsing the distance between skin and dress, painted surface and corporeal surface. It is this effect, not the woman's dress alone, that makes the transvestite's body look especially effeminate and brings it in line with the objectification of women's bodies as a 'passive' image, making the (female) body available to the (male) viewer. The effect is underscored by his make-up, which in comparison to the face of the woman on the left, and through difference in colour and brush strokes, is clearly shown as 'painted' on, so that the process of painting is foregrounded as an element of the transvestite's artificialness and gender ambiguity. Moreover, the material quality of the transvestite's transparent dress functions as a double surface that veils and exposes the surface of the painting and the surface of the male body at the same time—an effect that is especially visible in the lower half of the transvestite's body. Instead of presenting the male body as an impenetrable, black surface negating itself, Schad playfully reveals the male body through a layer of translucent paint. The materiality of painting, then, referenced by the transvestite's mask-like make-up—in conjunction with the materiality of the dress as a surface which at once both covers and reveals—is shown to be responsible for the artificial process of making-up and part of the performance of gender displayed here. In the same way the figures in the painting are not always what they appear to be, the 'realism' of the painting is exposed as artificial.

Whereas the women's clothing in these images lets the body shine through, men's dress is characterized by a variety of black evening outfits that mask the body almost completely. This does not mean that the bodies underneath these suits are de-eroticized, however. The male suit is not only part of the 'Great Renunciation' (Flügel 1930) in male clothing since the mid-nineteenth century, it is also a sign of phallic power. What is more, it evokes, as Anne Hollander has shown, an idealized, classical male body that combines male beauty, authority and sex appeal. But, just as the women's dresses do not guarantee a female body underneath or, as in the case of the baroness, women's dress does not necessarily indicate female heterosexuality, the men's tuxedos are equally unstable signs for male bodies and male heterosexuality.

In the count's portrait, this ambiguity is achieved by positioning him between the woman on the left and the transvestite on the right, suggesting his undefined sexual orientation. In the baroness's portrait, ambiguity is introduced by cutting off the heads of the men on either side of her, turning them into fragments. The body fragment of the figure to her right is also supplied with a manicured, female hand which destabilizes the gendered meaning of the tuxedo. Just as the transvestite is in drag, so could the 'man' on the baroness's right be female. Through his ambiguous treatment of the vestimentary signs of sexual orientation and gender, Schad suggests the potential homosexuality of the sitters, hitting the nerve of the contemporary discourse on transvestism, homosexuality and sexual identity. At the time of the painting's production in the mid-1920s, the discussion on sexual identity and gender in Germany was fuelled by the research of Berlin-based sexologist Magnus Hirschfeld, whose findings on transvestism showed that it was not a sure sign of homosexuality but could also be practiced by heterosexuals or bisexuals (Hirschfeld 1920: 236). In the 1920s, even within the homosexual scene, transvestites occupied ambiguous terrain. As Mel Gordon explains, 'Male transvestites projected a weak, jaded, and mocking reflection of same-sex male desire; a dangerous and irreparably haunting challenge to phallocentric gays and their Hellenistic theories of male supremacy and soldierly rectitude of man–boy love. Men in drag were regarded as Untermänner' (Gordon 2006: 120). By dressing the transvestite in women's fashionable evening clothes, which, unlike practical everyday wear for women, emphasized traditional femininity through the generous use of soft, shiny or see-through and flowing material, Schad makes the transvestite look like a parody of femaleness, ridiculing femininity as much as the attempt to look like a woman. 'Real' men, homosexual or heterosexual, could never be seen wearing translucent clothes, as this piece of advice from a men's magazine makes clear: 'A beautiful man impresses through his manly appearance, and if he has taste he circumvents everything, which emphasizes his body in a crude way. A transparent women's stocking can be charming. A transparent men's sock is ridiculous and therefore not elegant. Absolutely no female finesse! It discredits all masculinity' ('Editorial' 1917: 19, my translation).[7] Under no circumstances was the average man's skin to be put on public display and eroticized. Men's bodies were hinted at through the structured surface of the suit that offered a neutral surface. Nothing illustrates these rules better than the juxtaposition of the black-clothed, almost nonexistent body of the count and the rose-coloured body of the transvestite exposed by the flimsy, see-through material. Thus, women dressing up as men could play with or even aspire to the authority associated with men's clothing. Aspiring to or playing with femininity and femaleness, as we see in the rejection of transvestites by phallocentric gay male culture, is not something men should do (Gordon 2006: 120). Men dressing up as women caused unspeakable anxiety over sexual difference and loss of power, that, in contrast to women's masculine dress, 'could not be relieved through any promise of liberation, equality, and casual dressing' (Hake 1997: 188).

As has been proven by a wide variety of research on women's dress in the 1920s, fashion served a key function in the visual process of women's liberation and questions of gender and sexual identities (Hake 1997; Bard 1998; Kessemeier 2000; Follmann 2010). As Sabine Hake points out, 'Many descriptions of the so-called New Woman revolve around fashion... Fashion played an important role in defining modern femininity: as a marker of economic status and social ambition, as an expression of female narcissism and beauty, and as a focus of consumerist fantasies and commodified versions of the self' (Hake 1997: 185). With prewar *Reformkleidung* (reform dress) having paved the way for fashion to signal women's recently acquired literal and figural freedom of movement and the new introduction of ready-to-wear clothing, which made fashion available to a larger section of society, fashion 'came to be associated with a variety of causes, from the fight for sexual freedom and women's rights to the conservative campaigns against rampant consumerism and the Americanization of Germany' (Hake 1997: 185). In the years 1925 through 1929, when Germany enjoyed relative economic stability and Schad's portraits were painted, it was women's fashion that ignited debates about the problems of modernity and 'articulate[d] its contradictions in gendered terms' (Hake 1997: 185). Especially during the mid and late 1920s, women's fashion 'promised sexual liberation, social mobility and narcissistic gratification outside the confinements of traditional identity politics' (Hake 1997: 186). The most hotly debated look was the *garçonne* style, where elements of men's sporting, work and evening dress were adopted by women's fashion, producing a 'flirtation with masculinity' which 'involved a playful staging of identities that was predicated on the full achievement of gender equality, and given the imaginary nature of such assumptions, often highly ironical and self-reflexive' (Hake 1997: 196). Whereas this masculine look for women could already be adopted by certain movie stars such as Marlene Dietrich and other celebrities, causing scandals and much-wanted publicity, men dressing up as women in public remained unthinkable: 'Manliness was all the rage. The men of the twenties searched themselves for vestiges of effeminacy as though for lice' (Crisp 1983: 21). Men's cross-dressing was not part of the public fashionable world but was strictly confined to certain nightclubs, where it could clearly be seen as staged and therefore kept at bay. Schad sets the scene of the count's portrait in such a club when he comments that he had seen the transvestite in the Berlin nightclub Eldorado (Schad 1997). In the Eldorado, fashionable (mostly heterosexual) Berliners and international tourists were presented with equally fashionable transvestites. At the time, the Eldorado was described by a popular guide book about 'sinful' Berlin as a place where 'transvestites have been put on display for national and international tourists … A grande dance hall for an elegant audience. Smoking, evening cut and grande evening dresses—this is how the average person presents him and herself, the guests have come here to stare' (Moreck 1931: 180, my translation). This reveals that the Eldorado was not a club for transvestites, but a club mostly for heterosexuals to look at transvestites.[8] Without necessarily having to question one's own sexual orientation or even gender, the visitor to the Eldorado could experience a space where the world of sex and gender was turned upside down, a space where clothing did not signal one's sexual orientation or gender. The visitor enjoyed this spectacle of exotic deviance, like going to the zoo. Again, the guide book provides a good description of the Eldorado's atmosphere: 'This is right, one can read on the advertisements. An ominous slogan, which gets the imagination going. The place is a stage, only the absolute naive believe the transvestite's authenticity. Even the real transvestites, who make money with their sexual deviance, turn into actors here' (Moreck 1931: 180–1, my translation). And so could the visitors. In play with the real or fake transvestites, the visitors' dress loses its power to denote 'real' gender and sexual orientation, as well. In his portrait of the count, Schad leaves it up to the viewer to decide which stance to assume, whether to take the attitude of the distanced audience described above or to reflect on the gendering effect on one's own clothes. Thus, Schad's presentation of transvestism not only thematizes homosexuality but also raises the issue of heterosexuality as a construct. By making the baroness and count a 'couple', as well as showing each of them in a threesome of unclear sexual orientation, the dichotomy of male/female (husband/wife) is thrown into crisis, a crisis that has been described by Marjorie Garber as transvestism's key function. She writes, 'Transvestism is a space of possibility, structuring and confounding culture: [crisis is] the disruptive element that intervenes, not just a category crisis of male and female, but the crisis of category itself' (1997: 17).

To this crisis of gender and sexual identity can be added one of portrait painting, which was being challenged by photography as prime medium for portraiture and artistic expression in general. This crisis was seen to be connected to a destruction of male, bourgeois individuality through the effects of modernity. The rise of photography was considered to mirror this threat, producing nameless faces of types rather than individual beings (Meyer-Büser 1994: 85–9).

CONCLUSION

The 1920s were a time when the individual, gendered self-image was felt to be in flux, if not altogether in danger. Schad's portraits of the count and baroness address these fears on the level of gender identities in a medium that was equally under duress, using the tensions between painting and photography to make the crisis of gender identity visible. In this, fashion functions as an intelligent membrane that registers these tensions and provides the tenuous, transparent surfaces that negotiate between or collapse the body of the sitter and the materiality of paint, creating an ambiguous and productive illusion of appearances. In the dawning age of modernist fashion photography, Schad produced realist portrait paintings to convey the ambiguous potential of fashion and its relationship to gendered identity. Schad dealt with his media very much on a conscious level, pushing them to their limits: he used his knowledge of photography not to produce realist images but emphasized photography's painterly and tactile quality and photography's potential for abstraction. At the same time, Schad revives portrait painting and brings to the fore its ability to produce colourful, sensuous, multilayered, see-through or opaque surfaces, which seem to be hyperreal. Literally, the gendered, dressed body is seen to be a surface phenomenon. By looking at Schad's *Count* and *Baroness,* 'seeing through clothes' doesn't mean you see the truth or the core; instead you see just another surface open for interpretation.

ACKNOWLEDGEMENTS

For translation and comments, I thank Staci von Boeckmann and Shaun Cole.

NOTES

1. See Schad's commentary in Bezzola 1997: 104.
2. Kallai's thesis was discussed by Willi Baumeister, Wassily Kandinsky, Laszlo Moholy-Nagy and others.
3. By the 1930s, the photographic style of *Neues Sehen* made its way into fashion magazines as part of general reporting on lifestyle issues, travel and so on. It is only in the early 1940s that it is generally used in fashion photography. Because so many photographers who were working in the style of *Neues Sehen* (such as Martin Munkasci) were forced to emigrate to the United States in the 1930s, fashion photography in the style of *Neues Sehen* spread much more quickly in US fashion magazines such as *Vogue* or *Harper's Bazaar.*
4. Most artists who practiced this new realist painting were well aware of new developments in photography and used photographs for their work. Some of them were amateur photographers themselves. For a general overview of the connection of New Objectivity painting and photography in Germany, see Michalski 1992: 180–202.
5. For a detailed analysis of Schad's self-portrait, see Söll 2006.
6. This section of Schad's painting was used as cover illustration for the New York's Metropolitan Museum's catalogue of its show on German portrait painting of the 1920s in 2009 called *Glitter and Doom.* By focusing on the transvestite's face and dark spot, his potentially sick and sexually ambiguous body becomes the sign for Weimar Germany's demise.
7. Although this comment stems from 1917, it is equally valid ten years later at the time of the portrait's production.

8. In 1920s Berlin, transvestites had their own clubs, strictly divided into venues for homosexual or hetero-sexual transvestites. Since there were serious disputes between heterosexual and homosexual transvestites, they would not frequent the same bar; on this issue, see Herrn 2005: 142–3.

BIBLIOGRAPHY

Bard, C. (1998), *Les Garconne. Modes et fantasmes des Années folles,* Paris: Flammarion.

Bezzola, T., ed. (1997), *Christian Schad. 1894–1982,* Zürich: Wienand.

Bezzola, T. (2008), 'Lights Going All Over the Place', in W. Ewing and T. Brandow (eds), *Edward Steichen. In High Fashion, Seine Jahre bei Conde Nast 1923–1937,* Ostfildern: Hatje Cantz: 187–97.

Bruhn, W. (1926), *Das Frauenkleid in Mode und Malerei vom 18. Jahrhundert bis zur Gegenwart,* Berlin: Staatliche Kunstbibliothek.

Crisp, Q. (1983), *The Naked Civil Servant,* New York: Plume.

Dogramaci, B. (2006), 'Die Modefotografie der Weimarer Republik im Spannungsfeld zwischen Modegrafik und Fotoreportage', in U. Rütter (ed.), *Think while You Shoot. Martin Munkasci und der moderne Bild-journalismus,* Hamburg: Conference Point Verlag, 43–58.

'Editorial' (1917), *Die Herrenwelt,* February: 2.

Flügel, J. C. (1930), *The Psychology of Clothes,* New York: International Universities Press.

Follmann, S. (2010), *Wenn Frauen sich entblößen…Mode als Ausdrucksmittel der 1920er Jahre,* Marburg: Jonas Verlag.

Garber, M. (1997), *Vested Interests. Cross-dressing and Cultural Anxiety,* London: Routledge.

Gordon, M. (2006), *Voluptuous Panic. The Erotic World of Weimar Berlin,* Los Angeles: Feralhouse.

Hake, S. (1997), 'In the Mirror of Fashion', in K. von Ankum (ed.), *Women in the Metropolis. Gender and Modernity in Weimar Culture,* Berkeley: University of California Press, 185–202.

Herrn, R. (2005), *Schnittmuster des Geschlechts. Transvestiten und Transsexualität in der frühen Sexualwissen-schaft,* Giessen: Psychosozial-Verlag.

Hirschfeld, M. (1920), *Die Homosexualität des Mannes und des Weibes,* 2nd ed., vol. 3, Berlin: Marcus.

Hollander, A. (1993), *Seeing through Clothes,* Berkeley: University of California Press.

Holschbach, S. (2004), 'Fotografische Rollenporträts und medialer Transfer—Schauspielerinnen im Atelier des 19. Jahrhunderts', in S. von Falkenhausen (ed.), *Medien der Kunst, Geschlecht, Metapher, Code,* Mar-burg: Jonas Verlag, 205–15.

Kallai, E. (1927), 'Malerei und Fotografie', *i-10,* 4: 148–57.

Kessemeier, S. (2000), *Sportlich, Sachlich, Männlich. Das Bild der Neuen Frau in den Zwanziger Jahren,* Dort-mund: Ebersbach.

Lloyd, J. (2003), 'Christian Schad. Reality and Illusion', in J. Lloyd and M. Peppiatt (eds), *Christian Schad and the Neue Sachlichkeit,* New York: Schirmer Mosel, 15–28.

Meyer-Büser, S. (1994), *Das schönste deutsche Frauenportrait. Tendenzen der Bildnismalerei in der Weimarer Republik,* Berlin: Reimer.

Michalski, S. (1992), *Neue Sachlichkeit. Malerei, Graphik und Photographie in Deutschland 1919–1933,* Co-logne: Taschen.

Mirabile, B. (1997), 'Schad und Italien', in T. Bezzola (ed.), *Christian Schad. 1894–1982,* Zürich: Wienand, 155–64.

Moholy-Nagy, L. (1927), *Malerei, Fotografie, Film,* Munich: Langen.

Moreck, C. (1931), *Führer durch das lasterhafte Berlin,* Leipzig: Verlag moderner Stadtführer.

Ribeiro, A. (1999), *Ingres in Fashion: Representations of Dress and Appearances in Ingres's Images of Women,* New Haven, CT: Yale University Press.

Schad. C. (1997), 'Commentary to the Portrait of Count St. Genois d'Anneaucourt', in T. Bezzola (ed.), *Christian Schad. 1894–1982,* Zürich: Wienand, 118.

Schader, H. (2004), *Virile Vamps und wilde Veilchen. Sexualität, und Begehren und Erotik in den Zeitschriften homosexueller Frauen im Berlin der 1920er Jahre,* Königstein: Helmer Verlag.

Söll, Ä (2006), 'Stoffe, Narben, Nähten. Geschlechterdiskurse in Christian Schads Selbstbildnis von 1927', in S. Scholz und G. Engel (eds), *Kopf- und andere Tücher,* Berlin: Trafo Verlag, 103–16.

Waetzold, W. (1908), *Die Kunst des Porträts,* Leipzig: Hirt.

8

CAUGHT ON CAMERA
THE FASHIONED BODY AND THE CRIMINAL BODY
nilgin yusuf

Fashion. noun; a popular or the latest style of clothing, hair decoration or behaviour *the production and marketing of new styles of clothing and cosmetics *a manner of doing something.

Crime. noun; an action or omission which constitutes an offence and is punishable by law *Illegal activities *an action or activity considered to be evil, shameful or wrong.

—Definitions from the Oxford English Dictionary[1]

Fashion and crime are not words that are commonly associated;[2] they represent very different cultural and psychic spaces. Fashion is a sphere that is perceived as ephemeral and transient—constantly renewed and therefore perpetually optimistic. The word *crime,* on the other hand, occupies a darker territory; something hidden or submerged that we understand as negative or threatening. The definitions above, drawn from the Oxford English Dictionary, make explicit their polarities. We consider fashion to be generally legal (although child labour and counterfeiting are clearly not) while crime is unequivocally illegal. We regard fashion as visible, readable and on trend while crime is opaque, shadowy and off radar. Fashion is about the right and acceptable way to dress; crime is about the wrong, unacceptable way to behave. In the lexicon of meaning, these two words, *fashion* and *crime,* could not be further apart.

Yet, despite their disparate starting places, representations of fashion and crime have travelled a strikingly similar journey. It was the media theorist Marshall McLuhan (1964) who first put forward the idea that the medium is the message and through the examination of evolving media technologies, it is possible to map this unexpected relationship. It is the technological interface—or medium—that seals our relationship to these messages of fashion and crime. And central to this, it is image that joins these two diametrically opposed realms of light and dark. It is through the two-dimensional image, still or moving, that we understand, participate in, construct and consume our notions of what constitutes fashion and crime.

It was through researching postwar criminal iconography for a master's thesis that I became increasingly aware of the parallels between perceptions of crime and fashion. For instance both areas, commonly regarded as 'low-brow' in the cultural hierarchy, are imbued with ambivalence and suspicion. This ambivalence seems to generate a similar 'push pull' compulsion among its consumers who are drawn with a guilty pleasure to their subjects. It could be argued that both fashion and crime contain varying elements of drama and glamour which enthral legions of loyal fans. These devotees become hooked on their genres. Both readers of fashion magazines and crime thrillers scan respective texts, hungry for more information and clues. The question *What happens next?* is as important for readers of crime media as it is for decoders of fashion media.

By focusing on three types of photographic image—still, moving and digital—this interdisciplinary examination will demonstrate how changing mediums have been and continue to be vital to our understanding, perception and processing of visual representations of both fashion and crime. By looking at images, past and present, this empirical account, based on many years research into both fashion media and crime media, will attempt to extract some of the underlying processes involved in the production, construction and definition of these distinctly different categories, which create, on the one hand, the fashionable body and, on the other, the criminal or deviant body.

In 1971, Dick Hebdige wrote an essay on the British 1960s celebrity gangsters Ronald and Reginald Kray, who came to be known affectionately by the British public through their media relations as Ronnie and Reggie. In the essay, he noted that technology was able to transform and enlarge our sense of reality: 'The Kray Twins existed in the mid-1960s not merely as professional criminals, but as a living complex phenomenon, an organic myth nurtured by the press and public alike, until their actions ceased to have any meaning, outside of the theatre constructed for them' (Hebdige 1971: 11). The Kray twins make an apposite example to introduce this chapter because they embody the morphing of two worlds: fashion and crime. This was achieved not accidently but by a deliberate, slick campaign that involved both the creation of a sartorial image and the active nurturing of press and media. These two areas of mimetic 'practice' were informed by reading books about their heroes, of whom Al Capone was one.

Capone, a 1930s American gangster and bootlegger, is arguably the first criminal to understand the importance of public relations and reputation management (Bergreen 1994). While he headed up a reign of robbery and murder, he presented the outward appearance of a legitimate business man—even holding press conferences. Capone's image was vital to this strategy and beneath his expensive bespoke suits, it is rumoured that he always wore silk boxers. As Jonathan Raban noted in his essay on the Kray twins' image, 'Emporium of Styles', Ronnie was drawn to the retro culture of decades past, which included the purchase of a gleaming Pontiac and diamond cufflinks (see Figure 8.1). The Krays were obsessed by American culture, a popular theme at the time and the subject of some anxiety by conservative British commentators. The barbarians had broken through the gate. But for Ronnie Kray, his sartorial, American-inspired image was about playing a role, attaining respect from the establishment, intimidation of his peers and showing his ascent

8.1. Ron Gerelli and the Kray twins. © Getty Images

in the world. He wore 'gangster style clothes—dark double-breasted suits, tightly knotted ties and shoulder padded overcoats . . . it was a classic uniform, and he followed the books slavishly' (Raban 1988: 70).

The Kray image, while derivative, stood out and made for striking photographic images. As identical twins, Ronnie and Reggie seemed to play a trick with the camera to which the eye was always drawn. This phenomenon was closely examined in the context of their relationship as twins by Lorentzon and Jenkes (1997: 94). What, however, has often been overlooked in cultural readings of the Kray twins is their relationship to fashion and the media, both of which were compelling factors in their longevity and iconic elevation. Ronnie and Reggie Kray, symbolized by a pair of suits, were almost elegant and conveyed a touch of old-fashioned glamour. Culturally, the Kray twins also managed to pierce the upper echelons of fashion photography, selected by David Bailey for his coffee-table book *Box of Pin-ups* in 1965 and appearing in a *Sunday Times* supplement. Reggie Kray even commissioned Bailey to document his own wedding to Frances Shea (Bailey and Harrison 1983) which ended tragically with her suicide three years later. Their appearance in these

8.2. George Raft. © Getty Images

publications reinforced the popular narrative of social mobility and fluidity: anyone could make it. In the context of visual culture, the Kray legacy is one that illustrates the sublimation of crime into fashionable image. On the one hand, the Krays were professional and violent gangsters; on the other, they were sharp-suited celebrities à la mode. In 1990, the feature film *The Krays*, directed by Peter Medak, starred two other twins of popular culture (who a decade earlier had also been at the height of fashion), Gary and Martin Kemp, formerly of the New Romantic band Spandau Ballet. Appearing on screen in bespoke shirts and monogrammed shirts, Ronnie and Reggie Kray were once more visually reinvented for consumption by a new generation and would prove to be a fore-runner to the sartorial violence of directors such as Quentin Tarantino and Guy Ritchie. Despite having been locked away and out of the public gaze for decades, the image that the Krays had cre-ated, fuelled by media, continued to intrigue and draw in new audiences.

Two years before the Krays were imprisoned, another British duo were sentenced to life in prison. Ian Brady and Myra Hindley were tried in 1966 for the torture and death of three minors with more bodies to come. Myra Hindley's photograph became an iconic image, a mugshot that the tabloid *Sun* newspaper branded as that of 'The Most Evil Woman in Britain', as noted in Helen Birch's defining essay which presents a feminist critique of the construction of Myra Hindley's media representation. Birch sees the photograph as 'atavistic—drawing its power from potent symbols of wicked women from the Medusa to seventeenth century witches—and portentous—what kind of violent acts might women be capable of?' (1993: 32). The controversial mugshot was recreated by artist Marcus Harvey from children's handprints and that appeared in the *Sensation* exhibition at the Royal Academy in 1998, where twenty-seven years after Hindley had been imprisoned, it was pelted by eggs and ink by angry visitors. There have been some notable discussions about Myra Hindley's treatment at the hands of the legal system and the press from a gendered argument,[3] notably in Birch's chapter, 'If Looks Could Kill: The Iconography of Evil in Moving Targets, Women, Murder & Representation' (1993), but there is another aspect to the social and cultural opprobrium she generated, and it is one that has rarely been discussed or commented on because one assumes, on the grand scale of things, it is perceived as trite and irrelevant.

Myra Hindley's hair was a key signifier in her role as an abhorrent and deviant other and played an instrumental part in her descent. Even though it was Brady who was the arbiter and auteur of their terrible crimes, the greatest wrath was directed at Hindley, and this was not simply because of her gender but also because of her appearance, which seemed to draw out popular prejudices and deep-seated anxieties about the appropriate boundaries of female behaviour including those around sexuality, permissiveness, submissiveness, dominance and the 'maternal'. Hindley's court appearance was actually very conservative and business-like: neat, clean and well coordinated. Her two-piece suits and neat blouses should have formed the basis of a respectful and dignified image, but this was undermined by her hair, which was clearly dyed, peroxide blonde, and backcombed into a beehive. This was hair, perhaps reminiscent of tawdry working-class glamour, that could be legitimately despised. For the notorious mugshot, it was snapped tousled and unkempt, and for her various appearances in court, it was freshly dyed, in a whole sequence of colours, a subject grimly noted by the several journalists who observed the proceedings. 'Her hair, naturally brown, has been changing colour from week to week of the trial. First, silver-lilac, then bright canary blonde,' wrote Maurice Richardson of *The Observer* in his essay 'What Is One to Make of the Moors Murders?' (1966: 21). Quite why journalists should have been compelled to pass comment on this is interesting in itself. Did they see it as evidence of Hindley's concern with vanity over humanity? Was there some conscious or subconscious drawing on the tales of medieval witches, females who were able to change their appearance? A working-class woman who had always been concerned with matters of style, the idea of appearing in a public forum underdressed or with black roots on show would have been anathema to Hindley. The care that she showed towards her hair—the colouring, the teasing, the arranging—was about showing she wasn't the mugshot that had come to define her. Semiotically, this dramatically backfired even though the blonde beehive that Hindley presented was a fashionable style of the time. Outside the charged atmosphere of the courtroom, thousands of other women went about, at liberty with similar hair, having taken to heart Shirley Polykoff's slogan for Clairol: 'If I Only Have One Life, Let Me Live It as a Blonde'. For Hindley, who was soon to be sentenced to life and indeed would end her days behind bars, this singsong phrase took on a different significance. The slight Scottish chap called Ian Brady seemed to diminish while she in contrast seemed to grow in monstrosity. In the context of their crimes, her hair became grotesque; it had connotations of artifice and masquerade. Her hair was as fake as she was. Once she was behind bars, Myra Hindley chose to reject the peroxide and grow her hair to its natural brown colour, but newspapers would forever after choose to represent her with the criminal mugshot that evoked such negative feeling, thus maintaining the symbolic order in which she was placed. Our cultural relationship with the Krays and Myra Hindley was, as outlined in Hebdige's original thesis, defined by their—and our—relationship with the media. Our understanding of crime is, on one level, all about images. Even though these examples take place in the late 1960s, a time of modern mass media, the relationship between fashion and crime is deeper, goes back further and can be mapped across a number of historical fashion/crime junctures to reveal a sequence of compelling intersections and dialogues.

OBJECT: STILL IMAGE AS A WAY TO CATALOGUE THE OTHER

Flowing from the same source of modernity and city life, fashion and crime, though separated at birth, were all inextricably linked from the very beginning. The machine age of industrialization saw the dawning of modern fashion. Increased cycles of production and consumption, a move away from small rural to sprawling urban economies and greater contrasts of wealth and poverty created the social, cultural and economic conditions in which both crime and fashion were able to thrive. As Elizabeth Wilson established in her seminal account of modern fashion, 'Economic expansion was the basis for a revolution in customs, beliefs and daily experience; henceforth fashion itself was to become one medium for the values of modernity' (1985: 155). It was these very same conditions that spawned the birth of modern crime. *The Condition of the Working Class in England* by Frederick Engels linked 'urban immiseration (including crime) directly to capitalist expansion' (cited in Heywood 2004: 21). This was also when the first police forces were organized. Capitalism, consumerism, overcrowding, rich rubbing against poor, more goods on show, more need, more want—all of these factors lead to a rise in crime. New media technologies created popular narratives around both fashion and crime, which in the age of industrialization became both more visible and accessible. Printing presses enabled widespread distribution and dissemination of both fields, aided by faster, cheaper printing and rising levels of literacy. So, on the one hand, there were Penny Bloods or Penny Dreadfuls, eight-page booklets that created a vast new readership for cheap crime fiction (Flanders 2011: 58), and, on the other, for the audience that desired refinement and fashionability, there was a growing number of fashion magazines that presented to readers the sartorial choices of the day (North 2007: 20). But it was the arrival of the photographic image which transformed how people saw themselves and the world. In a previous age, the affluent and aspirational might have been reproduced in oil paint or watercolour, but in the nineteenth century it was the camera that was able to capture images of the fashionable. Photo-mechanical reproduction developed rapidly from Joseph Nicephore Niepce and Jacques Louis Mande Daguerre's experiments with camera obscura in the 1820s to the release in 1888 of the first Kodak camera (Finn 2009: 10). It was this idea that the camera could deliver the unmediated truth that was so novel and thrilling at the time. As Sontag noted, 'While a painting, even one that meets photographic standards of resemblance, is never more than the stating of an interpretation, a photograph is never less than the registering of an emanation (light waves reflected by objects)—a material vestige of its subject in a way that no painting can be' (1978: 81).

So it was increasingly the camera, not the easel, that captured the Sunday suits, best dresses and evening gowns of the fashionably attired. These would be reproduced and mounted into picture frames, on walls, in photograph albums and in lockets. At this time, the carte de visite became a popular form of photographic format. These small photographs (6.4 cm × 10.2 cm) were patented by the Frenchman Eugene Disderi in 1854 and traded among visitors and friends. Albums for collections and displays of carte de visites became popular in Victorian parlours and were eventually supplanted by the larger cabinet cards (11.4 cm × 16.5 cm) in the 1870s. The camera was an important tool in the armoury of the curious and acquisitive Victorians who, as consumers, collectors and archivists, were able to employ the camera, with its mechanical and chemical processes, to make sense of the rapidly changing world. There was a great Victorian appetite for organizing, labelling and cataloguing, and this extended to people and bodies. Everything that moved and everything that didn't move was routinely subjected to the camera's gaze: 'Unlike other forms of visual representation, the photographic image was considered to be a direct, unmediated copy or an index of its subject in the natural world' (Finn 2009: x–xi). Although the black and white of photography was supposed to represent truth and unmediated reality, it was only a 'more convincing illusion, selection and artifice lurking behind the seeming impartiality of the mechanical eye' (Wilson 1985: 158).

Through the camera's gaze, the viewer was able to observe others and was also given access to other worlds. The camera was the technological interface between both the rarefied and elitist world of fashion and style and the censorious vision of the criminal classes, which were routinely photographed as part of the identification and classification process that emerged in the nineteenth century: 'The new field of criminology developed contemporaneously with the rise of photographic portraiture and the police mugshot' (Finn 2009: 2). Both fashion and crime were objects of fascination for the viewer and both could be read through the social/cultural map of coded signs. It would, for instance, be clear to viewers if they were looking at an image of a fashionable woman. She would be recognized through her clinched waist, the fine fabric of her attire, details such as jewels or ribbons and a dressed hairstyle. But there was more to the fashionable portrait than glossy surfaces: 'Like the state, the camera is never neutral. The representations it produces are highly coded and the power that it wields is never its own' (Tagg 1988: 63–4). Fashionable portraits similarly served particular social functions, to illustrate social status, material wealth and conventional attractiveness and to embody notions of solvency, legitimacy, social acceptance and normalcy.

Images of criminals, on the other hand, were not intended for this purpose. The act of photographing and cataloguing criminals was part of the identification process that became established in the nineteenth century. The framing of the criminal, which took place in a legal or correctional facility, constituted the earliest *mugshots,* a term derived from the word *mug,* which was an eighteenth-century English slang word for *face.* Their primary purpose was to make visible the criminal and identify the wrongdoer, lawless and punishable. There could be no mistaking a fashion portrait for a criminal mugshot, although there are examples of criminals who were able to use a fashionable exterior as part of their guise. Thomas Byrnes' photographic journal published in 1886 entitled *Professional Criminals of America,* presenting a visual lexicon of working criminal types which included 'Sneak Thieves, Forgers and Boarding House Thieves', was intended to illustrate precisely this dangerous paradox and warn the law-abiding public to be on its guard. Criminal anthropology, a fashionable and seriously regarded science at the time, purported the view that criminality could be spotted through the physical body and facial signs; atavistic throwbacks such as lantern jaws or joined eyebrows were said to reveal a less-evolved individual. Cesare Lombroso was the father of criminal anthropology, and the camera was his most vital tool in 'proving' his theories, that criminals were 'more likely to have crooked noses, sloping foreheads, large ears, protruding jaws, and dark skin, eyes and hair' (quoted in Gibson and Rafter 2006: 9). Michel Foucault (1979) has argued that this form of othering is about power and social control, and Tagg developed this idea persuasively: 'The photograph is not a magical emanation but a material; product of an apparatus set to work in specific contexts, by specific forces, for more or less defined purposes. Photography is a medium that 'flickers across institutional spaces' (1988: 118).

So while plates of the fashionable body (see Plate 25a) and mugshots of the criminal body (see Plate 25b) may seem poles apart on the social register, their meanings interlocked to remind all viewers of the pecking order in which 'every portrait implicitly took its place within a social and moral hierarchy. The private moment of sentimental individualization, the look at the frozen gaze-of-the-loved-one, was shadowed by two other more public looks: a look up, at one's "betters", and a look down, at one's "inferiors"' (Sekula 1986: 16). Fashion photography and criminal photography existed together in a virtual space, where the good, bad, heroic and infamous of society coexisted. Through the process of visual objectification, photography served both honorific and repressive purposes. Deviance and normalcy helped to define one another.

GLORY: MOVING IMAGE AND SELF-IDENTIFICATION

With the development of moving pictures and cinema, people's relationship with their image, how they saw themselves and each other, changed again. As cameras and technology became increasingly sophisticated, it was cinema that was one of the greatest influences on fashion in the 1920s and 1930s, years that were defined by economic instability and the escapist allure of glamour. The movies had an enormously influential reach and influence. People flocked to them, not only to leave their everyday lives behind but to take instruction on how to be more glamorous. Wilson notes that 'the cinema with its much larger audience, was influential in creating new ways for men and women to move, dance, dress, make love, be...and the move to Hollywood began the process of glamourisation...promoting new ways of walking, sitting and using the hands, but also the development of styles to suit personalities' (1985: 169).

Whereas fashion magazines were a luxury for the middle classes, the movies were a more democratic form of mass entertainment, accessible across all classes; therefore, it was movies that informed most people's ideas of fashion, glamour and style. Movie stars gave ordinary people the visual language and confidence to create alternative identities and even had the power to instigate fashion and style trends. Theorizing this process as a type of identity formation, Finkelstein explains, 'As an audience, we learn to see ourselves on the screen and, in turn, the techniques of representation shape desires and pleasures and become constituitive elements in the invention and management of identity' (Finkelstein 2007: 17).

It is no coincidence that the first tranche of criminal celebrities—all American—coincided with the widespread popularization of cinema and the emergence of the crime movie as a significant genre of its own. Famous criminals such as Al Capone and John Dillinger and the duo of Bonnie and Clyde all picked up their ideas of image and how to dress through watching movies. John Dillinger was influenced by the gangster films he watched as a young man. Bonnie Parker of Bonnie and Clyde initially aspired to be a movie actress, and although she lacked the necessary talent, she did adopt the glamour, the make-up, the clothes, the pose. Parker was adopting the male gaze to repackage herself as a glamorous moll but extending this idea further still; there might also be argued an idea of the 'criminal gaze' (Gamman 2008: 222), whereby the act of watching stylized criminals on screen results in mimetic dress codes, gestures and ways of behaviour. Anecdotal evidence suggests that real-life criminals became better dressed through observing and then imitating on-screen criminals. Ronnie and Reggie Kray fuelled their visual imaginations by watching 1930s film noir and gangster movies, and it was through the close observation of heroes such as George Raft, James Cagney and Humphrey Bogart that, according to their 'official' biographer, John Pearson, they were able to piece together their own sartorial identities, ones that harked back to an age of male elegance (see Figures 8.1 and 8.2). Despite emerging in the 'swinging' 1960s, this pair of retro-gangsters seemed to capture the zeitgeist of sartorial male role play and dandyism. This seems to follow Finkelstein's theory that 'certain styles and self-fashioning in appearance, manners of speech and bodily gestures can be used to produce groups who recognize each other, who are, in effect, a community of practitioners. Popular culture thus functions as a toolkit for shaping identity' (2007: 12).

As argued in the earlier section, the criminal mugshot, which has become an icon of contemporary visual culture, is predominantly about power or, as Foucault would describe it, a 'microphysics of power' (Foucault 1979). It is about the harnessing of technology to make visible the criminal. Its stark parameters literally capture, label and contain the individual within its borders. It is celluloid captivity, the powerful seizing the powerless. But criminals such as Al Capone, John Dillinger, Charles Ponzi and the Krays seized control of the technology and turned the camera back on themselves. As directors and auteurs of their own image-making, this was not about the camera being used to incriminate and damn but to elevate and glorify. Moving pictures gave criminals a sartorial language and confidence which allowed them to create their own mugshots, managing their own image and by extension their public profile and reputation. Through the observation and imitation of on-screen style and glamour, some high-profile criminals became style icons on their own terms, repackaging themselves in a media-friendly way that saw their images become culturally significant. By styling their images with care, they were able to reposition themselves in the cultural hierarchy not as social outcasts but successful, aspirational and attractive figures. Criminals could be, and had become, fashionable.

Examples include characters such as John Haigh, who in the 1940s became known as the 'Acid Bath Murderer'. Before his arrest he was photographed by Angus McBean, Cecil Beaton's one-time assistant and a highly sought after portrait photographer of British society. In an image reproduced in *Murder with a Difference* by Molly Lefebure in 1958, he appears with slicked-back hair and a pencil-thin moustache arranged like a matinee idol—a dashing double of Clarke Gable. This portrait was commissioned by an older, wealthy woman called Barbara Stephens, who ended up in a vat of acid, as did all of Haigh's other victims, but the image lives on—a symbol of the danger lurking beneath a polished exterior, a perennial theme of modernist literature seen in many Victorian detective novels.

Originally from a poor Italian background, Charles Ponzi used his first earnings to reinvent himself as a glamorous man with a straw boater, malachite cane and winning smile. Many thousands of gullible investors, including many vulnerable immigrants, fell for this image and lost their life savings. The 'Ponzi' schemes, which he gave his name to, continue to feature intermittently in the news.

So cinema had taught criminals how to create their own mugshots, how to look like and behave like stars. Glamour was a technology, all its own, that could be utilized to form an alternative identity. As Goffman identified in *Performance of the Self in Everyday Life,* 'Once the proper "sign equipment" has been obtained and familiarity gained in the management of it, then this equipment can be used to embellish and illuminate ones daily performances with favourable social style' (1971: 42–6).

The portraits of criminals that were starting to circulate were perceived as glamorous, aspirational and attractive as images of fashion. The playing field had evened out; definitions had blurred. It wasn't about looking down at one sort of image and up at another. The movies had made the creation of aura a democratic right. Fashion through the movies was available to everyone, but the digital revolution would bring images of fashion and crime closer to everyday lives than ever before.

REVELATION: DIGITAL IMAGE TO FRAME PRACTICE, PERFORMANCE AND PROCESS

The digital revolution has seen the widespread democratization of information sharing. The fact that now anyone can use their mobile phone as a portable editing suite from which they can film, photograph, record and edit has created huge changes across society and culture. The arrival and proliferation of Internet technologies has seen the emergence of unschooled, instinctive or intuitive communicators. Fashion bloggers have, through the democracy and accessibility of the Web, become viable and sometimes influential voices in the blogosphere (Rocamora 2011). The phrase 'citizen journalist' has come to connote a participatory, guerrilla or street journalism, whereby ordinary citizens can record news as it happens, visually or verbally, and then post this to the official or mainstream news outlets, in the form of photographs, film or text. Social networks are able to link all kinds of online communities, which are no longer restricted by geography or time. Twitter has also introduced a further outlet for actual news as it happens. This culture that we now inhabit, one of instant and widespread communication, has found equitable expression in both crime and fashion media. The idea of being able to view previously closed worlds and their inhabitants is a seductive one. Both crime and fashion have harnessed technology to display and perform their practices for the participatory pleasure of new audiences.

SHOWstudio, the online fashion portal started by fashion photographer Nick Knight, was the first to utilize the many editorial possibilities of the Internet. The name SHOWstudio was devised because of its objective to show the viewer fashion's metaphorical and actual studio and reveal aspects or processes that in the past would have remained hidden. Its mission statement at the time of writing is as follows: 'Inspired by the inherent generosity of the verb "to show" SHOWstudio opens up the studio of designers and artists allowing everyone to not only witness the creative process, but to respond and contribute creatively, documenting, commenting and evaluating the results'.[4]

This philosophy is reflected in a wide range of material. The project Sittings: Thirty Men (1 April 2005) saw stylist Simon Foxton style thirty male models as 'living magazine pages', as seen in Plate 26, which shows a male fashion model caught in his own private world while being publicly captured for a global fashion audience. Seated in front of a webcam, they became blinking, smirking, laughing humans, real people rather than two-dimensional representations. SHOWstudio has also been key in the pushing forward of live streaming, showing events as they happen, via webcam, to anyone who has the available technology and can log in to the right address. From international, large-scale events such as international designer catwalk shows through to more intimate collaborations such as photographic shoots, the fashion industry is allowing itself to be surveilled—by whoever chooses to watch. The process and the practice have become as important as the performance, spectacle or finished product. 'Behind the Scenes' as its own form of documentary genre has in fact become standard technological fashion fare, earning its own acronym, BTS—with many websites and online magazines offering this sort of material as an additional extra. Supporters of BTS feel that it makes the fashion industry more accessible and less elite. For fashion companies, this might mean they can reach more people and generate increased interest and income. Critics of BTS say that much of the material is tedious, difficult to watch and pointless. If you remove fashion's illusion and magic, what is left?

SHOWstudio's on-screen strapline is 'the home of fashion film', and this medium has been innovatively employed to show fashion as it happens, to draw viewers closer. Most typically and influentially, the camera is trained on fashion shoots as they happen, to document the creative process. Once, fashion processes had been a closed window that viewers could only press their noses against. But the hypertextual richness of interactive, online media means the window is now open and can be climbed through, allowing viewers a different, possibly more meaningful, engagement with fashion.

There has been a huge amount written about surveillance society and technology being used against individual or civil liberties (see Davies 1996), but digital technology has also been used as a tool by law-breakers to promote their own messages and/or narrate their own dramas (see Plate 27). The history of communication technology as a criminal interface presents a fascinating historical perspective on crime. In the 1960s, Ian Brady and Myra Hindley used technology not only to record the cries of a child who was being abused but also to photograph their subjects and each other. This was irrefutable evidence that lead to them both being imprisoned for life. Snuff movies also document the process of an individual being killed in real time on film. So while technology has always been enthusiastically embraced by the criminal contingent (everything from cars to phones and walkie-talkies), what has changed today is the speed, the scope of the audience and the potential to network and mesh with other like-minded individuals. The same media that is facilitating a global village of switched-on fashion fans is doing exactly the same with many pockets of criminal life.

So, image as revelation in the criminal context can include incidents of happy slapping—acts of violence that are recorded on mobile phones and are then shared among networks—and perhaps the most disturbing images of all, films of hostage takings. These images 'reanimate that extremely violent and graphic form of political theatricality which Foucault assigned to predisciplinary society and which he named "the spectacle of the scaffold"' (Mackenzie 2009: 339). Described by sociologist Mark Juergensmeyer as 'performance violence' and 'a theatre of terror' (cited in Mackenzie 2009: 339), these digital dramas can only exist in our minds and lives because of the new modes of transmission made accessible through the digital revolution, part of the 'worldwide electronic network of cameras, screens, databases, processors and editing boards' (Mackenzie 2009: 340). While it might make us uneasy to juxtapose these mediated images of fashion and crime, it could be argued that in the context of new technologies, both the new communicators of fashion and of crime are using digital platforms and expanded audiences to present and perform their practice and impress their viewers with the authenticity (and theatricality) of their processes and practices. It could be argued that both groups aim to amplify their message and increase their visibility and status within specific groups.

CONCLUSION

Media is central to our understanding, construction and consumption of fashion. It is the engine that thrums across the capitalist system, proliferating vast quantities of imagery across a growing number of platforms: print-based, televisual and digital. Through image, fashion has become part of the spectacle of all of our everyday lives, however remote our actual participation might be. Through fashion media, we are informed of prevailing taste and aesthetics, what is considered sartorially acceptable and desirable and by extension what is regarded as déclassé or démodé.

Similarly 'media portrayals of crime and violence have become part of the spectacle of everyday life' (Kidd-Hewitt and Osborne 1999: 1). From TV's criminal reconstructions to its many forms of dramatic entertainment including movies and docudramas, from lurid, sensational accounts of real crime in newspapers to the groaning shelves of crime fiction, this media informs us of 'the normative forms of behaviour' (Cohen 1972: 15) what is acceptable and what is not and repeatedly reminds us what the consequences are for those who flout the rules. It could therefore be argued that both fashion media and crime media have a similar social and cultural purpose: to present and promote the hegemonic ideal, to discipline the minds and bodies of potential dissenters, to encourage compliance and to deter out of the box thinking.

Springing from the same well of modernity and created using the same tools, images of both fashion and crime repel and compel us in equal measure. As this chapter shows, the imaging of fashion and the imaging of crime have much in common. Crime, like fashion, has been catalogued and labelled, displayed and glorified, revealed and exposed. Both have gone from object to subject, from beguiling surface image to three-dimensional, interactive experience. Both fashion and crime media have hawked their own celebrities and icons, which we have greedily consumed. These divergent forms of information, entertainment and spectacle echo each other. But without the media technologies that have framed, given life to and defined its meanings, this bizarre parallel universe of fashion and crime would not have been possible.

NOTES

1. Oxford English Dictionary Online, http://www.oed.com.
2. Although phrases such as 'crimes against fashion' and the 'fashion police' used in contemporary vernacular allude to the unspoken laws that govern 'appropriate', 'correct' or 'tasteful' dress.
3. See also Heidenshon 1985 and Kennedy 1993.
4. 'About SHOWstudio', http://showstudio.com/about.

BIBLIOGRAPHY

Bailey, D. and M. Harrison (1983), *Black and White Memories: Photographs, 1948–1969,* London: Dent.

Bergreen, L. (1994), *Capone, the Man and His Era,* London: Macmillan.

Birch, H. (1993), 'If Looks Could Kill; the Iconography of Evil', in H. Birch (ed.), *Moving Targets: Women, Murder and Representation,* London: Virago.

Byrnes, T. ([1886] 2000), *Professional Criminals of America,* New York: Lyons Press.

Cohen, S. (1972), *Folk Devils & Moral Panics: The Creation of the Mods & Rockers,* London: MacGibbon & Kee.

Davies, S. (1996), *Big Brother: Britain's Web of Surveillance and the New Technological Order*, London: Pan Books.

Finkelstein, J. (2007), *The Art of Self Invention, Image and Identity in Popular Visual Culture*, London: I.B. Tauris.

Finn, J. (2009), *Capturing the Criminal Image, from Mug Shot to Surveillance Society*, Minneapolis: University of Minnesota Press.

Flanders, J. (2011), *The Invention of Murder, How the Victorians Revelled in Death and Detection and Created Modern Crime*, London: Harper Press.

Foucault, M. (1979), *Discipline and Punish: The Birth of the Prison*, Harmondsworth: Penguin,

Gamman, L. (2008), 'On Gangster Suits and Silhouettes', in M. Uhlirova (ed.), *If Looks Could Kill, Cinema's Images of Fashion, Crime and Violence*, London: Koenig Books, 218–29.

Gibson, M. and N. H. Rafter (2006), *Criminal Man, Cesare Lombroso*, Durham, NC: Duke University Press.

Goffman, E. (1971), *Presentation of Self in Everyday Life*, London: Penguin.

Hebdige, D. (1971), *The Kray Twins: A Study of a System of Closure*, Birmingham: University of Birmingham.

Heidensohn, F. (1985), *Women and Crime*, New York: New York University Press.

Heywood, K. J. (2004), *City Limits: Crime, Consumer Culture and the Urban Experience*, London: Cavendish Publishing.

Kennedy, H. (1993), *Eve Was Framed: Women and British Justice*, London: Random House.

Kidd-Hewitt, D. R. and R. Osborne, eds (1999), *Crime and the Media, the Post-modern Spectacle*, London: Pluto Press.

Lefebure, M. (1958), *Murder with a Difference*, London: Heinemann.

Lorentzon, J. and C. Jenkes (1997), 'The Kray Fascination', *Theory, Culture & Society*, 14/3: 87–107.

Mackenzie, J. (2009), 'Abu Ghraib and the Society of the Scaffold', in P. Anderson and J. Menon (eds), *Violence Performed*, London: Palgrave Macmillan, 338–56.

McLuhan, M. (1964), *Understanding Media: The Extensions of Man*, London: Routledge.

North, S. (2007), 'From Neoclassicism to the Industrial Revolution: 1790–1860', in L. Welters and A. Lillethun (eds), *The Fashion Reader*, Oxford: Berg, 20–33.

Raban, J. (1988), *Soft City*, London: Collins Harvill.

Richardson, M. (1966), 'What Is One to Make of the Moors Murders?', *The Observer*, 8 May: 21.

Rocamora, A. (2011), 'Personal Fashion Blogs: Screens and Mirrors in Digital Self Portraits', *Fashion Theory*, 15/4: 407–24.

Sekula, A. (1986), 'The Body and the Archive', *October*, 39 (Winter): 3–64.

Sontag, S. (1978), *On Photography*, London: Penguin.

Tagg, J. (1988), *The Burden of Representation: Essays on Photographies and Histories*, Basingstoke: Macmillan.

Wilson, E. (1985), *Adorned in Dreams, Fashion & Modernity*, London: Virago.

9

GUERRILLA MEDIA
TOWARDS A MEDIA THEORY OF FASHION
friedrich weltzien

On the first of May 1971, an explosion destroyed the fashionable Biba Boutique on London's Kensington High Street. A terrorist group calling themselves the Angry Brigade claimed responsibility with a pamphlet entitled *Communiqué 8*. The very same group had also executed a bombing attack in November 1970 on a BBC broadcast truck in front of the Royal Albert Hall during the Miss World Contest. The communiqué read as follows:

> If you are not busy being born you are busy buying.
>
> All the sales girls in the flash boutiques are made to dress the same and have the same make-up, representing the 1940's. In fashion as in everything else, capitalism can only go backwards—they've nowhere to go—they're dead.
>
> The future is ours.
>
> Life is so boring there is nothing to do except spend all our wages on the latest skirt or shirt.
>
> Brothers and sisters, what are your real desires?
>
> Sit in the drugstore, look distant, empty, bored, drinking some tasteless coffee? Or perhaps BLOW IT UP OR BURN IT DOWN. The only thing you can do with modern slave-houses—called boutiques—IS WRECK THEM. You can't reform profit capitalism and inhumanity. Just kick it till it breaks.
>
> Revolution. (Angry Brigade 1971)[1]

Following this claim, the intention of the Biba bombing was neither a merely political one nor was it religious (like the mass of suicide bombings committed in recent years, even in London).

The communiqué states that this assault was justified by a judgement about fashion. In the eyes of the Angry Brigade, dress and 'make-up, representing the 1940s' is reason enough to attack.

Can a bombing be a fashion medium? What is fashion media anyway? In the following, I want to address these questions along the pathways of media theory. I want to scrutinize the ways in which the historical period of the Biba bombing differs from today's perspective. It is not so much about fashion and terrorism; it is more about the definition of fashion media.

FIRE BOMBINGS AS FASHION MEDIA

In the late 1960s and early 1970s, a variety of terrorist cells spread throughout Europe. Opposition to the United States' involvement in the war in Vietnam made left-wing and communist groups popular among many Western, and mostly young, people. The anticapitalist idiom made the term *fashion* synonymous with the industrial class system of exploitation and consumption, accountable for the alienation and suffering of countless humans as well as animals. By that, fashion became a major target of self-appointed revolutionaries of the class struggle. The rather negative connotation of fashion in this context is based on its notion as an instrument of power, conveying and enforcing normative rules of the establishment. The Miss World Contest—attacked by the Angry Brigade and several feminist activists—was viewed as a 'cattle market' that degraded women. The left-wing critique on capitalism during the 1970s and 1980s saw followers of fashion to be remote controlled, uniformed. In the diction of the Angry Brigade, the choice was clear: being part of the establishment or being part of the revolutionary force. Within this model the Biba boutique was a representative of establishment.

The first attacks by the terrorist group Rote Armee Fraktion (RAF) in Germany in April of 1970 were fire bombings on department stores in Frankfurt. By hitting such places of consumption, it meant to strike the heart of capitalism. Both the Angry Brigade and the RAF pursued a strategy of the city guerrilla like the heroes of revolution did in Latin America. According to Che Guevara, 'the guerrilla fighter is a social reformer' making use of any artifice and stratagem that is at his hands (Guevara and Davies 1997: 52). Thus *guerrilla* means to use the enemy's infrastructure for executing tactical operations, a hit-and-run strategy of singular actions.

In his ancient book *Art of War,* the Chinese general Sun Tzu (Sun 2005) advises the combatant to become familiar with the habits of his opponent: know your enemy. Following this advice, the Angry Brigade necessarily had to learn about fashions in dress and make-up and seemingly found out that there was a preference for the style of the 1940s. From this point on, a guerrilla fighter had to be a specialist in questions of style. But what does it mean to use a lipstick colour or wear a skirt with the silhouette of the time of the Second World War? Does this necessarily mean that this person will be a capitalist, a fascist or, at the very least, a bellicist? The anarchist guerrilla must admit that this was also the style of the resistance. So it is highly questionable whether this is a good criterion to tell friend from foe. And what exactly is the problem: to dress up in nostalgia or to buy the latest fashion? However this crude argument is to be understood, one thing is clear: fashion obviously became a highly political issue during the 1970s. Punk dwelled on this way of thinking by coining the slogan 'fuck fashion' only a few years later.

BODY EXTENSIONS

To me the crucial question is: How can this situation be judged from the point of view of media theory? One of the most influential intellectuals addressing this problem was the Canadian communication theorist Marshall McLuhan. As one of the fathers of media theory, his ideas were groundbreaking. In his classic book *Understanding Media: The Extensions of Men,* first published in 1964, McLuhan gives a definition of *medium* in his terms. Any device that is able to change the ways of social life is called a medium. Railways or electric light, for instance, are media because men are able to behave differently with this technical support—to work at night, to name only one of innumerable consequences. According to this definition, a medium always is an 'extension of men' as it expands the possibilities and adds completely new opportunities to the spectrum of human action (McLuhan [1964] 2003).

McLuhan points out that it is irrelevant who is sitting in this or that train. To understand the effect of electricity on human society, it is not important to know exactly what is lit by each light-bulb. The fact that there is a railway or electric light per se changes our habits and our society. The topic of each single phone conversation or the programme on different television stations is not important: the fact that we can talk to somebody far away or that we can watch moving pictures right in our living room affects our social behaviour.

In that sense, clothing is an important medium to McLuhan:

> Clothing as an extension of our skin helps to store and to channel energy, so that if the Westerner needs less food, he may also demand more sex... Clothing, as the extension of the skin, can be seen both as a heat-control mechanism and as a means of defining the self socially. In these respects, clothing and housing are near twins, though clothing is both nearer and elder. (McLuhan [1964] 2003: 163)

Clothing—as one of the historically oldest media of mankind—not only increased the reproduction rate by cutting calorie requirements, but it also allowed the human species to colonize places that would be too cold or too dry to survive without this artificial body extension. Moreover clothing, by protecting the body, provides support in executing particular actions, such as fighting animals (or each other) in a more efficient way. Clothing clearly brings many advantages to those who have a better or more appropriate dress and deeply changes any social habit. This is still true with fire fighters, divers or astronauts, who depend on their special work uniforms, and athletes, who break running, swimming or skating world speed records because of specific textiles or footwear.

To McLuhan, clothing is a vehicle of communication but not in the sense of a specific dress expressing, for example, the belonging to a certain class or group of people—like a uniform or the style of the 1940s.[2] 'Clothing and housing as extensions of skin and heat-control mechanisms, are media of communication... in the sense that they shape and rearrange the patterns of human association and community' (McLuhan [1964] 2003: 168). To McLuhan, the individual style, the colour of a shirt, the condition of jeans and sneakers, the logo on a suit's label does not matter. Consequently to him but unfortunately for us, fashion is not a topic of scientific investigation. *Communiqué 8* clearly posits that clothing governs the way of social behaviour far beyond the point of the function of a heat-control mechanism. An appropriate dress code will enable otherwise impossible courses of action and allow access to places that are not only defined by environmental conditions.

FASHION AND ART

Despite McLuhan's underdetermination of fashion, a media theory of fashion on the fundament of his writings can be developed with the help of another term: *art*. During the advent of a new medium, the patterns of human community change. This process of transformation comes to rest through defining a new environmental system, which will be stable as long as there is no other medium introduced into society. But what happens to the previous environment? Does it just vanish? Not according to McLuhan's theory:

> The older systems are transformed into art forms, ... the new environmental system turns the old environments into antienvironments. That is one way of perceiving what a work of art is. Art as an antienvironment is an indispensible means of perception, for environments, as such, are imperceptible. (McLuhan 2005: 3)

In his 1966 text, *The Emperor's Old Clothes,* McLuhan argues that the unchanged environment in the terms of a normative media habit is invisible. We just blindly make use of what is available. The old environment can be brought into visibility as an antienvironment. The instrument of making visible is what the Canadian thinker calls art.[3]

Each medium 'creates an environment by its mere presence' (McLuhan [1964] 2003: 8). Clothing produces an environment; towards this environment we are blind. The extension of the skin in order to control body heat is imperceptible. Dressing differently, dressing consciously, makes clothing visible: fashion makes clothing visible. Fashion is an art form as far as it makes us aware of the fact that clothing is a vehicle of communication—regardless of the individual style or meaning or content of that communication. In other words, fashion is a medium because it changes one form of clothing into an antienvironment on behalf of another form of clothing. To McLuhan, dressing up in the style of the 1940s during the 1970s would not be so much an unprogressive, reactionist political statement but the artful transformation of an old system into perceptibility. Fashion like art can reconcile history with the present as we learn to see only with the help of the contrasting agent of transformation.

But what if no one recognizes the uniformly dressed up sales girls in the 'flash boutiques'; what if fashion is not making things visible? What if it takes a bomb exploding on Kensington High Street to make people aware of this fact? Well, then of course a bombing is also a medium. So this is what makes the Biba bombing interesting from the point of view of media theory: two media in confrontation; the struggle of media.

HYBRID AND HUBRIS

In *Understanding Media* McLuhan had already thought about such a case. In the chapter called 'Hybrid Energies', he delivers the following description of what happens when two media melt into each other and form a new device different from both of the sources:

> The hybrid or the meeting of two media is a moment of truth and revelation from which new form is born ... The moment of the meeting of media is a moment of freedom and release from the ordinary trance and numbness imposed by them on our senses. (McLuhan [1964] 2003: 80–1)

The hybrid reveals the force of life; it is a wake-up call to rescue us from drowning into the boring routine of the ordinary—a statement that sounds quite similar to *Communiqué 8*. Theory and terror meet in the discovery that we all are to be saved from a life of grey, from emptiness, boredom, numbness, blindness and heteronomy. When fashion and bombing meet, they will potentiate each other. Professionals in this area of potentiated visibility again are artists: 'Artists in various fields are always the first to discover how to enable one medium to use or to release the power of another' (McLuhan [1964] 2003: 79)—artists or small children.[4] Like a chef de cuisine, the artist combines the ingredients at will: 'In our age artists are able to mix their media diet as easily as their book diet' (McLuhan [1964] 2003: 78).

Fashion relates to clothing like art relates to media: it makes its vehicle visible. That might be a reason why fashion has to change constantly: to wake us up from our numbness. The Angry Brigade was convinced that dressing up in the style of the 1940s was a retrogression and would slow down the process of change, the process of making visible and by that prolong the state of numbness. A bomb might therefore be the medium of choice to accelerate transformation.

Apart from the hubris that lies in both McLuhan's and the Angry Brigade's exclusive access to the truth, *Understanding Media* gives no clear distinction between terrorism and art.[5] Art as an instrument of antienvironment necessarily has an impact on society:

> The art object is replaced by participation in the art process...The artist leaves the Ivory Tower for the Control Tower, and abandons the shaping of art objects in order to program the environment itself as a work of art. It is human consciousness itself that is the great artefact of man. (McLuhan 2005: 14)

Two years before the first man landed on the moon, McLuhan liked to think that in the space age even 'the planet has become an antienvironment, an art form, an extension of consciousness' (McLuhan 2005: 10). Marshall McLuhan was up to date with contemporary developments in art as he was aware of performance art and land art, which produce situations and environments much more than traditional works of art that had the goal of eternal significance. Fashion fits perfectly into this concept. It is not this or that style that counts—because each single manifestation will soon be out of fashion again—but fashion as a social phenomenon, fashion as a medium; fashion as fashion proved to be stable.

FLESH LIGHT

Marina Abramovic is one of the most well-renowned performance artists today. She began her career in the former Yugoslavia and moved to Amsterdam during the early 1970s, just as the Angry Brigade and the RAF committed their attacks against fashion. In November 2005, she recreated seven of her own and other artists' performances at the Guggenheim Museum in New York in a show entitled *Seven Easy Pieces*. Abramovic cares about the history of performance art and questions today's use of images produced back then:

> Today, there are so many young performance artists who repeat different performances from the seventies without giving credit to the original source. Even the fashion and advertising industries consciously or unconsciously use images from well-known performances. (Abramovic 2007: 10)

One good example of fashion using a strong image of art (which Marina Abramovic could not have known of when she made this statement) was the garb that Stefani Joanne Angelina Germanotta (aka Lady Gaga) wore at the 2010 MTV Video Music Awards: a gown by the Los Angeles designer Franc Fernandez made completely of beef steak (Plate 28). Together with shoes, bag and hat, Lady Gaga was dressed from head to toe in raw meat (Roberts 2010; Winterman and Kelly 2010). To use meat as material for clothing is not an original idea from Fernandez. Instead, he refers to an artistic strategy that originated in a work by the Czech-Canadian artist Jana Sterbak in 1987. *Vanitas—Flesh Dress for an Albino Anorectic* was a dress made out of 60 pounds of salted flank steak that could be worn by a mannequin (Plate 29). The formal similarities to Fernandez's 2010 meat dress are so striking that it is hard to think that neither Fernandez nor Lady Gaga had any knowledge of Sterbak's *Vanitas* piece.

Lady Gaga refers to Sterbak's intentions insofar as she recalls a feminist interpretation of her meat dress in interviews, an interpretation that was strong in *Vanitas* from 1987 as well.[6] But as Marina Abramovic had mourned in advance, Lady Gaga never gave credit to the original source. In her work, Sterbak connects more and different aspects of art, such as the relation between performance and dress, as well as the use of edible materials for art which had previously been addressed by some Fluxus artists such as Joseph Beuys (see Novero 2010). Moreover, the title *Vanitas* points not only towards the baroque topic of the fugacity of all worldly belongings but also to eating disorders such as anorexia or bulimia, which have been argued to be triggered or supported by the presentation of thin fashion models via media. She follows the track of charge against fashion: Jana Sterbak (as well as Marina Abramovic) carries on the tradition of a critical attitude towards fashion as social criticism.

Fernandez and Lady Gaga hijacked an antifashion statement in favour of a highly glamorous red carpet entrance. That turns McLuhan's argument upside down. From his point of view, art is the ultimate state of perceptibility. It cannot be made more visible by putting it into a new context. Art cannot be transformed into an anti-antienvironment; art already is the terminus. So, what can be learnt from this case? One conclusion could be that Jana Sterbak's *Vanitas* is not a piece of art, or that McLuhan's definition is insufficient—which I do not want to believe. Another solution to this problem is to account Lady Gaga's performance as art. A third way would be to see the meat dress as the melting of two media: fashion and performance art together form a hybrid.

It is one thing to develop the concept of the meat dress and to exhibit it in a context clearly marked as a field of art—a white cube gallery for instance. But it is a totally new situation to wear such a dress at an eminent social event like the MTV Awards. It took the artist (or the small child) Lady Gaga to become aware of this new environment and make the dress virtually visible to the world. Fashion's ability to adopt and incorporate even its antonym proves that fashion is a medium in its own right. It is not tied to certain contents.

It not only takes courage to do what Lady Gaga did, it also takes some artistic intelligence to develop such a plan. Fashion as medium demands creativity not only on the side of the designer but also on the side of those who actually wear the garments. Lady Gaga meets McLuhan's requirements to abandon 'the shaping of art objects in order to program the environment itself as a work of art. It is human consciousness itself that is the great artefact of man' (2005: 14).

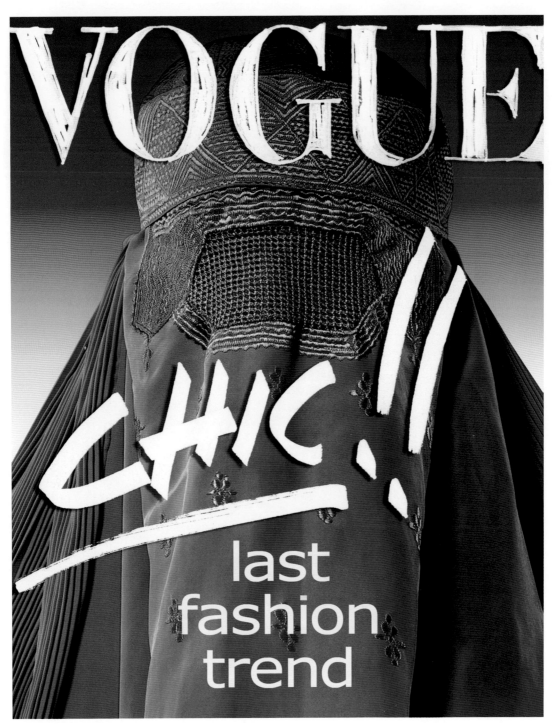

Plate 17. Flavio Lucchini, *Vogue* cover, 2011. © Flavio Lucchini

Plate 18. Flavio Lucchini, *Next Prada?*, 2011. © Flavio Lucchini

Plate 19. Adolf Menzel, *Das Ballsouper*, 1878. © Staatliche Museen zu Berlin, Nationalgalerie/Jörg P. Anders

Plate 20. Jakob Seisenegger, *Portrait of Charles V with a Dog*, 1532. © Kunsthistorisches Museum, Vienna

Plate 21. Christian Schad, *Count St. Genois d'Anneaucourt,* 1927. © Christian Schad Stiftung Aschaffenburg/ADAGP. Courtesy Centre Pompidou, MNAM-CCI, Dist. RMN-Grand Palais/ Georges Meguerditchian

Plate 22. Christian Schad, *Baroness Vera Wassilko,* 1926. Private collection

Plate 23. Christian Schad, *Miss Mulino von Kluck,* cover of *Die Dame*, 1930. © bpk—
Bildagentur für Kunst, Kultur und Geschichte, Berlin

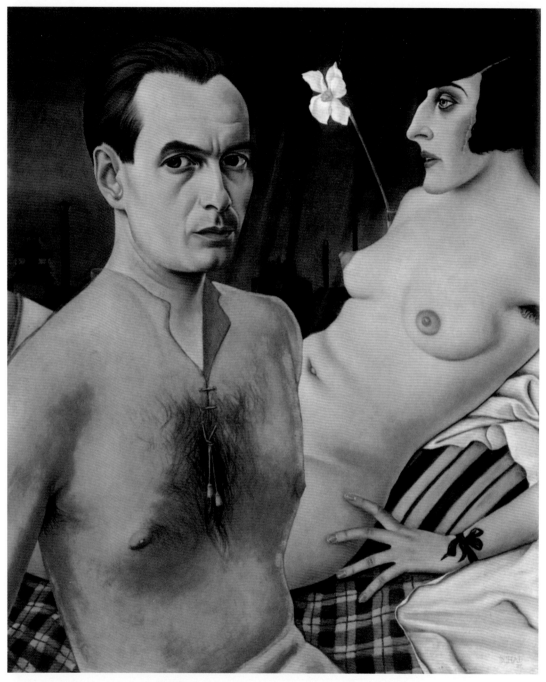

Plate 24. Christian Schad, self-portrait with model, 1927. © bpk—Bildagentur für Kunst, Kultur und Geschichte, Berlin

Photograph of Prisoner.

Lucy Freeman

Plate 25. (a) Victorian women's fashion. Courtesy Victorian Image Collection (www.victorianimagecollection. co.uk) (b) Prisoner Lucy Freeman, mugshot, Cambridge, 1875–77. Courtesy Mary Evans Picture Library

Plate 26. Webcam still from Thirty Men model Matthew Gidding and shoot by Simon Foxton for SHOWstudio. © SHOWstudio

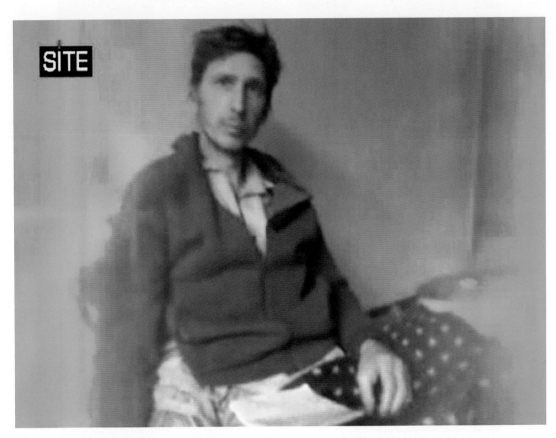

Plate 27. Hostage image screen grab of French journalist. © Getty Images

Plate 28. Pretty in pink: Lady Gaga wearing a dress by designer Franc Fernandez at the 2010 MTV Video Music Awards. With kind permission of picture-alliance dpa

Plate 29. We happened to meet the meat twenty-three years before: Jana Sterbak, *Vanitas—Flesh Dress for an Albino Anorectic,* as shown in Toronto, 1987. With kind permission of Jana Sterbak

Plate 30. The texture of communism: film still from *Sasa Kovacevic: I'm a Good Socialist*, 2009. With kind permission of Sasa Kovacevic

Plate 31. A moving still: film set shot from *Sasa Kovacevic: I'm a Good Socialist,* 2009. With kind permission of Sasa Kovacevic

Plate 32. *Dansa serpentina*, 1900. Courtesy Filmoteca de Catalunya

I'M A GOOD SOCIALIST

As a kind of conclusion, I want to present another example to show that clothing doesn't necessarily have to leave the textile behind to become fashion as an art form. Additionally. I think that this example shows how far the medium of fashion film is able to pronounce the mediality of fashion itself.

Like Abramovic, the designer Sasa Kovacevic was born in Yugoslavia, a country which now no longer exists. He studied fashion at the Berlin Weissensee School of Art and runs a label called Sadak. His first breakthrough came during the 2009 Berlin Fashion Week with his 2009/10 collection, called 'I'm a Good Socialist'. This collection was presented in the form of a fashion film which he titled *Ex-land*. In his designs, Kovacevic refers to material, pattern, texture and colour, style and silhouette of the now vanished former socialist country of Yugoslavia but also refers to regional traditions of Serbia and the cultural horizon of the Balkans (Plate 30). Having worked for some years at the textile department of the Beograd Museum of Cultural History, he is familiar with the socialist as well as the traditional fabrics of the region.

Video is important for Sadak, as this small business does not have the financial power to realize full-size fashion shows. Fashion film as a genre is characterized by a very short length of time, between one and five minutes long. Unlike a commercial spot, in fashion films there mostly is no spoken word, either by one of the protagonists or from an off-screen voice. Moreover, the atmosphere is emphasized in opposition to a narrative. The story just offers a frame or a carpet for creating a certain mood. Fashion film is unlikely to replace the catwalk, but in the age of the Internet and YouTube it is a complementary medium of growing importance to fashion photography.[7]

In *Ex-land,* Sasa Kovacevic tells a story of a fictitious country, showing the governor or president and his wife as well as some of the inhabitants dressed in his collection. Kovacevic even wrote a state constitution formulating that clothing, turned into fashion, enables people to define their very own point of view and by that strengthen the idea of individuality and democracy. In his visual language, he uses quotations from several cinematic genres such as science fiction and thrillers. He also makes use of artistic strategies: big pictures of the president and the first lady of Ex-land hanging on the wall seem to be a tribute to the concept of the tableaux vivant (Plate 31). The video artist Bill Viola transformed the tableaux vivant into something that has been called 'moving paintings': pictures that move only slightly (for instance the dress or hair blowing in the wind, the lips moving) but without any formal change to the structure or composition of the picture in whole, as he did in 1995 with *The Greeting*. One might refer to such films as 'moving stills' as the pictures seem to belong to a longer movie with which we are unfamiliar. Fashion film has much in common with moving stills as they are mostly based on a static framework or structure—although the camera and/or the protagonists can move through this space of static action.

BEYOND NUMBNESS

Film undoubtedly is a medium. To use it in order to show a fashion collection makes fashion film a hybrid media. As Sadak's collection 'I'm a Good Socialist' is very much concerned with communism and its dogma of fashion as degenerated bourgeois expression, Kovacevic also incorporates a historical antifashion statement into haute couture (see Bartlett 2010). Fernandez and Lady Gaga reassess the language of protest against fashion and transform it into the *dernier cri*. Kovacevic is doing something similar. Like an act of guerrilla tactics, designers as well as fashion users take over the infrastructure of their enemies to demonstrate the power of fashion as a medium of communication, legitimated by the very mechanisms of high culture. This means there are infinite possibilities of combination, of inventing and reinventing, of assessment and reassessment of clothing. Sasa Kovacevic believes in the power of fashion. To him, fashion is a medium of social reformation. But unlike the 1970s revolutionaries, his understanding is more democratic and lacks the hubris of a dogmatic specification in style and meaning.

Fashion film as a hybrid helps supersede bombings. We are not numb but sovereign. The future is ours.

NOTES

1. See Carr 1975: 103 and Hecken 2006: 92–3. There have been fourteen published communiqués related to the Angry Brigade. The complete texts are online: http://recollectionbooks.com/siml/library/AngryBrigade/Communiques.html, accessed 1 December 2011.
2. Regarding differences in the concept of *meaning* in fashion, see, for instance, Barnard 2002 and Rubinstein 1995.
3. But not the only instrument: 'Science, quite as much as art, is concerned with the construction of anti-environments' (McLuhan 2005: 10).
4. According to McLuhan, also another group of people is able to see new environments: 'Only small children and artists are sensually apt to perceive the new environment' ([1964] 2003: 4).
5. The Russian artists group Voina ('war') around Oleg Vorotnikov, based in St Petersburg, clearly demonstrates how up to date this discussion is. The spectacular performances are claimed to be art but function as anarchist provocations of Russian state authority—for instance setting a police car on fire such as on New Year's Eve 2012, called *Cop's Auto-da-fe, or Fuck Prometheus*. Most of the recent performances are filmed and can be seen on YouTube.
6. For feminist notion of Sterbak's art, see Milroy 1991. On Lady Gaga's concept of the meat dress as an expression of female self determination, see Roberts 2010 and Winterman and Kelly 2010. There were several other artists using the idea of a meat dress, for instance, the Milan-based artist Robert Gligorov (*Waiting,* 1997). Two photographs show a man wearing a jacket made from meat: in the first, the meat is in a rather fresh state; in the second, a few days later, there are maggots feeding on the jacket. The Chinese-born artist Zhang Huan, in his 2002 performance *My New York,* put on a muscle suit made from raw meat and walked the streets of New York City. As far as I know, neither Gligorov nor Huan have given credit to Sterbak.
7. See, for instance, SHOWstudio (http://showstudio.com/) or A Shaded View on Fashion (http://www.ashadedviewonfashion.com/).

BIBLIOGRAPHY

Abramovic, M. (2007), *Seven Easy Pieces,* Milan: Charta.
Angry Brigade (1971), *Communiqué 8,* 1 May, http://recollectionbooks.com/siml/library/AngryBrigade/Communiques.html, accessed 1 December 2011.
Barnard, M. (2002), *Fashion as Communication,* London: Routledge.
Bartlett, D. (2010), *FashionEast. The Spectre That Haunted Socialism,* Cambridge, MA: MIT Press.

Carr, G. (1975), *The Angry Brigade. The Cause and the Case,* London: Gollancz.

Guevara, E. and T. M. Davies (1997), *Guerrilla Warfare,* Lanham, MD: Rowan & Littlefield.

Hecken, T. (2006), *Avantgarde und Terrorismus,* Bielefeld: transcript.

McLuhan, M. ([1964] 2003), *Understanding Media. The Extensions of Man,* Corte Madera, CA: Gingko Press.

McLuhan M. (2005), *The Emperor's Old Clothes,* vol. 20, Corte Madeira, CA: Gingko Press.

Milroy, S. (1991), 'The Flesh Dress. A Defence', *Canadian Art,* 8/2: 71–2.

Novero, C. (2010), *Antidiets of the Avant-garde. From Futurist Cooking to Eat Art,* Minneapolis: University of Minnesota Press.

Roberts, L. (2010), 'Lady Gaga's Meat Dress Divides Opinion', *The Daily Telegraph,* 14 September, http://www.telegraph.co.uk/culture/music/music-news/8001267/Lady-Gagas-meat-dress-divides-opinion.html, accessed 1 December 2011.

Robinson, H., ed. (2001), *Feminism-Art-Theory. An Anthology. 1968–2000,* Oxford: Blackwell.

Rubinstein, R. (1995), *Dress Codes. Meanings and Messages in American Culture,* Boulder, CO: Westview Press.

Sun Tzu (2005), *The Art of War,* translated and annotated by L. Giles, El Paso, TX: El Paso Norte Press.

Winterman, D. and J. Kelly (2010), 'Five Interpretations of Gaga's Meat Dress', *BBC Online,* 14 September, http://www.bbc.co.uk/news/magazine-11297832, accessed 1 December 2011.

WEBSITES

Sadak, http://sadak.de/sadakpress.html, accessed 1 December 2011.

A Shaded View on Fashion, http://www.ashadedviewonfashion.com, accessed 1 December 2011.

SHOWstudio, http://showstudio.com, accessed 1 December 2011.

10

THE FASHION FILM EFFECT
marketa uhlirova

The 'digital age' has brought about considerable shifts in how fashion today is produced, represented, consumed and experienced and, consequently, in our understanding of its very culture. One important form to crystallize amidst these transformations is the fashion film. While the practice of showing fashion through the moving image (and sound) is hardly new, the phenomenon of the fashion film as a widespread form driven and controlled by the fashion industry has only gained momentum in the last decade. Just as twentieth-century fashion lent itself to powerful mediation by photography and the fashion show, twenty-first-century brands now keenly embrace fashion film's reaestheticizations. So much so that the fashion journalist Suzy Menkes (2010: 15) recently declared that 'movies have become the hottest new fashion accessory...for the YouTube generation'. At first glance, 'accessory' seems a fitting way to put it—unlike photography, film is not quite vital to the system, and it remains to be seen if it ever will be. Film is unlikely to challenge photography's dominant position as the most convenient visual mode of representation/communication across the fashion media. Yet, together with email, websites, e-commerce, social media, blogging, live streaming and other dynamic forms of digital communication and exchange, the fashion film has already reshaped the industry in more than one way, and this transition is still very much ongoing. The moving image has proven to be an enticing alternative to other forms of (re) presentation because it has a capacity to open fashion to a performative dimension with a different kind of sensorial and experiential complexity. The fashion film is so ubiquitous and seemingly indispensable today that one imagines the cultural critic Roland Barthes would have to incorporate it into *The Fashion System* (1967). He could hardly afford to ignore 'moving image clothing' as an additional signifying structure, distinct from 'real clothing', 'written clothing' and (static) 'image-clothing'. Fashion film's recent proliferation on the Internet and beyond has demanded that we seriously rethink what role the moving image can play within fashion, and it has, arguably, also reinvigorated a critical interest in the historical impact of cinema on the fashion industry (and vice versa).

In an attempt to better understand this fashion film phenomenon, it is perhaps unavoidable to first ask about its legitimacy as a genre and how such a category might be conceptualized in what is a rather chaotic field. Elsewhere I have outlined a brief, introductory history of the fashion film as a kind of cinema, linked to the fashion industry, that during the course of the twentieth-century evolved in many different modes and eventually exploded with the development of digital technologies. Such a history is to act as a reminder that the rhetoric of newness that often accompanies the contemporary fashion film is not always justified. In that spirit, I have also suggested some ways of framing the fashion film in a broader sense, within intermedial practices and discourses of fashion, cinema, art and the new media (Uhlirova 2013). At the heart of my enquiry here is the question of what film can do for fashion that other media and forms can't. Rather than attempting to interpret individual works in any depth, I consider the recent fashion film phenomenon more globally, as a social, cultural and technological construction and a field that stems from the collective more than any particular individual's contribution. I will explore some of the specificities of the 'film effect', especially as it forms a synergy of sorts with the 'fashion effect', and link these to the conditions of viewing in the 'digital age'.[1] Because the fashion film has asserted that movement and rhythm are among the key instruments of imaging contemporary fashion, it may be particularly illuminating to compare its aesthetic strategies with those of some subgenres in early cinema which, over 100 years ago, first foregrounded the performance and the experience of costume in motion.

I would argue that as an institutionalized cultural form, the fashion film had a curiously delayed emergence. Although it had existed in different guises throughout the twentieth century—the very label 'fashion film' was already used in connection with Pathé newsreels in 1911 (*The Bioscope*, quoted in Leese 1976: 9)—it finally achieved a 'cultural fit' and widespread adoption by the fashion industry in the 2000s. Thus my focus here on the fashion film in the 2000s is not arbitrary. To frame the phenomenon this way proposes to understand it, firstly, as a form that is generated and quintessentially owned by the fashion industry—fulfilling almost exclusively its creative and business needs—and, secondly, as a form that should be situated within the context of the digital technologies with which it has largely been produced and disseminated. This means acknowledging that rather than the origination and development of a form, it is the process of its solidification within certain conditions of its diffusion that amounts to a transformative cultural and social force. The electronic and, increasingly, digital technologies effected crucial changes in the practices of exhibiting and accessing film material, dispersing fashion-as-moving-image in multiple contexts, from the common practice of recording fashion shows for documentation, to television, fashion retail, exhibitions and events. But it was the growing accessibility of the Internet, combined with its increasing capacity to store and play audiovisual content, that made the fashion film finally enter the public consciousness as a distinct category of both the fashion image and the moving image. Key to this change was the placement of the fashion film in various 'online archives' (be they participatory or curated) that can be freely accessed at any time. Arguably the first and most important such online platform has been Nick Knight and Peter Saville's SHOWstudio, which has since 2000 produced and diffused the fashion film globally, exploring aesthetic possibilities and establishing conventions of this Internet 'genre'. The fashion film, then, has come into its own at a time when the very technologies and the spectatorial experience of the filmic and the cinematic were being transformed by the technologies and viewing/user modes of the electronic and especially the digital—a time that Steven Shaviro has characterized as 'witnessing the emergence of a different media regime' (2010: 2).

THE FASHION FILM AS A GENRE?

As a heterogeneous cultural form with no clearly predefined stylistic criteria or conventions, the fashion film eludes any attempt at a neat classification as a genre. Formally, fashion films have relied on a range of filmmaking techniques, from stop-motion and computer animation to variously processed live-action footage and combinations thereof; they have borrowed—and often combined—conventions of other genres and modes of production, including music video, avant-garde and experimental cinema, video art, documentary film, dance film and commercial; they have ranged from non-narrative to those that have a (usually basic) narrative scaffolding; they have included a whole spectrum of approaches from mimetic representation to its simulation to abstraction. They have varied from big-budget to virtually no-budget productions, from commissions by brands to individual, free-floating pieces; they have been made by individuals as well as teams of experienced fashion image-makers, filmmakers, animators and postproduction specialists. Fashion films have been circulated through a wide range of spaces, real and virtual, most prominently on websites but also in fashion show tents, cinemas, museums, galleries and retail environments. Exploratory and visual effects–driven films have coexisted alongside films that adopt more standard journalistic formats—interviews and profiles, reportage on the catwalk, backstage, beauty and the red carpet—which are now integral to online fashion and lifestyle magazines such as *Vogue.com*, *Elle.com* or *T Magazine*. All these types of the fashion moving image—prolific, diverse, multifunctional and unregulated as they are—attest to the great multiplication and diversification of the moving image in the 'digital age'. But are they all 'fashion films'?

Perhaps characteristically for a form that didn't develop in any programmatic way—one that wasn't spoken for by a single collective—the fashion film and the debate about it are surrounded by a certain messiness, with a staggering plurality of views as to what exactly constitutes it. The more secure its place is within the fashion industry (that, for one, is hard to argue with), the more question marks seem to hover over its definition and its place within the histories of cinema and the new media. Given that the majority of fashion films are shot, produced and circulated digitally, can we still consider the fashion film as part of the cinema tradition? As the new media theorist Lev Manovich (2001: 302–3) notes, digitally produced cinema is in its essence painterly, graphic and artificial. It is aesthetically based on special effects (which, as in animation, are largely manually constructed and manipulated) rather than the indexical, photographic 'reality-effect' of cinema proper. Is the fashion film, then, a form of digital (or electronic) cinema, with its new aesthetic derived not only from the possibilities of the electronic image but also from the new viewing experiences of the contemporary moving image culture? Or is it premature to overemphasize the departure of the digital from the (analogue) cinematic, to see it as a rupture with the old rather than its transformation and continuation, especially as the two are still profoundly intertwined and hybridized?

Somewhat predictably, there are also the familiar art-and-commerce disagreements: does the fashion film have artistic merits or is it just a new kind of (formulaic) advertising? Has it developed film/computer language towards new aesthetic or social possibilities, or is it for the most part fulfilling the precoded functions of the 'apparatus(es)'?[2] The proximity of the fashion film to advertising is particularly hard to unpack given that the category of the fashion film seems to be seamlessly applied to more direct kinds of advertising and, at the same time, to work that is demonstrably more invested in authorial expression than in generating promotional benefits for products or brands. The fashion film doesn't always blatantly implicate the viewer as consumer and has, generally, a greater degree of autonomy from the fashions it displays or connotes, as it is less concerned with social and psychological processes of identification, persuasion and reassurance than is the case in more conventional advertising. And therein precisely lies its appeal for brands who are certainly not blind to the new marketing trends that eschew conventional advertising in favour of a more authentic experience. The fashion film thus sits somewhere on the margins of conventional advertising, and where it is a promotion, it remains less direct and less governed—perfectly in tune with an increasingly media-savvy spectator/user who is in control of what to view and how. One thing is certain: the fashion film enters a value system where it is considered on its own terms, while, in an inverted logic, it becomes a commodity to be consumed in its own right.[3]

Failing to establish a clear corpus of the fashion film by such criteria as formal and physical properties, mode of production and effect, could we classify it by its most obvious property—its subject matter? Even that is not so simple. Through numerous interviews conducted with fashion image-makers and commentators including Diane Pernet, Adam Mufti, Kathryn Ferguson and Hywel Davies, the journalist Kirsty Blake Knox (2010) has shown that there was no clear consensus as to whether the fashion film's 'raw material' was fashion at all. Indeed, 'atmosphere videos' that accompany fashion shows are not necessarily of or about fashion; they only begin to signify fashion in the right context. Although rarer, this can also be true for stand-alone promotional films. One of the most striking recent examples is the short animation *Wonderwood* (2010), made by the Brothers Quay to promote Comme des Garçons' fragrance of the same name. The 'allegorical' animation may have been made in direct response to the product which it was to promote—the Quays took the perfume's smell as their point of departure and tried to evoke the lush essence of an enchanted wood—but it showed nothing identifiable as 'fashion'.[4]

Such practice of subordinating and even completely abandoning the fashion subject is certainly nothing new, as it already became standard in fashion photography in the previous decades.[5] When Barthes wrote about fashion photography in the 1960s, he argued it was a distinct genre possessing its own unique lexicon and syntax (1983). By the late 1980s, however, this view became increasingly difficult to sustain, for fashion photography had become highly hybridized—'dirtied' with a growing stock of 'alien' photographic genres and styles. Two major exhibitions which commented on this tendency within contemporary fashion photography, *Chic Clicks* (ICA Boston, 24 January–5 May 2002) and *Fashioning Fiction in Photography Since 1990* (MoMA, 16 April–28 June 2004) made the same point: in the 1990s, fashion photography no longer strove to fulfil its 'principal' task to illustrate the proper subject of fashion, the 'theater of clothing' (Lipovetsky 2002: T10). Instead, the photographers' self-expression and exploration came to be valued more highly, especially by the more progressive fashion and lifestyle magazines such as *Purple, i-D, Self-service* and *Dutch*. This shift, it was argued, made fashion photography come closer to the contemporary lived reality (Lipovetsky 2002; Kismaric and Respini 2004) while also becoming more and more art-like (Lehmann 2002; Kismaric and Respini 2004)—hence (it was implied) its rightful place in fine art establishments.

Like fashion photography, the fashion film appears to be something of an ubergenre, an umbrella term that accommodates, and breaks down the boundaries of, a great variety of existing genres. Such openness of parameters and a genuine sense of exploration of possibilities are also actively encouraged by the various platforms that commission and exhibit it, keen as they are to emphasize the value of artistic originality. At the same time, the fashion film is, inevitably, undergoing a process of acceptance and institutionalization—of 'stabili[sing] its own ways of being and doing'—while also becoming a 'social institution' as 'a coordinated complex of objects, behaviours and expectations' (Cassetti 2009: 59). This kind of self-management and self-regulation of the fashion film has been especially apparent since its entering the 'mainstream' between 2008 and 2010, with fashion journalists and big brands becoming increasingly important agents to coshape the field and the discourse. If we accept the fashion film as a genre, we have to accept a notion of a genre not as a static set of stylistic or material commonalities but as an ever-evolving historically bound category which is fluid and at times even self-contradictory. Arguably, the fashion film is most coherently bound by its belonging to the fashion industry and by its (multiple) functioning within it. Ultimately, however, the methodological question remains of how inclusive or exclusive the fashion film as a genre should be. If it is limited to the more exploratory production led by visual effects, as I am inclined to apply it, we may learn something about its aesthetic strategies—but how are we to think of what is left behind? If, conversely, it includes all the journalistic formats that are being produced, leaving only fashion as a common turf, just how useful can the category be to any understanding and interpretation of it?

THE FASHION FILM EFFECT

Since so many fashion filmmakers have a background in the fashion industry, and so have cultivated specialist knowledge and an appreciation of clothing and accessories, it is hardly surprising that they are largely motivated by the desire to demonstrate how these are made, to show the complexities of their detail and functionality. As Nick Knight noted about one of his first films, *Sweet,* he wanted to

> show how much effort, and even pain, goes into making a single dress. I wanted each garment to seem precious, like an art form...I'm well aware of the fact that fashion is ultimately disposable—but I'm lucky enough to be able to work with people who prove there's more to it than that. (quoted in Frankel 2000)

Similarly, Ruth Hogben said of her 2009 collaboration with Gareth Pugh (Figure 10.1):

> You've got to try and...mak[e] sure people can see the clothes. The clothes are just as important as the [filmmaker's] concept; everybody has to see what the clothes are, what they're made out of and how they move. (quoted in Ferguson and Bradley 2009)

10.1. Frame enlargements from Gareth Pugh, autumn/winter 2009. © Ruth Hogben / Art + Commerce

In a didactic sense, then, film can direct attention, show a multiplicity of angles, illustrate a way of folding or magnify detail. Crucially, it can also re-present clothing as a living organism. As Hogben observed:

> [Pugh's] clothes are not about one simple movement (walking up and down the runway). As you saw in the film, the big coat changes form and becomes a kind of ladybird. I think it was really exciting for him to be able to see in more than one way. (quoted in Ferguson and Bradley 2009)

But such notions of film as a moving study or illustration of fashion are only part of the story. Equally important is film's capacity to extend the properties of physical garments into new mental spaces where experimental effects of impressionistic and poetic cinema play a significant role—as do the qualities of sound and rhythm. And for this, the predisposition of digital cinema as a painterly medium is ideal. Hogben's own work transforms live footage of dressed bodies in motion into multilayered imagery, synchronizing visual rhythms with musical ones. Such an approach characterizes the fashion film as a simultaneous exploration of the properties of cinema and fashion. Film transports the sartorial into a persuasive illusory world that has the dual effect of offering new knowledge and defamiliarizing. Film furnishes different experiences and at the same time poses different spectatorial demands. As it moves, it also moves the spectator.

The fashion film's emphasis on the display of clothing in motion echoes that of early cinema's serpentine dance and the trick film of the late 1890s and early 1900s. It was the serpentine dance in particular, as filmed at Edison Manufacturing Company, Gaumont, Pathé-Frères, American Mutoscope and Biograph and other companies, that most prominently centred on costume as a fitting physical manifestation of motion and time (Gunning 2002; Lista 2006a: 353–7, 2006b; Uhlirova 2011).[6] A distinct subgenre of 'dance subjects', it capitalized on the international stage successes of the American dancer Loïe Fuller, mechanically reproducing the swirling and undulating movements of many of her imitators (that included Annabelle Whitford Moore, Crissie Sheridan, Teresina Negri and Bob Walter). In these short films, costume became a visualization of continuity—it presented itself in a permanent state of flux, with shapes rhythmically appearing and disappearing, momentarily 'solidifying' into flowers, waves, whirls or flames (Figure 10.2). Fuller herself had emphasized the constant metamorphosis of forms with the use of coloured lights and other stage effects, and similarly, the serpentine films were typically enhanced by colours, applied by hand or, later, stencilling.

Following Fuller, cinema embraced costume as a device that can mesmerize and hypnotize the spectator, a dramatic and radiant entity with a potential for engendering multiple forms and optical effects. Cinema proved that it could mimic, more or less successfully, the spectatorial pleasure of Fuller's distinct choreography of effervescent, ever-evolving form. Costume, movement and time appeared to form an indivisible unity in the serpentine dance, and through the protean veils of the earliest films, cinema already anticipated its capacity to not only record (register) but also generate imagery. This interest in costume as a site of instability and constant transformation continued in Georges Méliès's and Pathé's trick films and 'féeries'[7] such as *The Wonderful Living Fan* (*Le Merveilleux éventail vivant*, Méliès, 1904), *Rajah's Casket* (*L'Ecrin du rajah*, Gaston Velle, 1906) and *Transformation* (*Métempsycose*, Segundo de Chomón, 1907), where the physical movement of the serpentine dance gives way to the 'magical' movement of substitution though editing. Méliès, and Pathé filmmakers after him, conceptualized the film camera as a pleasure-loving eye

10.2. Frame enlargements from Annabelle Whiteford Moore's serpentine dance dir. William Heise/W.K.L. Dickson for Edison Manufacturing Company, c. 1895. Courtesy Archives françaises du film / CNC

that lavishes on the spectacular metamorphoses of material splendour, and once again, it is the costume that typically becomes the principal variable, mutating into multiple incarnations before the viewer's eyes.

Much like the fashion film, early cinema did not allow for elaborate narrative development (although narrative certainly was not completely excluded) and instead strategically focussed on display. André Gaudreault and Tom Gunning have called this tendency 'the cinema of attractions' and argued it was ruled by an impulse to make visible, to exhibit (Gaudreault and Gunning 1986). Although the term *cinema of attractions* described the early period of cinema (until c. 1906–7), Gunning (1990: 60–1) soon allowed for its wider applications, naming, among others, avant-garde and experimental film. Over the last two decades, film scholars have applied Gaudreault's and Gunning's influential theorization to examine a range of non-narrative film as well as non-narrative sequences within narrative film. Among others, the model of attractions has also recently been used to interpret fashion-related films such as newsreels and fashion sequences in fiction films (Hanssen 2009; Evans 2011). The contemporary fashion film too can be situated within this theoretical delineation as it clearly privileges a cumulative display of tableaux and effects (usually accompanied by asynchronous sound) over linear narrative with diegetic sound.

Although there are many affinities between the fashion film and early cinema worth examining, it is the problem of costume in movement and its relation to stasis that I want to emphasize here. There is a striking similarity in how both early cinema and the fashion film emerged out of an impulse to animate a world that was for the most part mediated through static imagery (although in both cases this was already anticipated by existing practices within visual culture). Indeed, some of the early SHOWstudio productions mine the aesthetic of what Penny Martin calls 'moving stills' (2009: 55). Films such as SHOWstudio's *Shelly Fox 14,* Nick Knight's 2002 Warhol tribute *More Beautiful Women,* Nigel Bennett's 2004 *Martin Margiela AW 2004* and Jean-François Carly's 2005 *I Feel* engineer, very much from the photographer's viewpoint, a dialogue between photographic immobility and cinematic movement and time.[8] Tellingly, early cinema was often referred to as 'animated photographs' or 'animated pictures', a fact that betrays early film culture's reluctance to dissociate its new mode of representation from the old ones based on stillness. This early terminology reveals an understanding of cinematic movement as mechanically reconstructed from static images, not as the seamless illusion of continuity its effect produced. Fluid movement was not seen as cinema's ontological essence but, rather, a surplus value added to pictures, especially photographs. Yet, fluidity of movement was precisely what early film practices and discourses were fascinated with. Following the many protocinematic devices (zoetrope, praxinoscope, the magic lantern and so forth), early cinema called attention to the illusion of movement—this time more seamless than ever—and its dizzying potential to surprise and amuse spectators. As cinema emerged into the late nineteenth-century culture of popular attractions (originally considered, as it was, among subjects of popular scientific amusement), the notion of animated photographs also evoked the awe-inspiring miracle of the inanimate coming to life that cinema audiences experienced.[9] Through movement and time, film undeniably foregrounds the quality of presence (although, admittedly, this presence can be theorized from several perspectives). As Roland Barthes (1978: 45) and Christian Metz after him (1974: 5–8) have noted, the 'having-been-there' of a photograph gives way to the 'being there of the thing' in film or, as Vivian Sobchack (2009: 73) has it, the moment of the photograph is replaced with the momentum of film. And because of the impossibility of fixing and owning film as a discreet, portable image/object, it also makes it less prone than a photograph to being had, to becoming fetishized (Metz 1985).

There is, of course, a fundamental difference between how early cinema strategically approached dress in movement and how the contemporary fashion film does. While early cinema mobilized costume (through dance or tricks, for example) in order to show what the moving image can do, the fashion industry has utilized movement (including that of the camera, editing or effects) in order to show what clothing can do. Yet, beyond this difference, both produce a similar result, what I call the *fashion film effect*, in that they present clothing as an elastic, polymorphous and unstable entity. No longer possessing a fixed form, the physical fashion object becomes less of an objective certainty. Its potential to be endlessly reconstituted in space and time imbue it with new defining values of visuality and transitionality. Both early cinema and the fashion film also accentuate the surface, the skin of the screen, on which the kinetic and spectacular images 'parade' and accumulate. This is where images of fashion are pushed towards the spectator, their fashion-filmic materiality and texture magnified in their capricious fluidity. Fashion on the screen produces a unique, emotionally charged overlapping (layering) of two materials, the sartorial and the cinematic, what Giuliana Bruno (2011: 95) has called 'the fashioning and wearing of the image' or, to extend the Deleuzian concept (1983), a kind of fashion-image-movement.

But for this materiality of the surface to reach its tactile and emotional potential, for it to assert its presence so as to touch the spectator, the experience of the electronic/digital screen is more limiting when compared to the projection-based cinema experience (analogue or digital). And since the performative aspect of projection/display is such a vital part of cinema, the transition from cinematic to electronic is as critical with regard to the shifts in the spectator's experience as it is with regard to the shifts in the aesthetic of the film object itself. It is principally a question of two aspects of the viewing experience that have profoundly changed both the object and the spectatorial habits and expectations: firstly, the inferior image quality on the electronic screen that, even at its best, compromises image resolution and depth of colour and, secondly, the fragmentary viewing modes enabled by cable television, video and the Internet. The electronic and the digital have generated a new regime in which the spectator becomes a spectator-user, exercising a greater-than-ever control over film viewing while at the same time facing a greater degree of acceleration and distraction. Importantly, this is also a regime which violates the notion of 'cinematic time' that characterizes traditional film viewing. Nathalie Khan has recently drawn on Lev Manovich's concept of a 'permanent presence' to describe the floating existence of fashion films online, '[un]restricted by time or space in which the image[s are] shown' (Khan 2012: 237). It is perhaps not too far-fetched to claim that today's uberavailability of film (DVDs, online) has paradoxically recast film in cinematic projection as 'the real thing', as somehow possessing the quality of aura (which, following Walter Benjamin, seems an absurdity).[10]

The omnipresence and saturation of the moving image in electronic media has not always been interpreted as a positive force. Already in the mid-1990s, Suzy Menkes (1995: 47) observed that the recent 'fashion's TV [and video] frenzy' (one that she put down to cable television especially) made fashion seem faster and more disposable than ever. She also noted that designers were now 'play[ing] to the cameras', privileging theatrical effect and entertainment over the 'real thing'—the clothing itself. The film theorist Vivian Sobchack (2009: 79–81) has, equally gloomily, described the electronically disseminated image as simulated, atomized and merely skin-deep, in its 'simultaneous, dispersed, and insubstantial transmission across a network'.[11] Locating the electronic image (and the electronic experience) within the postmodernist framework, she has argued that space 'become[s] abstract, ungrounded, and flat—a site for play and display rather than an invested situation in which action "counts"' (Sobchack 2009: 79–81).

This would suggest that, evocative and thrilling as it may be, the fashion film cannot really *matter* to us in the same way in the virtual electronic landscape of our computer screens as it can in the cinema, that it cannot be as fully absorbing or feel as physical. In some ways, the not-so-precious digital experience of the fashion film echoes the nonimmersive spectatorship of the cinema of attractions where visual pleasure was not (yet) locked into coherent fantasy worlds (that came to be emphasized by the narrative mode but also the cinema as a particular kind of space), worlds that would unleash the psychic mechanisms of desire and identification. The contemporary fashion film, too, is part of a distracted milieu in which we, as the viewers/users, are exposed to an abundance of appealing imagery that fight for our attention while being easily ruptured and even cancelled out by each other. Postmodern critics such as Sobchack are probably right in implying that this milieu produces short-lived audiovisual intensities whose experiences are equally short-lived. Whether we take a dismal view or not, the fashion film (somewhat like the music video) is undeniably symptomatic of our contemporary moving image landscape, the (new) media regime that raises some pressing questions about just how it might coshape twenty-first-century culture.

ACKNOWLEDGEMENTS

Some of the ideas that I develop in this chapter stem from a conversation between Caroline Evans, Penny Martin and myself in 2009 about the inherent similarities between the contemporary fashion film and the early cinema of attraction. I would like to thank both for their comments on this text.

NOTES

1. Christian Metz, Jean-Louis Baudry and other film theorists have considered cinema in terms of what unique effects it produces, or what it does as a medium, beyond its 'reality-effect'. More recently, Sean Cubitt has in his ambitious study *The Cinema Effect* (2005) posed this question anew, with regard to the entire history of cinema, including digital cinema.

2. From early on, Manovich (2001) has shown how computer software programmes and packages cleverly embed avant-garde aesthetic strategies in their menus and commands.

3. In *The System of Objects,* the cultural theorist Jean Baudrillard has already made this point about advertising. He was concerned with its 'dual status as a discourse on an object and as an object in its own right' and its dual function as *imperative* and *indicative* (2005: 180). Following Barthes, he notes that advertising is not merely functional but also creates an extra universe of 'pure connotation' (Baudrillard 2005: 178–9), which in itself becomes the object to be consumed.

4. One might, of course, ask what exactly are the fashion markers in most conventional perfume commercials, given perfume and smell are such abstract entities. The bottle itself? Images of glamour, beauty, desire, sex? The Comme des Garçons film seems to be a rare example of a perfume commercial that attempts to illustrate an essence of the thing rather than a promise it makes.

5. This is also true for other imagery produced and commissioned within the fashion industry. Comme des Garçons' own ad campaigns or their *Six* magazine from between 1988 and 1991 are good examples.

6. The term *serpentine dance* is used here as a common denominator for a number of specific choreographies based on a similar principle, including the butterfly, fire, lily, lotus and scarf dance.

7. The cinematic féerie (fairy play) developed from the stage féerie, a genre that was especially popular in France during the nineteenth century, with an equivalent in the English pantomime. The féeries dealt with fantastical and supernatural subjects and were especially distinctive for their spectacular displays and magical transformations, with great emphasis on production values, including costumes. For more on early film costume as a cinematic spectacle and the aesthetic of opulence, see Uhlirova 2011.

8. In her recent article on the digital fashion film, Nathalie Khan (2012) too considers the contemporary fashion film as transitional between stillness and movement; she also believes that the contemporary fashion film must be understood vis-à-vis the fashion photograph. I would like to thank her for sharing her article with me prior to publication and comparing notes.

9. The act of coming-to-life was in fact thematized in early cinema, most notably by Méliès who had paintings and objects routinely transform into living, breathing creatures. Also see Barthes 1981 and Metz 1985 on the conceptualization of the photograph as death-like and the cinema as life-like.

10. In Benjamin's account, film was precisely one of the prevalent modern media of mass reproduction associated with the loss of the aura. See especially his critique of the 'ultraconservative' notions of film as being in any way sacred or supernatural (Benjamin 1999: 221). Yet, Benjamin was largely concerned with the absence of the *real* that film—itself a copy—can only represent; he couldn't see the cinephile point of view that film stock, despite its status as copy, may have intrinsic artefact value attached to it, that cinema viewing, as experience, may be the authentic reality, and that the film image may acquire an auratic presence of sorts as it travels in real time from a projector to a screen.

11. Sobchack (2009) puts special emphasis on the network's character as flimsy and insubstantial, as opposed to being a grounded and physical presence. Drawing on Fredric Jameson (1984), she sees electronic space as affect-free, as both disorienting and liberating of centred subjectivity—what Jameson described as a peculiar kind of euphoria.

BIBLIOGRAPHY

Barthes, R. (1978), 'Rhetoric of the Image', in *Image, Music, Text,* New York: Hill and Wang.

Barthes, R. (1981), *Camera Lucida,* New York: Hill and Wang.

Barthes, R. (1983), *Fashion System,* New York: Hill and Wang.

Baudrillard, J. (2005), *The System of Objects,* London: Verso.

Benjamin, W. (1999), 'The Work of Art in the Age of Mechanical Reproduction', in H. Arendt (ed.), *Illuminations,* London: Pimlico, 211–35.

Bradley, L. and K. Ferguson (2009), 'Birds Eye View 2009: Panel Discussion', SHOWstudio, http://showstudio.com/project/birds_eye_view_2009#discussion_transcript, accessed 22 January 2012.

Bruno, G. (2011), 'Surface, Fabric, Weave: The Fashioned World of Wong Kar-wai', in A. Munich (ed.), *Fashion in Film,* Indianapolis: Indiana University Press, 83–105.

Cassetti, F. (2009), 'Filmic Experience', *Screen,* 50: 1.

Cubitt, S. (2005), *The Cinema Effect,* Cambridge, MA: MIT Press.

Deleuze, G. (1983), *Cinema 1: L'Image-mouvement,* Paris: Minuit.

Evans, C. (2011), 'The Walkies', in A. Munich (ed.), *Fashion in Film,* Indianapolis: Indiana University Press, 110–34.

Frankel, S. (2000), 'Sweet', SHOWstudio, 10 November, http://showstudio.com/project/sweet#essay, accessed 2 February 2012.

Gunning, T. (1990), 'The Cinema of Attractions: Early Film, Its Spectator and the Avant-garde', in T. Elsaesser (ed.), *Early Cinema: Space, Frame, Narrative,* London: BFI Publishing, 56–61.

Gunning, T. (2002), 'Loïe Fuller and the Art of Motion', in R. Allen and M. Turvey (eds), *Camera Obscura, Camera Lucida: Essays in Honor of Annette Michelson,* Amsterdam: University of Amsterdam Press, 75–90.

Gunning, T. and A. Gaudreault (1986), 'Early Cinema as a Challenge to Film History', in W. Strauven (ed.), *The Cinema of Attractions Reloaded,* Amsterdam: Amsterdam University Press.

Hanssen, E. F. (2009), 'Symptoms of Desire: Color, Costume and Commodities in Fashion Newsreels of the 1910s and 1920s', *Film History,* 21/2: 107–21.

Jameson, F. (1984), 'Postmodernism, or the Cultural Logic of Late Capital', *New Left Review,* 1/146: 53–92.

Khan, N. (2012), 'Cutting the Fashion Body: Why the Fashion Image Is No Longer Still', *Fashion Theory,* 16/2: 235–50.

Kismaric, S. and E. Respini (2004), *Fashioning Fiction in Photography Since 1990,* New York: Museum of Modern Art.

Knight, N. (2009), 'Foreword', in *SHOWstudio: Fashion Revolution at Somerset House,* London: Somerset House, 3.

Knox, K. B. (2010), *Having the Stars,* MA diss., Central Saint Martins College of Art and Design, University of the Arts London.

Leese, E. (1976), *Costume Design in the Movies,* Bembridge: BCW Publishing.

Lehmann, U. (2002), 'Fashion Photography', in U. Lehmann (ed.), *Chic Clicks: Commerce and Creativity in Contemporary Fashion Photography,* Boston: Institute of Contemporary Art.

Lipovetsky, G. (2002), 'More Than Fashion', in U. Lehmann (ed.), *Chic Clicks: Commerce and Creativity in Contemporary Fashion Photography,* Boston: Institute of Contemporary Art, T10.

Lista, G. (2006a), *Loïe Fuller, danseuse de la Belle Epoque,* Paris: Hermann.

Lista, G. (2006b), 'Loïe Fuller and the Cinema', *Cinegrafie,* 19 (The Comic and the Sublime): 297–313.

Manovich, L. (2001), *The Language of New Media,* Cambridge, MA: MIT Press.

Martin, P. (2009), 'SHOWstudio: A Revolution in the Making', in *SHOWstudio: Fashion Revolution,* London: Somerset House, 54–9.

Menkes, S. (1995), 'Fashion's TV Frenzy', *New York Times,* 2 April: 47.

Menkes, S. (2010), 'Fashion Films Become the Hottest New Accessories', *International Herald Tribune,* 18 May: 15.

Metz, C. (1974), 'On the Impression of Reality in the Cinema', in *Film Language: A Semiotics of the Cinema,* New York: Oxford University Press, 3–15.

Metz, C. (1985), 'Photography and Fetish', *October,* 34: 81–90.

Shaviro, S. (2010), *Post-cinematic Affect,* Ropley: O-Books.

Sobchack, V. (2009), 'The Scene of the Screen: Envisioning Cinematic and Electronic "Presence"', in R. Stam and T. Miller (eds), *Film and Theory: An Anthology,* Malden, MA and Oxford: Blackwell Publishing, 67–84.

Uhlirova, M. (2011), 'Costume in Early Cinema: The Aesthetic of Opulence', in M. Uhlirova (ed.), *Fashion in Film: Birds of Paradise* [exhibition catalogue], New York: Fashion in Film and Museum of the Moving Image.

Uhlirova, M. (2013), '100 Years of the Fashion Film: Frameworks and Histories', *Fashion Theory,* 17/2: 137–57.

Section 3

NEW MEDIA

11

FASHION MODELLING, BLINK TECHNOLOGIES AND NEW IMAGING REGIMES
elizabeth wissinger

The air outside the tents at New York City's Fashion Week crackles with energy. Paparazzi, fashion students, film crews, fashion reporters and curious onlookers jumble together as fashionistas and their acolytes in sky-high heels totter by. Models, still in their wild hair and make-up from the runway, stop amidst calls of 'Over here!' and 'Just one more!' to pose obligingly for the battery of flashing cameras before disappearing into the black cars waiting to whisk them off to their next show. The excitement is palpable. I am on a research mission, milling around in the crowd outside the tents during New York City's Fashion Week, drinking up the energy—an energy that taken on new significance since the Internet has become a part of our daily lives.[1]

This chapter examines the impact of the international imaging systems of cable television and the Internet on modelling. I argue that these technologies represent a new imaging regime, a notion that builds on poststructuralist feminist Patricia Clough's idea that the dominant mode of imaging and the dominant forms of power are connected within a specific 'regime of representation' that enforces particular social and cultural practices (Clough and Halley 2007: 16). Examining this shift, via a study of modelling work, reveals changing understandings of not only work, the body and consumption but also practices that make up the fabric of our everyday lives.

THE BLINK

The imaging regime dominated by the Internet has changed many things. In a world now punctuated by pop-ups, pings and tweets, we relate to images differently. Images dance at the margins of our vision whether we are at work or at play. With the dawn of this imaging regime in the late 1980s and early 1990s, attention spans have been overwhelmed, pathways of suggestion have proliferated and the volatility of markets has reached a rapid boil.

Journalist Malcolm Gladwell's notion of the blink (2005) is useful for conceptualizing this volatility, a time of speed-up on various fronts, not the least of which is the velocity and number of images flooding our lives, creating what Herbert Simon predicted would become a 'poverty of attention' (Simon 1971: 40–1). Characterized by speed, the regime of the blink has produced a veritable explosion in the availability of information, moving faster than the human ability to process it, requiring new techniques of attention to manage the flow. Communications scholar Brian Massumi claims the kind of 'networked jumpiness' typical of this regime facilitates forms of 'affective attunement' (2005: 32, 44). In what cultural geographer Nigel Thrift has likened to the sylvan flashes of a school of fish, we flit from one image to the next, with little time for conscious reflection and at times without registering what we actually see (2008: 236).

What happens to the image-making industry in a world where modern capitalist practices have recreated the means of perception so often that our 'social, urban, psychic, and industrial fields' are 'saturated with sensory input' (Crary 1999: 13)? The need to create an image that cuts through the noise has changed the modelling industry in ways indicative of larger trends affecting work, the body and culture that point to not only new structures of attention but also new structures of production. Looking in particular at why fashion models tend to be so thin, and so monochromatically white, raises questions about structural shifts that affect not only the appearance of models but also the meaning of work and bodies more generally.

There are several reasons for this, and I will examine each in turn. First, the regime of the blink has influenced the structure and function of the fashion show in a manner that pulled for a 'bleaching' of the catwalk, aiding and abetting the phenomenon of the ever-shrinking model body. Related to this, the Internet's globalizing tendencies have facilitated the influx of new models from all over the globe, as access to images of fashion has heightened knowledge about and interest in working in the industry. The larger pool of aspirants facilitated 'scouting' (that is searching for) models in destinations ever-farther from the fashion capitals of New York, Paris, London and Milan, contributing to the shortening of model careers and, consequently, increasing the competition for jobs, exacerbating the precarious nature of getting and keeping a job in modelling. This scenario, increasingly the problem for jobs in general, is one that the modelling industry nonetheless glamorizes. Third and finally, in the regime of the blink, models sell us a life engaged with technology that productively focuses our energy, where we freely give away our leisure time in a manner that can be measured and organized for profit.

The effects of the regime of the blink are thrown into sharp relief when comparing watching a fashion show in person, as models come and go, up and down the catwalk, to watching the Victoria's Secret Fashion Show. Each demands a different way of attending to the event. The Victoria's Secret show, a televised event with simultaneous webcast, shaped by a breathless pace of quick cuts and wild camera angles, is paced so fast it is sometimes hard to know where to look. It organizes bodies in space and time very differently than the fashion show's traditional form.

The delirium of the fashion world has not always spun at such a frenetic pace, however. From its inception in the early 1900s, the fashion show, or 'parade' as it was called at the time, was an exercise in regal glamour. Often sober affairs, models struck dramatic poses and walked sedately, reflecting the social status of their clientele. The show was about buying the fashions on parade. Models sometimes held a small card denoting the model number of the gown they wore, for ease of ordering. Unscripted, often without set pieces or music, their sole purpose was to show the fashions to the clientele.

In mid-century America, fashion's pace overall moved more slowly, from the shows to career arcs, to the news of fashion itself. Fashion news took months to arrive from Paris, the centre of the fashion world at the time. We did not have 24/7 news coverage allowing access to fashion weeks from around the globe; in fact 'fashion week' only happened in the big three of the fashion nexus: Paris, London and New York (unlike the myriad of fashion weeks today, from Shanghai to Sao Paulo). Only in March of 1953 was *Vogue* magazine able to publish its first 'international' fashion issue—made possible by the new jet travel—in which, 'for the first time in one issue we can report on couture collections in five countries' (McLuhan 1964: 212).

Up through the 1980s, many models' careers were longer and slower-paced as well. While some models worked for only a short time before marrying out, 1940s and 1950s queens of the modelling world Dorian Leigh and Suzie Parker both reigned for at least a decade. Similarly, the supermodels who came to prominence while the regime of the blink was still in its infancy in the 1980s seemed to be the last hurrah for the long modelling career. More recently, according to one respondent, the owner of a New York modelling agency I interviewed for part of my study, a long career even for a successful model in high fashion is three to five years. This shortening of careers is due in part to the need for 'stimulation', as the owner of a New York model agency put it:

> Of course, [the Internet] speeds things up, everything is accessible. So because everything is accessible and you might see the same faces because of the accessibility, you might have to make it more cyclical. You know, the cycle of new faces—oh, who's she? You know, she's a new face. You know, it's all about stimulation.

He connected the idea of being 'cyclical' to the increased need for more new faces in the industry, making it difficult for any one model to achieve much staying power.

The need for stimulation has not only shortened careers, it has made them harder to get. Reality television shows such as *America's Next Top Model* and websites such as Modelina.com and Style.com, which cover the industry in detail, have increased familiarity with the industry, swelling the ranks of aspiring models and increasing competition. On top of this growing interest, the Internet has made it easier to find potential models in far-flung places, causing a broader and faster influx into the industry of aspirants from all over the globe, as this agent pointed out:

> You used to be able to send scouts and maybe wait a week or two for an image to come by, not because there weren't any computers, it's because you wanted the right photos to sell, [which took time.] [Now it's] pretty much live and you do video streaming, you know exactly what you're getting into. And that's instant and that's why the world is open, that's why you can find a girl in Riga, Latvia or you can find a girl, you know, anywhere in the world, you know, Sao Paulo—Sao Paulo's good—and Peru. You know, in a little mountain in Peru you can find a girl.

With the globe as your scouting grounds, a new girl who could be the next big thing might be just one scouting trip away. This attraction to and availability of the new detracts from the energy and time that an agency might have spent working with the young women, or girls, as they are called in industry parlance, that they already have on their rosters. The general consensus among my respondents was that not many models have time to build careers, and although there are exceptions to this rule, on the whole, new models tend to either make it right away or drop out.

Not only is there a hunger for new faces—wrought by the instant overexposure made possible by the 24/7 availability of fashion images on the Internet—but also the competition for attention has intensified as the viewing public becomes increasingly distracted. Consequently, the regime of the blink shortens attention spans. While advertisers once assumed viewers would take the time to read the text of an ad to get information about the product, images now try to make an instant impact, without necessarily explaining what's for sale. As 'show, don't tell' has become the name of the game, brand advertisements for luxury fashions evoking a mood or a feeling depict models in various states of undress, or enact attention-getting scenarios, with text showing only the name of the brand or just enough information to catch a distracted look.

As the public's 'networked jumpiness' has increased, measures to ensure the marketability of a model's image have become somewhat draconian. Digital imaging's rise as a dominant regime fanned a long-standing desire, evidenced in the history of photographic retouching, to manipulate appearances. While photo retouching has always been a given in fashion photography, after the 1990s, Photoshop took off. Pixilated thighs were shaved thinner; splotches erased; and pores, under-eye circles and wayward hairs magically disappeared. This new digital unreal created a tension between the fashion images in circulation and the real people they supposedly represented, resulting in an even stronger push for models to embody an increasingly impossible look. As one model agent told then top model Coco Rocha when she weighed just 108 pounds, 'You need to lose more weight. The look this year is anorexic. We don't want you to be anorexic; we just want you to look it' (Herbst 2008). When fashionable equals thin, then looking thin from every angle becomes the Holy Grail for those caught up in producing the tsunami of images brought on by the cable and Internet revolutions. Achieving the fashionable look demanded producing a look that stood out and caught the attention of an increasingly fickle public, as well as maintaining the kind of body that looked like it had already been Photoshopped.

To argue that the regime of the blink fosters this type of cultural attention deficit disorder lends a new perspective on the recent moral panics about the changing look of models on runways and in magazines. These panics have centred on two aspects of models' bodies. The first focus has been on how thin they are, as evidenced by the public outcry against too-thin models that stimulated some efforts at regulating the fashion shows in terms of the body mass index of the models that were hired. The second has looked at what fashion journalist Guy Trebay has dubbed the 'bleaching of the catwalks'—evidenced by the lack of models of colour on the runways—which garnered media attention in the last few years (2007).

Feminists such as Sandra Bartky (1990), Naomi Wolf (1992), Susan Bordo (1993) and Sut Jhally and Jean Kilbourne (2011) have attributed the slender model body to an effort by patriarchal power, incensed by threats to its dominance, to keep women frail and easily controlled. Bodily aesthetics emerge not only from gendered power relations, fashion's dictates or the inexorable processes of consumerism—the level of technological development at any given time shapes them as well. This approach complicates these usual explanations for the bleaching of the catwalks and models' shrinking girth to include the influence of developments in imaging technology as a causal factor.

Looking to patriarchy, for instance, cannot fully account for the fact that models' bodies have gotten smaller since the 1930s. Figure 11.1, culled from my research tracking the body measurements reported in the model agency annuals listing all of the available models for that year, documents this trend. As the graph illustrates, the bust, waist and hip sizes of models from the 1930s to the present has shrunk, both in terms of the range of sizes in working models, from tallest to shortest, and their bust, waist and hip measurements.[2] While contemporary models are taller, their measurements have stayed similar to those of their much shorter counterparts from previous eras (Twiggy, for instance, measured 31–22–32 inches [79–56–81 cm] but was only 5 feet 6 inches tall, a proportion that looks very different on a woman of 5 feet 11 inches [180 cm]).

In 1930, the most powerful modelling agency in the world, run by John Robert Powers, presented models such as Betty Marr, who, while tall enough, at 5 feet 9 inches, weighed in at a portly, by today's standards, 135 pounds [61 kilograms], with the generous proportions of 35-inch bust, 29-inch waist and 38-inch hips [89–74–97 cm] (Powers 1930: 7; first on the chart in Figure 11.1). By the 1950s, models slimmed down considerably, yet Dorian Leigh, one of the most famous models of the era, was only 5 feet 4 inches [163 cm]—three inches shorter than today's minimum standard. It was only after the 1960s and the dawn of television—when the art and artifice of the

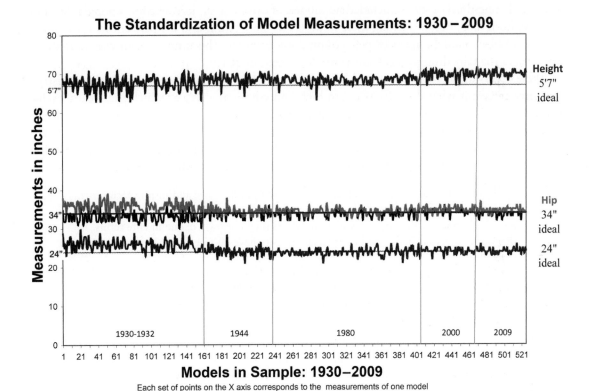

11.1. Model measurements. Data compiled from annual rosters of the John Robert Powers (1930, 1932 and 1944), Ford (1980), Elite (2000) and Wilhelmina (2009) agencies

corseted 1950s model gave way to the model in motion, looking fashionable at any time, from any angle—that model bodies settled into the narrow frame that we are accustomed to today.

After the global imaging tsunami of cable technology and the Internet came into play in the 1980s and 1990s, however, this attenuation became ever more extreme. Currently, there are plenty of girls with Twiggy-like measurements, such as Danielle Dwyer, who was listed on Elite's website as having a 33–23–34 inch [83–58–86 cm] figure, but at 5 feet 10 inches [178 cm] her frame is much longer than her 1960s counterpart. Model manuals from the 2000s explain that while the required height to model is strictly 5 feet 7 inches [170 cm] and above, 'fashions change … less than ten years ago, the ideal model was a size 6' (Bean and Bidner 2004). However, one model agent observed, 'During most recent seasons, all my designers want size 0 to size 2 models … the girls were still just as tall, but they were tiny. They had to fit in the sample clothes, and they had to look good' (Bean and Bidner 2004: 61). Has patriarchy become that much more powerful, since the 1930s, when a wider variety of bodies were acceptable (as per Figure 11.1)? Or is there something else going on?

Similarly, although public data are difficult to obtain, since modelling agencies don't make a habit of publicizing how many models of colour they have on their rosters, and the US Department of Labor has not tracked this data, there is clear evidence that models of colour have been under-represented in fashion in recent decades. After press coverage drew attention to the issue, *Women's Wear Daily* tracked the race of models on New York Fashion Week's runways in 2007 and found fully one-third of shows included no models of colour at all. Jezebel.com, a popular fashion and feminism blog, began tracking these numbers in 2007 and found a 6 per cent increase in the number of black models, up to 18 per cent on 2008 runways. This improvement was short-lived, however, as the tally dropped back down to 16 per cent in 2010.

These observations are corroborated by sociologist Ashley Mears's findings about the industry's tendency to favour what she calls 'size zero high-end ethnic models', by which she means 'exclusively Anglo-looking' models who are exceedingly thin (2011: 171). Mears argues that, contrary to popular belief, fashion models are not selected on the basis of their good looks. In fact, in the face of enormous uncertainty, the fashion elite tends to adhere to pre-established conventions, looking to past successes to determine what look to promote for the future. Mears explains,

> Producers in the field of high-end fashion are attempting to awe and inspire each other. They choose models principally because they *do not* have anything in common with the average shopper … they prize distinction, which they narrowly define in elite terms. In this world, everyday bodies and their racial diversity have no place. (2011: 206–7)

While racism has been a constant in the industry, there have been moments—such as the flourishing of several black modelling agencies in the 1940s (Summers 1998; Haidarali 2005, 2007; McAndrew 2010) and the number of black runway models, such as Pat Cleveland and Bethann Hardison, who 'dominated the runways' in the 1970s (La Ferla 2011)—when black models have come to the fore. Advertising and fashion have never been stable businesses, however, and in the speed-up that comes with the regime of the blink, the level of uncertainty and volatility in the industry has increased. Further, the kinds of technologies that shrink distance and accelerate time typical of this regime have also made large mergers and acquisitions possible in the fashion world, reducing the space available for artistic expression while increasing the demands to meet commercial needs (Agins 1999). These changes led to a new pressure on creatives in the industry to produce a saleable or safe look, shrinking opportunities for models of colour.

Thus, while Mears attributes the phenomenon of the 'bleaching of the catwalks' to the competition for status, I also see the influence of new media technologies, which push the fashionable ideal to the most slender and whitest extreme. In the competition for attention within the regime of the blink, this look's historic roots also come into play. In order to be read as fashionable, starting in the 1960s and accelerating into the 1980s, fashion images have tended to take long-entrenched cultural understandings of what is, exactly, a fashionable 'look' for a model to new levels of uniformity. Current cultural understandings of the fashionable look took root when modelling became a profession in the 1920s, a time when the reigning aesthetic was the pale and lithe figure of the flapper (see Plate 33). The white and slim image was also fashionable at the moment when photography became a vocation, a conjuncture that linked the fashionable body and the slender body, cementing the two ideas together in the popular consciousness. While the variety of body types for working models covered a wider range of sizes in the 1920s and 1930s, the overall impression was of a slim, lithe figure.

Identifying this cultural imprinting does not discount the fact that demands of status were also at work. As historian Lois Banner has pointed out, the slender, lean lines of the flapper connoted class exclusivity, the exact opposite of the generous and sexualized proportions of the silent screen stars, such as Theda Bara, who appealed to the masses (Banner 1984) (see Figure 11.2). Arguably, concerns about status were in play not only with regard to the slenderness of the new model image but also in the game to project a 'high-end', white ethnicity. As historian Elspeth Brown has documented, it was in this era that projecting an 'elite hauteur' associated with whiteness became part of the couture model's standard repertoire, in which 'the subdued gestures of the couturier model performed a corporeal language that consolidated a discourse of Anglo-Saxon white supremacy for its elite viewers' (2009: 267).

While, at the outset, the 'model' image was pale and lean, until the regime of the blink, a relatively wide variety of sizes existed within this ideal. The speed-up in our exposure to images, however, caused by developments in imaging technology typical of the regime of the blink, pushed the general ideal of the tall and slender body towards an extreme limit, resulting in an attenuation of this bodily ideal, calling for models to become ever more lean, pale and long. In the current imaging environment of shortened attention spans, designers and fashion purveyors increasingly seek to find models that project an image that is very white and thin in order to be read as fashionable in a split second.[3]

The 'mediatization' of everyday life which characterizes the regime of the blink fostered the development of an increasingly digital and information-based economy, in which symbolic production, immaterial and affective labour (where the product is not an object but rather an experience, a meaning or an association) have gained currency. This type of production emerges most readily from the globalized, flexible, volatile environment of work common in developed economies, and in this environment, careers tend to be made or destroyed in the space of a blink. Adapting to this environment, the model is as an ideal worker, willing to submit herself to a precarious position in a volatile industry, in fact glamorizing this precarity. Models report having to work all of the time to 'keep ahead of the jobs until they dried up', as one female fashion model explained who travelled so often, she was in her apartment 'one night a month'. Or, as another put it, 'I always felt as though my last job was my *last* job.' At the same time, shows such as *America's Next Top Model*, *The Model Life*, *Scouted* and *Make Me a Supermodel* in the United States, along with highly publicized

11.2. Silent screen star Theda Bara

model search contests and media treatments of model's lives, depict this feeling of uncertainty and precariousness as a form of adventure and a source of excitement.

Not only do models glamorize an organization of work predicated on precarity, but also living 'the life' of modelling has become a job requirement for many models, in which models try to be 'in the know' about the latest styles, present themselves in line with the current bodily ideal, and make it look fun in the process. Marketers play on this attraction to the fashionable life, providing it as the raw material that consumers can then use to build communities—of fans or of people who are 'with it', or know about fashion. An effervescent value resides in something as fleeting as an experience, a mood or a feeling, and recent changes in technology, which track mouse clicks and tweets and mine digital profiles to track our interests and affections, have made stimulating and measuring the movement of these energies profitable.[4]

The foundations for the economics of affect and production were laid in the regime of the blink as the boundaries of bodies became more porous, amplifying the affective to flow between them.[5] Idealizing a merging with technology—both in practice and in the images it produced—the growth of the fashion industry, and the popularity of modelling in particular, helped further attune the public to the rhythms of affective production. The digital technologies that made the regime of the blink possible drew the public even further into the matrix, and models played in instrumental part in creating 'affective economics' in which trademarks become 'lovemarks' and play a large role in our everyday lives (Jenkins 2008: 68–70).

Glamorizing the fashionable lifestyle, models not only benefit the fashion and cosmetic industries for which they work, they help interest audiences in fashion more generally, selling fashion as a way of life through reports about where they shop, where they eat, what events they attend and, of course, what they wear. In recent years, this 24-hour exposure of every aspect of their lives has become a part of the job. The result? Modelling work doesn't just sell products, it draws publics towards being regulated by fashion, engaging with its rhythms, aligning with its needs. This kind of regulation feeds a kind of biopolitics of beauty, organizing individuals not only as consumers with desires but also as populations ready for transformation, always already in need of that makeover.[6] Engaged in this manner, publics interact with visual, surveillance, medical and productive technologies, creating value during both leisure and work time. As we turn to the screen to find the information we need to achieve our new look and as we email, blog or tweet about what we want to buy, to be or to achieve, we intimately engage with screen technologies that organize bodies in time and space in a manner that is beneficial to capital.

As desire for community is directed towards predetermined ends, consumers produce themselves as attentive audiences, delivering themselves for free as marketable units of attention to the market. One belongs to this world by means of using commodities associated with it—connected by advertisements in which models appear—and the 'model life', which participants in the modelling world work so hard to produce. This lifestyle is then packaged and sold to us as a commodity, an experience that can be had for the price of our attention. Subsequently, our era has seen the shift from modelling to sell products towards working to 'model' a lifestyle that it would benefit the forces of, power and profit to adopt.

In the regime of the blink, the look of fashion models has changed in response to the demands of this new imaging structure, which increased competition to achieve the right look at the expense of diversity in skin colour and body type. Further, the population of models has changed as the Internet has given freer access to fashion images, garnering more interest in the industry while also granting more access to model aspirants, increasing the breadth and range of the scouting system. Both of these changes have increased the competition for jobs and shortened models' careers. Finally, as the Internet increasingly weaves itself into our daily lives, the modelling lifestyle now includes a need to appear hooked up and in the know, as models not only walk runways but also tweet about it from backstage, post informal candids during their downtime at photo shoots, or appear on their way to fashion shows or in the street in various street-style blogs. Elucidating these changes not only reveals important structural shifts in the modelling and fashion industries, but it also uncovers some significant shifts in the organization of work, consumption and body/technology networks that are increasingly affecting our ability to connect with others, make a living and retain some autonomy in the process.

NOTES

1. This chapter is based on a research conducted on the New York modelling industry. The data for this article came from a larger study (Wissinger forthcoming), for which I interviewed thirty-four models (twenty-six female and eight male), six modelling agents (or 'bookers' as they are known in the industry), one casting agent and one production assistant; forty-two interviews in total. Semistructured and conducted in public places, interviews lasted between one and two hours. I asked respondents how they had got into the modelling industry, what types of clients they worked with, how they felt about the opportunities available to them, and their experience of the industry more generally; the rest of the interview was open-ended. Taped with consent, transcribed and manually coded, interviews were conducted during the periods 1999–2004 and 2007–10. The sample ranged from sixteen to twenty-eight years old for the models; the other workers tended to be slightly older, mostly in their thirties and forties. The sample's racial composition was predominantly white, with one female Asian model, four black female models, one black male model, one black female model agent and two female models as well as one model agent of Hispanic origin, reflecting the white bias in fashion modelling my respondents described.
2. Measurements from John Robert Powers's annuals dated 1930–32, volumes 6–8, Ford Models' annual, 1944, and Wilhelmina agency annual, 2000.
3. I am speaking about broad trends here, and there are always exceptions to the rule. *Vogue Italia's* 2008 all-black issue, Diane Von Furstenberg's use of a majority of black models for her spring 2010 collection and Miuccia Prada's use of voluptuous models in her collection that same year come to mind (see http://nymag.com/thecut/2010/02/today_in_curvy_news_shapely_de.html, accessed 19 August 2013). These efforts at diversity have arisen in part, however, in response to the trend I am identifying here, not as an argument that disproves it.
4. See Entwistle 2002 for a full elaboration of the notion of effervesence.
5. Not exactly instinct, prior to emotion, affective energy is part of the atmosphere in the room, the mood or attitude in a crowd, or the intake of breath at the sight of a beautiful or striking image that impacts the individual and changes his or her inner state. Sometimes affective energy moves so quickly we aren't sure what has happened to us; we just know something has changed. Sweaty palms make us realize we are nervous; a pulsing temple betrays our anger. When one is tuned into affective flow, one goes with gut reaction, the viscerally felt impulses that guide actions whose causes, upon reflection, we are hard-pressed to explain. Affect is not emotion but the changes in the body prior to realizing one's emotional state; it is an energy that flows between bodies, not belonging to any body in particular.
6. The phrase 'biopolitics of beauty' was inspired by Zylinska's article (2009), 'Of Swans and Ugly Ducklings: Bioethics between Humans, Animals, and Machines'; see also Meredith Jones's (2008) *Skintight: An Anatomy of Cosmetic Surgery.*

BIBLIOGRAPHY

Agins, T. (1999), *The End of Fashion: The Mass Marketing of the Clothing Business,* New York: William Morrow.

Banner, L. W. (1984), *American Beauty,* Chicago: University of Chicago Press.

Bartky, S. L. (1990), *Femininity and Domination: Studies in the Phenomenology of Oppression,* London: Routledge.

Bean, E. and J. Bidner (2004), *Complete Guide for Models: Inside Advice from Industry Pros,* New York: Lark Books.

Bordo, S. (1993), *Unbearable Weight: Feminism, Western Culture, and the Body,* Berkeley: University of California Press.

Brown, E. (2009), 'De Meyer at *Vogue:* Commercializing Queer Affect in First World War-era Fashion Photography', *Photography & Culture,* 2/3: 253–74.

Clough, P. T. and J. O. Halley (2007), *The Affective Turn: Theorizing the Social,* Durham, NC: Duke University Press.

Crary, J. (1999), *Suspensions of Perception: Attention, Spectacle, and Modern Culture,* Cambridge, MA: MIT Press.

Entwistle, J. (2002), 'The Aesthetic Economy: The Production of Value in the Field of Fashion Modelling', *Journal of Consumer Culture,* 2/3: 317–39.

Gladwell, M. (2005), *Blink: The Power of Thinking without Thinking,* New York: Back Bay Books.

Haidarali, L. (2005), 'Polishing Brown Diamonds: African American Women, Popular Magazines, and the Advent of Modeling in Early Postwar America', *Journal of Women's History,* 17/1: 17–37.

Haidarali, L. (2007), 'Is It True What They Say About Models?: Modelling African American Womanhood on the Eve of the Civil Rights Era', *Atlantis: A Women's Studies Journal,* 32/1: 144–55.

Herbst, K. (2008), 'CFDA Panel on Skinny Models: Coco Rocha Admits to Using Diuretics', *The Cut,* 6 November, http://nymag.com/thecut/2008/06/cfdas_takes_on_the_tooskinny_m_1.html, accessed 12 August 2013.

Jenkins, H. (2008), *Convergence Culture: Where Old and New Media Collide,* New York: New York University Press.

Jhally, S. and J. Kilbourne (2010), *Killing Us Softly 4,* Northampton, MA: Media Education Foundation.

Jones, M. (2008), *Skintight: An Anatomy of Cosmetic Surgery,* Oxford: Berg.

La Ferla, R. (2011), 'On the Runway. An Uptick, but Is It Enough?' *New York Times,* 23 September, http://runway.blogs.nytimes.com/2011/09/23/an-uptick-but-enough/, accessed 1 March 2012.

Massumi, B. (2005), 'Fear (the Spectrum Said)', *Positions,* 13/1: 31–48.

McAndrew, M. (2010), 'Selling Black Beauty: African American Modeling Agencies and Charm Schools in Postwar America', *OAH Magazine of History,* 24/1: 29–32.

McLuhan, M. (1964), *Understanding Media: The Extensions of Man,* 2nd ed., New York: New American Library.

Mears, A. (2011), *Pricing Beauty: The Making of a Fashion Model,* Berkeley: University of California Press.

Powers, J. (1930), *John Robert Powers Model Agency,* vol. 6, New York: John Robert Powers.

Simon, H. A. (1971), 'Designing Organizations for an Information-rich World', in M. Greenberger (ed.), *Computers, Communication, and the Public Interest,* Baltimore: Johns Hopkins University Press.

Summers, B. (1998), *Black and Beautiful: How Women of Color Changed the Fashion Industry,* New York: Harper Collins.

Thrift, N. J. (2008), *Non-representational Theory: Space, Politics, Affect,* London: Routledge.

Trebay, G. (2007), 'Ignoring Diversity, Runways Fade to White', *New York Times,* 14 October, http://www.nytimes.com/2007/10/14/fashion/shows/14race.html?pagewanted=all, accessed 30 July 2013.

Wissinger, E. (forthcoming), *Fashion Modeling in the Age of the Blink,* New York: NYU Press.

Wolf, N. (1992), *The Beauty Myth: How Images of Beauty Are Used against Women,* New York: Anchor Books.

Zylinska, J. (2009), 'Of Swans and Ugly Ducklings: Bioethics between Humans, Animals, and Machines', *Configurations,* 15: 125–50.

12

FASHION FILMS, BLOGS AND E-COMMERCE

THE PUZZLE OF FASHION DISTINCTION IN CHINA

simona segre reinach

Chinesepeoplehavenostyle[1] is the name of a blog discussing contemporary Chinese fashion designers, along with all the most relevant news concerning fashion theory and fashion events. One of the recurrent topics is China's relationship with Western fashion and Western brands. I met the creator of the blog, Timothy Parent, a cheerful Korean-American young man with a degree in fashion theory from Harvard, at the Younik boutique on 18 on the Bund in Shanghai. At the time, April 2010, he was director and consultant of the store. The Younik store was one of the few stores, if not the only, presenting exclusively high-end Chinese fashion designers such as Uma Wang, Mary Ching, Stephan Cheung, Pari Chen and Ni Hua. Some of the younger designers had been discovered by Parent, and he explained the way they work, their approach towards fashion, where they have their products manufactured and how they have built their network of craftspeople and artisans.

According to Parent, high-end Chinese fashion was ready to become an alternative to the invasion of Western brands, to what he calls the 'cultural imperialism' of fashion brands in China. Korean fashion is too marketing oriented, Parent explains—it all looks the same—and Japanese fashion is elitist. Chinese fashion, on the other hand, is both beautiful and democratic, according to Parent. He mentioned precious capsule collections, pieces produced in limited runs, which are manufactured by artisans to emphasize their sartorial competence. Yet these Chinese brands are not as expensive as global luxury brands. That's why Parent defines Chinese couture as a sort of contemporary haute couture that could satisfy the current craving for unique luxury—a sort of democratic offering in the competitive world of global fashion.

However, Chinese designers have not really reached the global scene yet, unless they are based somewhere else, especially in the United States, where second-generation Asian-American fashion designers have entered New York's fashion industry since the 1990s (Tu 2011). Moreover, among Chinese consumers, wearing a piece of carefully chosen, branded Western fashion 'gives face' or status to a still insecure consumer, maintains Parent. In China, Chinese designers still follow the powerful Western brands, as do Chinese consumers. But according to Parent, this is going to change soon; it is a matter of time. The young and educated Chinese consumers, he explains, are ready to understand the value of a good piece of Chinese fashion; meanwhile, Chinese fashion will also become known outside of China.

The recognition of Chinese fashion needs to come both from outside and from within China (Finnane 2008) in order to overcome the stereotype of a Chinese 'lack of taste' and the bad connotation of 'Made in China' (Segre Reinach 2011). That's why Parent chose the provocative named for his blog. Style is the capability of choosing and mixing garments in order to perform oneself; being fashionable is sporting a brand that reassures you about your taste, and in the case of the Chinese, gives you 'face', or respectability. I do not know if the Younik store is still selling only Chinese fashion and expressing all the nuances of contemporary Chinese style. In 2009, it wasn't clear whether the owner of the shop intended to continue with Parent's strategy or if he was going to add Chinese objects, such as jade vases in the Yu Gardens style, that are consciously manufactured and marketed to please foreign customers.

Where does the weak self-esteem of both Chinese designers and Chinese consumers towards their own sartorial capability come from? What prevents Chinese fashion from being as prestigious as Japanese and Western fashion? I will start to answer with a digression from further back in time: the tale of the Chinese tailor (Toynbee 1993). The episode, which was included by André Chih in his book *The Christian Occident Seen by the Chinese in the Late 19th Century* (1961), was 'discovered' by Chih in the diary (published in Taipei in 1954) of Ku Hung Ming (a Malaysian Chinese man of letters, 1857–1928):

> There once was a European who wanted a new suit. Since there were no European tailors in China, he called in a Chinese tailor and asked him if he was able to copy and sew a European suit. The tailor said he could make it up, if he provided him with a model. The European found an old, worn-out suit and gave it to him. After a few days the tailor brought the new suit. The European examined it and found it perfect. The only thing was that on the shoulders of the suit the tailor had made a hole, and mended it with a patch. The European asked him why. The tailor replied, 'I followed the model exactly'. Today, the narrator comments, 'China seeks to imitate the West in everything, without understanding the reason why.' (Canfora in Toynbee 1993: 104, my translation)

As I found in my fieldwork in 2002 to 2009[2] in Italy and in China, copying without creativity, as in the story of the late Chinese tailor, was a leitmotif in many interviews with Italians who did joint business with the Chinese in the textiles, garment, and fashion industries—as if Chinese design didn't exist and the Chinese could only copy from somebody else.[3]

One manager in a joint venture noted:

> The real competitive advantage of Italy is in design; in the capacity to be creative in production of clothing. It will be many years before the Chinese are up to understanding the language of style. (2008)

Declarations such as 'Creativity is something you are born with, you can't be taught it' or 'The Italians have fashion in their DNA' (manager of a Sino-Italian joint venture, 2008) rely on orientalist stereotypes to maintain precise relationships of power within these joint ventures with China. If style cannot be learnt or taught, or if it is a question deferred in time, those deciding and commanding can only be Italian:

> We firmly maintain the controls. There are Italian technicians and Chinese technicians, but chosen by us. We have appointed the financial director, the heads of marketing, control, planning and sales. Only production is left entirely up to the Chinese partner. (Entrepreneur and owner of a joint venture 2009)

Over the course of the eight years of fieldwork, many factors changed in the relationship between the Italians and Chinese. One of the most important changes was a consequence of China's transition from a source of outsourced production ('China, apparel house to the world') to a market for luxury brands. 'Made in China' has become 'Made for China'. This change is also visible in the ideas which the Italians have of the Chinese:

> Twenty years have been like centuries. Today everything is different. Chinese clients are demanding and are fully aware of the quality of the product. We definitely no longer need to tell them how to wear a tie or a jacket. They know perfectly well. (Entrepreneur and owner 2008)

Still, 'tasteless' Chinese can show their good taste, so to speak, only by choosing Italian garments.

The apologue of the Chinese tailor has its roots in the colonial milieu of European concessions in China. The 'imperialism of Western brands', to quote Parent again, fits very well with the image of a colonial Shanghai made up of beauties and spies, of slim *qipaos,* mysterious alleys and led-astray army men, as can be seen in the advertising images of many Western luxury brands in China. But the imperialism of Western brands also refers to a more recent stereotype: 'China, the factory of the world', where most of the garments are manufactured following instructions from foreign companies. This image links the colonial *fantasmagories* to the aftermath of the politics of Western aesthetical denial in the years of the Cultural Revolution (Segre Reinach 2012).

Fashion culture in contemporary China offers a composite picture made up of these different but complementary stereotypical imaginaries. As Alex Balasescu writes:

> Making types is the essence of any myths of alterity. The encounter with otherness is managed through the construction of taxonomies. 'Type' is the result of an empirical generalization, but also an ideal of the observer. The poor cousin of 'type' is the 'stereotype', a type that is no longer scientific, a type that entered the popular use and lost its explanatory value. In this way, stereotype is closer to cliché, and it is less useful to recognize and even to desire difference, but it is more used in order to summary dismiss that difference through the process of simplifying and framing it…There is an undeniable link

between the colonial advent, and the creation and proliferation of stereotypes emerged out of the encounter with the Other. (Balasescu 2001: 1)

The absence of China from the life and culture of the Western world in the years after the Second World War—when fashion acquired a relevant role in popular culture (from the 1950s to the 1980s)—have contributed to the picture of China as a country incapable of expressing style. The first years of exposure to Western fashion tell a story of a country which suddenly discovered beauty, style and aesthetics, as if China had not existed before the years of turmoil of the Cultural Revolution. The two main stereotypes, the colonial imaginary, on the one hand, and the aesthetically deprived country, on the other, mix together to produce a repository ready to use for Western fashion communication in China.

In this chapter, I analyse the different communication approaches to fashion in China. I first propose a classification among Western brands in China (and about China). Then, I analyse Chinese blogs and their rhetorical tactics. Whereas Western luxury brands rely largely on stereotypes, Chinese bloggers deconstruct these stereotypes to reveal the very many streams that compose the identity of contemporary Chinese fashion.

WESTERN BRANDS

In the global scenario of fashion communication by Western brands, I have singled out three different approaches of advertising that have—in different ways—China at their core. Italian companies tend to essentialize both 'Made in Italy' and 'Made in China' so that the truth of one reinforces that of the other one. Global French luxury brands, on the other hand, are more likely to play with new forms of orientalism by referring to the colonial atmosphere of 1930s Shanghai. Whereas Italian companies theorize the inability of the Chinese to 'have style', to market their 'Made in Italy' fashions, French luxury groups draw on oriental style through the cliché of the Shanghai of French Concession (1849–1946), when the city was defined as the 'Paris of the Orient', to sell their brands.

Type One: Naturalization of Taste

Naturalization of taste is a strategy put forward mainly by Italian companies. I propose three images as examples of naturalization of taste: one from the Sharmoon/Zegna website, one from the Piombo spring/summer 2008 catalogue and one from the Baldassari 2008 catalogue. These brands are purposely designed for the Chinese market. In different ways, they all essentialize an Italian lifestyle which flows from the Tuscan Hills to olive oil, Roman *dolce vita*, the Renaissance.[4]

Sharmoon is a brand of menswear made by the Sharmoon company in Wenhzou (where the garment factories give the people a good amount of economic clout in Italy; see Gardner 2010) in a joint venture (50 per cent) with Ermenegildo Zegna. A sample image from the Sharmoon website shows what is clearly an Italian location, possibly a village on Lake Como. One can see the houses, trees and mountains of a typical Italian landscape. All the models appear stereotypically Italian.

Piombo is also an Italian menswear brand, bought by Zegna to be sold in China. Some images from the Piombo catalogue draw on the theme of the dolce vita to convey a more general sense of Italian lifestyle that links Rome to Florence, Siena and Pisa. In other words, the Roman dolce vita, in a catalogue clearly written by someone who has no knowledge of Italian geography or thinks that geography is not the point, becomes a Tuscan getaway:

> Nevertheless, Tuscany is much more than only Rome and Florence. Each town in this region has its individual charm and joie de vivre. Pisa has its leaning tower that dips further every year, Siena gothic palaces and local Palio feast are festive and welcoming, Alba's precious truffles make for a delectable risotto and Lucca's operatic forte is an auditory delight. (Piombo catalogue, spring/summer 2008: 37)[5]

The peak of essentialist advertising is for the Maurizio Baldassari campaign, whose claim 'Pure Italian Expression' is applied to a brand, Maurizio Baldassari, that doesn't even exist in Italy but was created especially for the Chinese market.

What these three visuals that celebrate the Italian lifestyle[6] do not say or hide is evident in the double message of two other advertisements. One is what is called, in marketing terms, 'institutional advertising'.[7] Used to promote Italian fashion internationally, 'If You Speak Fashion You Speak Italian' was put forward by Ice[8] in 2009 for the United States (Segre Reinach 2010). The other one is an advertisement from a series put forward by Italian entrepreneur Carlo Chionna. It stresses a commonly shared thought in Italy about the Italian economic crisis being caused by 'Chinese unfair competition'.

On the one hand, we have the confident superiority as in Bourdieu's theory on social distinction (2010) represented in the statement 'If You Speak Fashion You Speak Italian'. On the other hand is the 'Roman gladiator' invented by entrepreneur Carlo Chionna, prepared to do anything to save 'Made in Italy' from the barbarians. Chionna has discussed in many interviews 'his fight against Chinese unfair competition'.[9] In the advertisement, Chionna is acting as Russell Crowe in the film *Gladiator* (see Plate 35). Barbarians, it is suggested, are foreign producers, such as China.

Concerning 'unfair competition', of which the Chinese are often accused, it is important to remember that, according to Lisa Rofel,

> dumping accusations displace the boundary between legitimate and illegitimate capitalism. These accusations remind us that the heart of capitalism rests in unfair competition. China has become a particularly compelling target of dumping accusations. Thus, the negotiations over China's entry into the World Trade Organization (WTO) reveal an unstable process of conflict over what counts as beneficial and proper, or, conversely, adverse, unacceptable, and even immoral capitalist practises. (Rofel 2007: 160)

Italian manufacturing of garments has been outsourced to China since the end of the 1980s. And since the 1980s, the Italian silk industry (the Como district) has been declining, as gradually the production of silk in China provided the highest-quality silk finishing, such as dying and printing. At the same time, Chinese immigrants to Italy engaged in garment manufacturing, especially in what is called fast fashion. Italy and China have therefore, since the 1980s, been in a very peculiar fashion relationship (Segre Reinach 2005).

Type Two: Neo-orientalism

While Italian companies essentialize 'Made in Italy', most French luxury brands claim their superiority by playing with a shared colonial imaginary. The rhetorical construction of these brands directly interacts with orientalist stereotypes, drawing on a constellation of assumptions underlying Western attitudes towards China. They do not use orientalistic issues directly, though. But, overturning, aestheticizing or reinventing these advertising images effectively reaffirms them.

Such is the case with David Lynch's film for Lady Blue Shanghai Dior. The female character is Western, French actress Marion Cotillard, while the man is Chinese, in a sort of reverse Madame Butterfly. Another Dior campaign by the Chinese photographer and artist Quentin Shih plays with the stereotype of Western individuality versus a featureless Chinese mass (see Plate 36). Chinese journalist Jenny Zhang wrote a commentary on this campaign in *The Guardian*:

> Given the history of Orientalism in Western sartorial practice is it any surprise that Christian Dior's latest ad campaign, 'Shanghai Dreamers' shot by Chinese artist, Quentin Shih, features a series of photos where a strikingly-styled white model clad in Dior couture towers over rows of digitally reproduced Chinese women and men dressed in cultural revolution drag? And no, your eyes have not deceived you—the Chinese people in the background literally all look the same. (Zhang 2010)

In the case of Karl Lagerfeld's film *Paris–Shanghai: A Fantasy*, by reinventing orientalist stereotypes the director and designer transform recent Chinese history, from the early twentieth century to Mao's era, into a sort of soap opera.[10] Again, Zhang commented sharply on the film in which

> a fictionalised Coco Chanel visits the Shanghai of her dreams. It is precisely nothing more than a dream, because in what other reality could 1960s Chinese labour camp workers possibly be played by Danish supermodel Freja Beha and Lagerfeld's French muse Baptiste Giabiconi? In one scene, Lara Stone as Coco Chanel informs the two actors that 'the Chinese invented quilting', followed by one of the Chinese labourers lamenting: 'I much prefer to have blue jeans.' The message couldn't be clearer—the Chinese are ignorant of their own history, desire to imitate the west, and need a cultured European to educate them. (2010)

And note that the two 'Chinese' actors speak fake Chinese.

Type Three: Accommodation

The third type I would name *accommodation* (*accomodatio* in Latin) as a tribute to the Jesuit Matteo Ricci, who was born in Macerata Marche in 1552 and died in Beijing in 1610. Ricci was the founder of Jesuit China Mission. The Jesuits' approach in China in the sixteenth and seventeenth centuries was to become Chinese to conquer the Chinese (that is to convert them to Christianity). Ricci's followers had the deliberate intention of completely de-Westernizing themselves to make a Confucian adaptation of their style of life, patterns of thought, preaching and worship. From the text by Father Le Comte, a French Jesuit who participated in the 1687 French Jesuit mission to China under Jean de Fontaney, I quote:

> We have to be barbaric with barbarians and civil with civilised peoples; we have to live a normal life in Europe and a profoundly austere life in India: we have to be elegantly dressed in China and half-naked in the forests of Maduré. In this way it will be easier to introduce the one, unchanging gospel into their minds. (Le Comte [1697] 2000: 98, my translation)

An example of accommodation can also be found in Hermès's latest strategy to launch a brand which is defined as 'completely Chinese for the Chinese'.[11] The brand's name is Shang Xia, and its first boutique opened in Shanghai on 16 September 2010. The media reported the news as follows:

> While Hermès is behind Shang Xia, the brand itself was started from scratch with the Chinese market fully in mind. Headed by creative director Jiang Qiong'er everything from the design to the materials, manufacture, marketing and management will be local.[12]

ADAPT VERSUS ADOPT: CHINESE BLOGS AND THE PRODUCTION OF FASHION

China is in a very advertising-heavy, brand-building phase with a potentially outsized e-commerce market, and the momentum for both brand-building and e-commerce advertising dollars is in the direction of social networks. With this in mind, Weibo[13] may well be the perfect place for global fashion brands to test and learn what resonates with their Chinese Internet fan base (Peng 2011).

I would lastly like to discuss Chinese brands as they are represented in blogs and e-commerce. There is a vast literature on blogs; however, there is no space to discuss it in this chapter (see Rocamora 2011). What I would like to stress though is the importance of alternative fashion information provided by blogs in relation to the stereotyped and somehow fixed ways of communicating the privilege of luxury brands. In the work by media scholar de Kloet, I have found the theoretical framework through which to interpret Chinese blogs. In a very interesting article on conceptual art in China, de Kloet shows how the focus on the banal, mundane and quotidian in Chinese art leads to a significant rupture from more historically and ethnically charged contexts (de Kloet 2010). De Kloet calls the actions of artist Pak Chuen a tactics of the banal and the mundane in the sense that they are firmly located in the here and now. The same strategy allowed the Hong Kong brand G.O.D. to gain prestige and recognition over the more conventional Shanghai Tang, as scholar Wessie Ling (2011) depicted in an article on Hong Kong consumers. These tactics provide a background, writes de Kloet, that may help to move away from the overcoded language of ethnicity and Chineseness. I found de Kloet's remarks very useful also for fashion—which is even more ethnically charged than art (2010).

Analysts have recently identified a new demographic of Chinese bloggers: young consumers, especially women, who readily spend on luxury goods and have begun sharing their style online, opening their closets and photographing themselves in their latest purchases. Following Jing Daily's suggestions,[14] I looked at five Chinese blogs: Nels Frye Stylites in Beijing, Fossilized Seed, Nini, Iris and Sammy. Some of these blogs present Chinese street style; others are more fond of international styles or comment on international brands. Many blogs play on the concept of East meets West or global-local. Everyday activities are mixed with conventional and unconventional fashion pictures in the typical language of fashion blogs and fashion networks to conjure the process of change through which Chinese fashion is gaining agency. 'Creative China', to follow Michael Keane's suggestions (2009), in fashion is to be found in the 'banal' activities of fashion blogs.

I was particularly struck by young designer Qinliumei. On his website and blog, he writes:

> My mother is an old tailor, she worked in a clothing factory in the last 10 years' time. one year's ago, she Retired. three months ago, I help her open a small tailor's shop, made all kinds of chinest style clothes.
> Hello every one. Welcome you come to this little shop, all clothes can be made in your own size, so all the clothes will fit you.[15]

The way Qinliumei revisits old and new stereotypes of Chinese fashion is fascinating. Qinliumei, apparently working in the register of the banal, forces us to see these stereotypes through a different perspective, as a way to dissolve them. The tailor is Qinliumei's mother. She used to work in a factory and not in an artisan atelier, but she quit the factory to work with her relatives. They make hand-made, made-to-measure garments—a local style that has become international on the Etsy.com platform.

In these blogs and microblogs, through very simple and banal everyday activities, the Chinese make their mark not just as manufacturers or as consumers of 'ruxury'[16] goods—that is just passive followers of European luxury; they are, instead, producers (and hence authors) of fashion.

The transition to 'creative China' lies not only with the international recognition of Chinese design in high fashion—which is only part of the game—but also with the 'small actions', so to speak, through the Web, of microblogging activities, where *adaptation* is a more suitable word than *adoption:*

> Adaptation involves interpretation or translation and transformation. The process is creative and refers specifically to actively engaging with a set of operations or ideas that modify an existing product or concept into a new one. (Ferrero Regis 2013: 7).

As Basile Zimmermann maintains, websites and Web pages are fundamental to anyone interested in global design 'as they are at the same time circulating inside and part of the structure of an international network: the Internet' (2011: 153). Moving away from terms such as appropriation, imitation, and copy offers, as fashion theorist Tiziana Ferrero Regis (2013) has pointed out, a better opportunity to understand fashion as a major global cultural form and institution. *Adaptation* is possibly a better word than *appropriation,* as it rejects the notion of a prior given original culture. The writing of most histories of sartorial exchange, writes Ferrero Regis, 'is particularly important to start moving towards an understanding of fashion as a place of exchange and hybridity instead of bricolage and pastiche' (2013: 5). The recontextualization of the sources of inspirations, which is precisely what is happening in sartorial relations, shows that the notion of exchange—described by de Kloet as 'the contradictory array of practices, experiences and pasts—which is after all what we normally call creativity' (de Kloet 2006: 3)—is more appropriate than pastiche and bricolage, which imply a one-way relationship between the West and the rest. Pastiche and bricolage are part of a Eurocentric discourse on fashion.

The narratives of the blogs go beyond the ethnic confines that characterize the communication of Western luxury brands. Chinese fashion cannot be described as subordinate—despite its well-known desire for Western luxury brands—when China is a leading economy and when the Western world is obsessed with China at least as much as China is obsessed with Western brands.

As a conclusion, I would therefore suggest it might be useful not to consider Western fashion and Chinese fashion as two separate entities either in conflict or collaboration. We should refuse the politics of polarity as we should also refuse a single perspective on global fashion. Asymmetrical relations of power cannot be ignored. The strength of stereotyping, in a world of images such as fashion cannot be underestimated either. Global fashion goes beyond the local and the international, and it is better understood as a multifaceted space in which different forces meet and whose boundaries and meanings are constantly shifting. As Peter McNeil writes, 'We might not require that nasty linguistic construction the "glocal" in order to understand that centre-periphery and metropolitan provincial binaries have never been neat nor simple one-directional flows' (2011: 149). Global fashion communication—in all its forms—proves to be a unique heuristic device of the workings of global capital where a series of tumultuous confrontations take place, and it deserves more transnational research among fashion scholars.

NOTES

1. See http://chinesepeoplehavenostyle.com, accessed 12 July 2012.
2. This was a collaborative ethnographic study of the cultural production of transnational capitalism being forged by Italians and Chinese engaged in textile and garment manufacturing and distribution in China; with professor Sylvia Yanagisako and professor Lisa Rofel.
3. A similar comment on Chinese design is made by de Kloet (2006) discussing Jacques Herzog orientalistic comments on the building of the Beijing National Stadium in 2006.
4. 'Made in Italy' in fashion is a fairly recent concept consolidated during the 1980s to define the industrial prêt-à-porter (Segre Reinach 2010).
5. 'Dolce vita' comes from Federico Fellini's eponymous film (1960) which portrays the life of journalist and man-about-town Marcello, who struggles to find his place in the world, torn between the allure of Rome's elite social scene and the stifling domesticity offered by his girlfriend, all the while searching for a way to become a serious writer. Dolce vita has since lost its dramatic edge to assume only the mundane stereotype of enjoying life—being competent and stylish and a socialite. Rome is not in Tuscany but in Lazio, a different Italian region. Alba too is not in Tuscany; it is in the north, in Piedmont.
6. Many Chinese brands in China depict the Italian life: Giordano, Captaino, Ghepardi Italia, Chiosolato Italy, Saint Angelo, See Uomo—brands that I spotted at Nine Clouds department store in Shanghai in 2008.
7. The promotional message aimed at creating an image, enhancing reputation, building goodwill or advocating an idea or the philosophy of an organization instead of sales promotion.
8. Ice is the Italian Institute for Foreign Commerce (Istituto per il commercio estero).
9. See http://corrieredibologna.corriere.it/bologna/notizie/economia/2010/16-giugno-2010/crociata-manager-gladiatore-salvo-made-italy-1703208745475.shtml, accessed 13 July 2012.
10. The film is described as such by the Chanel company: 'We are in Paris in the 1950s, Coco Chanel is having tea with her friend, the Duchess of Windsor, who tells her about her adventures in China, a country Coco has never visited. Once her friend has left, Coco falls asleep on her sofa. She dreams of China, a fantastic and surreal place, blending her friend's souvenirs with memorable scenes from Classics of the

30s where she encounters their protagonists' (http://chanel-news.chanel.com/en/home.html, accessed 12 July 2012).

11. 'Hermès's China Brand Shang Xia to Launch Next Week: Watch for Jing Daily's Exclusive Coverage', http://www.jingdaily.com/en/luxury/hermes-china-brand-shang-xia-to-launch-next-week-watch-for-jing-dailys-exclusive-coverage/, accessed 27 January 2012.

12. Ibid.

13. Sina Weibo is a Chinese blogging platform.

14. 'China's Fashion Bloggers: Five to Watch,' 10 August 2010, http://www.jingdaily.com/zh/luxury/china%E2%80%99s-fashion-bloggers-five-to-watch/, accessed 12 July 2012.

15. As in the game of Chinese boxes, I reached Qinliumei's website from Bof.com, which had taken it from Jiang Daily (Jiang Daily.com), who had found it through Etsy.com. Etsy is a website dedicated to craft all over the world: 'Buy and sell handmade or vintage items, art and supplies on Etsy, the world's most vibrant handmade marketplace' (www.etsy.com). The English is reported as it is written on the website.

16. 'You all certainly know what luxury is, but have you heard of "ruxury"? Well if you haven't, it's simple: it's China's version of luxury. The name is admittedly not entirely of my own invention…Actually, I didn't come up with it at all. I first heard of "ruxury" from my two good friends Nani and Nicole, and they thought of it when they saw this store "R.luxury" in the French Concession and tried to pronounce the name. And hence "ruxury" as a term was born, but the practice has existed ever since Western luxury brands were introduced to the Mainland' (http://chinesepeoplehavenostyle.com/2011/08/08/ruxury-china, accessed 27 January 2012).

BIBLIOGRAPHY

Balasescu, A. (2001), 'Orientalism and Fashion Design', paper presented at Stereotyping Arabs, Lebanese American University, Beirut, November.

Bourdieu, P. (2010), *Distinction. A Social Critique of the Judgement of Taste,* London: Routledge.

De Kloet, J. (2006), 'Chinese Design-designing Chineseness', *IIAS Newsletter,* 41 (Summer).

De Kloet, J. (2010), 'Created in China and Pak Sheung Chuen's Tactics of the Mundane', *Social Semiotics,* 20/4: 441–55.

Ferrero Regis, T. (2013), 'Re-framing Fashion: From Original and Copy to Adaptation', in M. Vaccarella and J. L. Foltyn (eds), *Fashion Wise,* Oxford: Inter-Disciplinary Press, 343–57.

Finnane, A. (2008), *Changing Clothes in China: Fashion, History, Nation,* New York: Columbia University Press.

Gardner, B. (2010), 'The Merchants of Wenzhou', *Chinese International Business,* April.

Keane, M. (2009), *Created in China: The Great New Leap Forward,* London: Routledge.

Le Comte, L. (2000), 'Nouveau Memoires sur l'Etat présent de la Chine', in C. Ginzurb (ed.), *Rapporti di forza. Storia, retorica, prova,* Milan: Feltrinelli.

Ling, W. (2010), 'From "Made in Hong Kong" to "Designed in Hong Kong": Searching for an Identity in Fashion', in *Visual Anthropology,* 24/1: 106–23.

McNeil, P. (2011) 'Old Empire and New Global Luxury: Fashioning Global Design', in G. Adamson, G. Riello and S. Teasley (eds), *Global Design History,* London: Routledge, 138–49.

Peng, E. (2011), Fashion 2.0 Brands Experiments with Weibo, China's Answer to Twitter', *The Business of Fashion,* 8 March, http://www.businessoffashion.com, accessed 27 January 2012.

Rocamora, A. (2011), 'Personal Fashion Blogs', *Fashion Theory,* 15/4: 407–24.

Rofel, L. (2007), *Desiring China,* Durham, NC: Duke University Press.

Segre Reinach, S. (2005), 'China and Italy. Fast Fashion vs Pret à Porter. Towards a New Culture of Fashion', *Fashion Theory,* 9/1: 1–12.

Segre Reinach, S. (2010), 'Italian and Chinese Agendas in the Global Fashion Industry', in G. Riello and P. McNeil (eds), *The Fashion History Reader,* London: Routledge.

Segre Reinach, S. (2011), *Un mondo di mode. Il vestire globalizzato,* Bari: Laterza.

Segre Reinach, S. (2012), 'Chinese Fashion and the New Relation with the West', *Fashion Practice,* 4/1: 57–70.

Toynbee, A. (1993), *Il mondo e l'Occidente,* Palermo: Sellerio.

Tu, T.L.N. (2011), *The Beautiful Generation,* Durham, NC: Duke University Press.

Zhang, J. (2010), 'Chinese People as Identical Maoist Robots? Thanks for That, Dior. How Can the Fashion House Think It Is Acceptable to Make Such a Nakedly Racist Ad Campaign?' *The Guardian,* 30 August, http://www.guardian.co.uk/commentisfree/2010/aug/30/china-dior-fashion-ad-campaign, accessed 16 January 2011.

Zimmermann, B. (2011), 'Analyzing Social Networking Websites: The Design of Happy Network in China', in G. Adamson, G. Riello and S. Teasley (eds), *Global Design History,* London: Routledge.

WEBSITES/BLOGS

The Business of Fashion, www.bof.com

Chinesepeoplehavenostyle, www.chinesepeoplehavenostyle.blogspot.com

Fossilized Seeds, http://fsj.blogbus.com/

Iris, http://styleiris.blogbus.com/

Jing Daily, www.Jingdaily.com

Nels Frye Stylites in Beijing, http://www.stylites.net/

Nini, http://blog.sina.com.cn/u/1291021104

Sammy, www.wodeyichu.com/space/iam_smallfry

Vogue Italia, www.vogue.it

13

HOW NEW ARE NEW MEDIA?
THE CASE OF FASHION BLOGS[1]
agnès rocamora

INTRODUCTION

The 1990s saw the birth of blogs—a contraction of the terms *Web* and *log* shortened into its present form by blogger Peter Merholz in 1999 (Rettberg 2008: 26)—with their number soaring from 50 in 1999 (Kaye 2007: 128) to over 181 million by the end of 2011 (Nielsenwire 2012). When in 2003 the genre—a regular, often daily, online posting of one's musings on a variety of topics—was appropriated by a young American woman to document her style, the first blog devoted to fashion—nogoodforme—was created. The fashion blogosphere, now comprising both independent and corporate sites, has since rapidly expanded, with Blogger.com evaluating in 2011 that there are more than 2 million blogs 'with an industry of fashion' (Blogger 2011).

Blogs are generally included in the category new media, a term which, although in use since the 1960s, acquired high currency in the mid-1990s (Hui Kyong Chun 2006: 1). This categorization according to novelty has been debated by some, a question being, how new are new media? (see, for instance, Lister et al. 2009). As Fuery (2009: 20) notes:

> The new is a complex intersection of issues requiring recognition at a moment in time. It is not always—perhaps very rarely—something that appears for the first time. The new is not always new at all. One of the ways in which the new gains its status is the transformation of vision that allows us to see the new, and the social consequences that allow us to evaluate this status of the new.

In this chapter, I revisit this issue of the newness of new media in the light of fashion blogs to ask, then, how new are fashion blogs? Asking the question forces us to reflect on the particularities of blogs as opposed to the printed press, which also means gaining a better understanding of fashion discourse as articulated in the media. I first look at a key dimension of fashion blogs that constitutes a novel way of conveying fashion news, and a departure from the printed press: hypertextuality. I discuss 'the transformation of vision' of fashion it has supported, insisting on some of the changes fashion blogs have brought to the production, circulation and consumption of fashion discourse. Drawing on the work of Bolter and Grusin (2000), I then discuss some of the ways blogs have refashioned old media, incorporating some of their defining traits in their own digital pages, to then look at how the print media have in turn refashioned themselves by capitalizing on the success of blogs.

HYPERTEXTUAL FASHION

The blogosphere is a hypertextual space. Hypertextuality has come to commonly refer to the electronic linking of a wide range of written texts and images, brought together in a constantly shifting configuration of networks; that is the sense in which it is used in this chapter. A link—also called hyperlink—is one which allows Internet users to move through this configuration, jumping from one site to the other by clicking on the related signifier, usually a word displayed in a different colour, font or style. As Lister and colleagues (2009: 26) remind us, 'The prefix "hyper" is derived from the Greek "above, beyond, or outside". Hence, hypertext has come to describe a text which provides a network of links to other texts that are "outside above and beyond" itself'.

The term and essential principles of *hypertextuality* are not in themselves new. The concept, coined in 1965 by Theodor Nelson to refer to 'a body of written or pictorial material interconnected in such a complex way that it could not conveniently be presented or represented on paper' (Nelson cited in Rettberg 2008: 45), was actually pioneered in the 1940s by Vannevar Bush and his idea for a machine, the memex, that would store and link texts together in a manner akin to the way, Bush argued, the human mind works: through associations and connections (Bush 1945 cited in Landow 1997).

This idea at the core of hypertextuality, that texts are inscribed in a complex formation of texts, a network, that they connect to other texts and exceed their limits, is also present, Landow (1997) reminds us, in the work of Foucault, Derrida, Barthes and Bakhtin. Indeed, the latter's thinking behind the notion of intertextuality (see Bakhtin 1981)—a term coined later by Kristeva (1969)—finds a materialization in the hypertext. Academic writing itself, with its annotations, footnotes and endnotes, is premised on the practice of a degree of hypertexuality (Landow 1997: 4).

With the World Wide Web, however, and the blogosphere in particular, hypertextuality has materialized. It is the very structure blogs rest on. When the reader clicks on a link, images (both still and moving), words and sounds can come at once on the screen, quickly succeeding and completing each other, making of fashion blogs, in contrast with magazines, texts in perpetual movement, always new, never-ending. Indeed, although a magazine is always caught in a wider discursive formation, this formation is kept outside of the material boundaries of the magazine. The reader's experience of the text, here the magazine, is contained by its materiality, the limits of its pages. The network of texts the magazine is inscribed in can be invoked, but it can never be made fully present. With fashion blogs, however, a broad range of texts a post relates to can be made accessible by the 'here and now' of the Web.

Thus, the many sites, images and posts a blogger is referring to can appear on the screen at any time, taking over the text the reader had begun with, or rather turning it into a multilayered text whose many threads lead the reader towards a potentially unending flow of images, words and sounds. As Landow notes, hypertext 'creates an open, open-bordered text, a text that cannot shut out other texts' (1997: 80); it 'blurs the distinction between what is "inside" and what is "outside" a text', making 'all the texts connected to a block of text collaborate with that text' (1997: 83).

With blogs, the reading experience parts with traditional, linear, modes of engagement with the printed text, for a hypertext is nonlinear—that is 'an object of verbal communication that is not simply one fixed sequence of letters, words, and sentences but one in which the words or sequence of words may differ from reading to reading because of the shape, conventions, or mechanisms of the text' (Aarseth 1994: 51). Multiple entries and trajectories are possible, dependent on the reader's whims, making of the blogosphere a nonlinear space of interrelated textual nodes that can be read in any order, a feature that Manovich (2001: 77) also argues is characteristic of new media.

Although a magazine can be opened at any page, it is still premised on the idea of a linear organization of its content from page one to page 'x', with a sequence of sections generally shared by all magazines: contents, editorial, features and other articles, fashion stories, beauty pages. With blogs, there is no beginning and no end, only a moment in one's encounter with a text. As Bolter observes, 'Where printed genres are linear or hierarchical, hypertext is multiple and associative. Where a printed text is static, a hypertext responds to the reader's touch' (2001: 42). The centre can always be decentred; 'it never tyrannizes other aspects of the network in the way a printed text does' (Landow 1997: 85).

Thus, linking is one of the key traits distinguishing hypertexts from print technology (Landow 1994: 6). Where fashion magazines never refer to any other magazines—clearly implying their independence from the rest of print publications and a status as the one authoritative fashion source—linking 'produces a network organization' (Landow 1994: 24) whereby fashion blogs constantly relate to other blogs, be it through directly linking to them in a post or by including them in their blogroll, the list of blogs and the related links bloggers favour.

DECENTRED FASHION

A hypertext is a space where margins can be brought to the fore. It 'reveals differences that turn out to be, no longer, inevitabilities and invisibilities' (Landow 1997: 87). So does the fashion blogosphere. Objects, subjects which in a print magazine have been left outside its pages, excluded from its discourse, can in the fashion blogosphere become visible. Indeed, far from simply recycling or appropriating stories already covered by the traditional media, bloggers often generate new, alternative content, as Bruns (2005) notes of news blogs. Bloggers are not mere users of the Internet, they are producers, too ('produsers', as Bruns [2005] puts it), active participants in the creation of news, or citizen journalists, an idea I return to later.

In print media, the showcasing of designers is ruled by advertising: editorial pages have to feature the brands that have earned titles some income by advertising in their pages. Although numerous independent blogs have started monetizing their sites by way of banner ads, such ads are few, leaving bloggers more control over the content of their sites. A platform can be given to designers whose lack of economic capital has excluded them from the media, a space crucial to success in the field of fashion. The popular Susie Lau (Style Bubble) for instance, whose blog when finalizing this chapter (November 2012) featured only two ads—for Bumble and Bumble and for John Lewis—has made reporting on the margins of the field of fashion a crucial element of her popularity. In a 6 November 2010 post, for instance, she discusses the work of the little-known Anna Jazewitsch, whose 'first graduate collection...entitled "Oftimica" was a geometric and structured affair'. By clicking on the words 'Anna Jazewitsch' and 'Oftimica', the reader is given direct access to the designer's blog and to some images of her collection, some of which are also featured on Lau's blog. Lau says, 'I do get designers who contact me about their work, to get features on the blog, and I'm happy that they're approaching bloggers as well, because they recognise that it's a different platform and that their clothes aren't always going to be called in for magazines' (Lau cited in Hanssen and Nitzsche 2010: 15).

On her Punky B site, the French blogger Géraldine Grisey, another highly popular fashion blogger, often features little-known names such as Heimstone, a company launched in 2007 and embraced by independent bloggers. When in 2008 Grisey 'introduced' it to her readers by way of a video, many enthused about the label:

- 'Superb discovery show of Heimstone' (steph, 3 July 2008)
- 'I didn't know Heimstone and the clothes look really cool' (littlejujube, 3 July 2008)
- 'I knew Heimstone a little...but seeing the look of the two designers makes me feel like trying the whole look' (clémentine, 3 July 2008)
- 'HEIMSTONE, a label that will quickly grow' (Sophia, 3 July 2010).[2]

Decentring also informs the fashion blogosphere in its construction of a network of fashion cities. Where the field of fashion is dominated by Paris, London, New York and Milan—the cities the printed press almost exclusively focuses on—in the fashion blogosphere, these cities are only a few in a wider topography of fashion locales. This is particularly evident in the case of street-fashion blogs, blogs that report on fashion as seen on the streets of various cities across the world (see, for instance, The Sartorialist; Dublin Streets; Sofia Street Style). When accessing such blogs, readers enter a network of cities that covers a wide territory, where no particular cities dominate others but each is just a node, a moment, in a larger formation. Centres in hypertexts, we saw earlier, are always transient: 'As readers move through a web of network of texts, they continually shift the center—and hence the focus or organizing principle—of their investigation and experience' (Landow 1997: 36). As a new fashion blog replaces another to which it is linked, becoming the new centre of attention of the user, so, too, do the cities linked to change, endlessly reconfiguring the fashion map.

When the reader logs on to Style From Tokyo, for instance, Tokyo becomes the city at the heart of the fashion blogosphere. The 'world friend' section then allows the viewer to move to Amsterdam by clicking on Damstyle, which can then take him or her to Lisbon with fashionstreet-lisboa and from there to Moscow or Warsaw—and so on towards more destinations. In contrast with print fashion magazines, the fashion blogosphere allows a wide range of places to become visible, extending the boundaries of the geography of fashion. As Manovich (2001: 333) observes, with new media 'cultural possibilities that were previously in the background, on the periphery, come into the center'.

In the fashion blogosphere, the geography of fashion has been decentred but so has the geography of fashion tastemakers. Indeed, where until recently the sole influential fashion media intermediaries were those fashion journalists, stylists and photographers linked to established titles such as *Vogue, Harpers* or *Elle* and avant-garde niche magazines such as *Purple* or *Pop,* the rise of the fashion blogosphere has resulted in the coming to prominence and the growing influence of individuals who had no institutional affiliation to the field of fashion when they started their blog. The French Géraldine Dormoy, of Café Mode, writes that her blog 'aims at making you share my personal point-of-view on fashion. Not really a fashionista, I consider myself more passionately eager for info' (Dormoy 2012). Lau was working in digital media when she started Style Bubble (Plate 37) and defines herself as 'a freelance writer, full-time blogger and dabbling in all sorts of projects. I'm still a fashion-outsider' (Lau 2010), whilst one of the most famous fashion bloggers, Tavi, started her blog (Style Rookie) in 2008, when she was twelve years old, quickly rising to popularity.

The popularity of such bloggers has been greeted with intense criticism by fashion insiders. *ES Magazine* cites a fashion director:

> I complimented Tavi on her skirt and she told me it was vintage Prada. I said, 'It's not vintage, it's from the collection five seasons ago'. She was astonished that I remembered it—but of course I remembered it. This is my world. I remember everything. These bloggers, they don't understand about the history. (Godwin 2010: 14)

Similarly, according to Robert Johnson (cited in Mesure 2010), associate editor of men's magazine *GQ,* bloggers 'don't have the critical faculties to know what's good and what's not'. As Bridget Foley (2010) of print magazine *WWD* also puts it, implicitly contrasting traditional journalists' informed knowledge (such as those working for her title) with bloggers' lack of it:

> Are we in competition with bloggers? Absolutely. I'd like to think that knowledge of what you are writing is still considered important. I'd like to think that some bed of knowledge about a designer and the history of the house remain important. I think we are starting to feel a little backlash toward the whole immediacy of things.

Such statements must be seen in the light of what some have argued is a crisis of the 'expert paradigm' (Walsh cited in Jenkins 2006: 52). Jenkins puts it thus: 'Walsh argues that our traditional assumptions about expertise are breaking down or at least being transformed by the more open-ended processes of communication in cyberspace' (2006: 52). Deuze (2007: 112) talks about a 'liquefaction of the boundaries between different fields, disciplines, practices, and categories that used to define what media work was'. In the field of journalism, including fashion journalism, this is compounded by the absence of official credentials, the lack of an established educational trajectory and the lack of 'professional boundaries' (Carlson 2007: 265). As a result, 'the line between journalist and nonjournalist is perpetually blurry and dynamic' (Carlson 2007: 265), a blurriness that has paved the way for the concept of citizen journalism, mentioned earlier, and that has allowed independent fashion bloggers to enter the field of fashion and claim legitimacy.

Hypertext 'does not permit a tyrannical, univocal voice' (Landow 1997: 36). In the fashion blogosphere, this means a decentring of the voice of traditional fashion experts, print fashion journalists, whose authority has been displaced by the shifting into focus of other voices such as those of bloggers. Thus, 'the newness of new media', Fuery (2009: 21) writes, 'is not necessarily its technical inventions, it is the transformation of vision that affects how we make sense of, and even actually make, the world and its social orders'. The newness of fashion blogs partly resides in the shifting approach to fashion they have conveyed, a fashion that is not centred on established designers and key cities only or on the voice of the traditional expert but that echoes the openness and the decentredness pertaining to blogs' hypertextuality.

FASHION REMEDIATION

However, Bolter and Grusin (2000), drawing on the work of McLuhan (1967), remind us that new media may well transform established visions, but they never totally supersede old media, for a new medium always appropriates some of the characteristics of an older medium. Where McLuhan (1967: 15–16) argued that what characterizes all media is that 'the "content" of any medium is always another medium', Bolter and Grusin (2000: 15) note, 'What is new about new media comes from the particular ways in which they refashion older media and the ways in which older media refashion themselves to answer the challenges of new media.' They call this process 'remediation', a process whereby both new and old media represent and refashion each other.

Thus, the Web 'is the remediation of print' (Bolter 2001: 42), a process clearly at play between fashion blogs and print magazines. Bloggers, for instance, regularly borrow visuals taken from the printed press to illustrate a post, when they're not directly writing about and celebrating the visual in question. As Bolter (2001: 23) reminds us, remediation involves 'homage'. On 13 November 2010, for instance, Marie of Kingdom of Style congratulates *Harper's Bazaar* 'on such a captivating golden Christmas cover!' She adds—having reproduced the cover—'At Christmas…I want to feel the magic and the fantasy, that only a big glossy cover can convey. When I first saw this cover I actually gasped.' Marie's enthusiasm for *Harper's Bazaar* lends support to Rettberg's argument: 'While use of the Internet is clearly increasing, this does not seem to be at the cost of other media usage, which remains stable. It seems likely that some media are used simultaneously' (2008: 45). Jaja Hargreaves of July Stars, for instance, states that she reads

> a disconcertingly enormous amount of fashion blogs and magazines. Anything from French VOGUE, JALOUSE, PURPLE, SELF SERVICES, LULA, RUSSH, ENCENS, FANTASTIC MAN, MONOCLE, POP and NYLON to the more conventional fashion publications like ELLE, UK VOGUE, GRAZIA, and the style supplement of the FINANCIAL TIMES. (cited in Hanssen and Nitzsche 2010: 44)

Similarly, in her blogroll, Anabelle (Fashion Pirate) links to the magazines she reads, including *Pop, Vogue Nippon* and *Another Magazine.*

Fashion blogs also remediate print magazines by way of some of the poses personal fashion bloggers adopt when putting themselves into the frame of the computer screen, poses that evoke those of models in glossies. A recurring trope of fashion photography, for instance, is images of a model photographed from behind whilst walking away from the camera. Evans and Thornton (1989: 104) call it 'the disappearing woman' (see also Rocamora 2009: 126–55). The popular Rumi of Fashion Toast and Karla of Karla's Closet regularly utilize this type of shot. On 9 June 2010, for instance, Karla is shown using a zebra crossing in a New York street, a visual evocative of Williams

Klein's famous 1960 photograph of two models in Rome, the black-and-white lines of the zebra they are crossing a striking echo, as in the case of Karla's picture, of a pattern on their dresses. On 8 September 2010, Rumi is shown standing in the middle of a busy city road, her post reading, 'I decided that I like the backs of things more than the fronts of things'. In images set in city streets more generally, the bloggers are often shown taking long strides, another trope of fashion photography and one that—like much contemporary fashion imagery—constructs the street as a space of fashionable display (see Rocamora and O'Neill 2008; Rocamora 2009).

In many posts, bloggers are shown in movement, albeit frozen in time by the camera, but they are also featured at rest, on the street, often standing against a city wall, in a seemingly unelaborated pose reminiscent of the straight-up, a genre of fashion photography that came to prominence in the early 1980s in the British style press (see Rocamora and O'Neill 2008) and that bloggers—street-fashion bloggers in particular—have capitalized on. Indeed, British style magazine *i-D*'s first issue, August 1980, featured a spread entitled 'straight-up' showing full-length portraits of ordinary people seen on the street, a city wall as prop. In the 1990s, this take on style became the raison d'être of print magazines, such as *FRUiTS, STREET* and *TUNE,* exclusively devoted to fashion as 'found' on city streets, whilst also being regularly mobilized in the fashion pages of various other glossies and newspapers. Thus, when fashion blogs such as thesartorialist and facehunter took up the genre, it had already been a regular feature of the printed press.

The blogs, however, have given it a new visibility, to the point that it has become tightly associated with the fashion blogosphere as if no other media before it had represented it. Indeed, independent fashion blogs are often seen as the one space where real fashion, fashion as worn by real people, can be seen. In April 2006, a reader tells Susie Lau, 'I'm so sick of fashion magazines which are almost always overpriced boring commercials (except purple. i love purple). i'm so much more engaged by what real people think and wear. so thank you and keep up the good work' (Sarah). French blogger Betty (2008) puts it thus: 'People love to be inspired by real people and also they see that there is fashion in real life and not only in the magazines', whilst—according to Eirik Slyngstad and Andreas Schjønhaug of The Streethearts—'blogs are often started by ordinary people like you and me, and that makes them more real and effective for a large number of readers than magazines do' (cited in Hanssen and Nitzsche 2010: 73). The inside cover of Scott Schuman's 2009 book *The Sartorialist,* the print version of his eponymous blog, a phenomenon I return to later, reads, 'His now-famous and much-loved blog, the sartorialist.com, is his showcase for the wonderful and varied sartorial tastes of real people across the globe'.

The street-fashion images many blogs have championed have in turn become an influence on the printed press. Indeed, as mentioned earlier, remediation is a two-way process: new media borrow from and refashion old media, which in turn refashion new media to absorb some of their characteristics in their pages. Thus, 'newer media do not necessarily supersede older media because the process of reform and refashioning is mutual' (Bolter and Grusin 2000: 259). The British *Grazia,* for instance, has a section entitled 'Style Hunter', which clearly brings to mind the street-style blog Face Hunter. Like many other glossies, its website also hosts a range of blogs, now a common tool of corporate fashion.

Print magazines have also remediated fashion blogs by incorporating the latter's visuals and take on fashion in their own pages. This is the case, for instance, of the British *Elle*'s 'Show Me Your Wardrobe' section. The section is the print version of Jackie Dixon's eponymous blog, started in

2008. Some of the pictures she takes for it appear in *Elle,* and vice versa, with the British magazine also inviting readers to explore the blog by way of a 'for more, see showmeyourwardrobe.com' and the blog announcing in its digital pages the release of the newest *Elle* issue that features it. This collaboration between blog and print medium draws attention to a defining trait of today's media culture, that of convergence or 'the flow of content across multiple platforms and networks' (Jenkins 2006: 274). As Bolter also notes:

> In the late age of print, we see the move to heterogeneity and hybrid forms, including on-demand printing from digital databases, printed books and magazines that refer to websites, websites that preview and sell books, and so-called 'information appliances' that combine the characteristics of books, notebooks, and calendars…All such hybrids work against closure, because both in form and function they refer their users to other texts, devices, or media forms. (Bolter 2001: 79)

Among the hybrid forms Bolter evokes features the putting into print of a blog such as Dixon's, as do the book by-products of popular blogs. Indeed, 2009 saw the publication of *The Sartorialist,* which was followed in 2010 by Rodic's *Face Hunter,* both made of images previously published in the blogs. This remediation of fashion blogs into books is part of a wider trend that has seen the release of books based on blogs, with the 'blooker prize' aptly capturing the proliferation of this new hybrid form.

CONCLUSION

The blogosphere is rapidly changing. It is only by paying careful attention to its many texts, producers and consumers that current shifts in practices of media production, representation and consumption will be identified and understood, shedding light on the shifting nature of the contemporary field of fashion media. In this chapter, I have started addressing some of these shifts, shifts in the representation of fashion for instance, shifts in the coming to dominance of new tastemakers. Thus, I have paid attention to some of the defining traits of fashion blogs, to their novelty in contrast with print media—also arguing, however, with Bolter and Grusin (2000), that new and old media, rather than excluding each other, feed into each other. This process forces us to see their relation as one of codependence rather than pure rivalry, as one that can lead towards a constructive redefinition of each genre rather than the annihilation of the one by the other, contrary to the many apocalyptic statements on new media.

In the present chapter, I have focused on blogs as texts, privileging a textual analysis of fashion blogs. However, studies of the fashion media should not limit themselves to such an approach, as understanding media products means understanding not only their textuality but their modes of production and consumption, too. Such a project falls outside the remits of this article, but it is hoped that it will be undertaken in future times, through, for instance, ethnographies of fashion blogging and blog audiences. Only then will the full extent of the changes currently taking place in the fashion media be captured, shedding light on the shifting nature of the contemporary field of journalism and the redefinition of practices of production and consumption within.

NOTES

1. This is an edited version of an article the author published in 2012 as 'Hypertextuality and Remediation in the Fashion Media', *Journalism Practice,* 6/1: 92–106. She wishes to thank Routledge for the kind permission to reproduce a version of this article.
2. In quoting from blogs, grammar, spelling and stylistic choices such as abbreviations and capitalization are reproduced unchanged.

BIBLIOGRAPHY

Aarseth, E. J. (1994), 'Nonlinearity and Literary Theory', in G. P. Landow (ed.), *Hyper/text/theory,* Baltimore: Johns Hopkins University Press, 51–86.

Bakhtin, M. M. (1981), *The Dialogic Imagination,* Austin: University of Texas Press.

Betty (2008), 'Press' section, interview, *Express Australia,* August, http://www.leblogdebetty.com/, accessed 21 December 2009.

Blogger (2011), http://www.blogger.com/profile-find.g?t=j&ind=FASHION, accessed 11 May 2011.

Bolter, J. D. (2001), *Writing Space,* London: Routledge.

Bolter, J. D. and R. Grusin (2000), *Remediation: Understanding New Media,* Cambridge, MA: MIT Press.

Bruns, A. (2005), *Gatewatching,* New York: Peter Lang.

Bush, V. (1945), 'As We May Think', *The Atlantic Monthly,* 176/1: 101–8.

Carlson, M. (2007), 'Blogs and Journalistic Authority', *Journalism Studies,* 8/2: 264–79.

Deuze, M. (2007), 'Journalism in Liquid Modern Times: An Interview with Zygmunt Bauman', *Journalism Studies,* 8/4: 671–9.

Dormoy, G. (2012), 'L'Auteur', 2 September, http://blogs.lexpress.fr/cafe-mode, accessed 25 August 2012.

Evans, C. and M. Thornton (1989), *Women and Fashion,* London: Quartet Books.

Foley, B. (2010), '100 Years of WWD', *The New York Times,* 1 November, http://runway.blogs.nytimes.com/2010/11/01/100-years-of-wwd/, accessed 9 November 2010.

Fuery, K. (2009), *New Media,* New York: Palgrave.

Godwin, R. (2010), 'Blog and Be Damned', *ES Magazine,* 27 August: 13–16.

Hanssen, K. and F. Nitzsche (2010), *Fashion Blogs,* Zwolle: d'JongeHond.

Hui Kyong Chun, W. (2006), 'Introduction', in W. Hui Kyong Chun and T. Keenan (eds), *New Media, Old Media,* London: Routledge, 1–10.

Jenkins, J. (2006), *Convergence Culture,* New York: New York University.

Kaye, B. (2007), 'Blog Use Motivations', in M. Tremayne (ed.), *Blogging, Citizenship, and the Future of the Media,* London: Routledge, 127–48.

Kristeva, J. (1969), *Séméiôtiké,* Paris: Seuil.

Landow, G. P. (1994), 'What's a Critic to Do?' in G. P. Landow (ed.), *Hyper/Text/Theory,* Baltimore: Johns Hopkins University Press, 1–48.

Landow, G. P. (1997), *Hypertext 2.0,* Baltimore: Johns Hopkins University Press.

Lau, S. (2010), 'FAQ', Style Bubble, http://www.stylebubble.co.uk/style_bubble/faq.html, accessed 18 December 2010.

Lister, M., J. Dovey, S. Giddings, I. Grant and K. Kelly (2009), *New Media: A Critical Introduction,* London: Routledge.

Manovich, L. (2001), *The Language of New Media,* Cambridge, MA: MIT Press.

McLuhan, M. (1967), *Understanding Media,* London: Sphere.

Mesure, S. (2010), 'Fluff Flies as Fashion Writers Pick a Cat Fight with Blogger', http://www.independent.co.uk/life-style/fashion/news/fluff-flies-as-fashion-writers-pick-a-cat-fight-with-bloggers-1884539.html, accessed 6 March 2011.

Nielsenwire (2012), 'Buzz in the Blogosphere', 8 March, http://blog.nielsen.com/nielsenwire/online_mobile/buzz-in-the-blogosphere-millions-more-bloggers-and-blog-readers/, accessed 2 September 2012.

Rettberg, J. W. (2008), *Blogging*, Cambridge: Polity.

Rocamora, A. (2009), *Fashioning the City*, London: I. B. Tauris.

Rocamora, A. and A. O'Neill (2008), 'Fashioning the Street', in E. Shinkle (ed.), *Fashion as Photograph*, London: I. B. Tauris, 185–99.

Rodic, Y. (2010), *Face Hunter*, London: Thames and Hudson.

Schuman, S. (2009), *The Sartorialist*, New York: Penguin.

Sundar, S., H. Edwards, Y. Hu and C. Stavrositu (2007), 'Blogging for Better Health', in M. Tremayne (ed.), *Blogging, Citizenship, and the Future of the Media*, London: Routledge, 83–102.

14

THE MODEST FASHION BLOGOSPHERE
ESTABLISHING REPUTATION, MAINTAINING INDEPENDENCE
reina lewis

The numbers of women wanting to dress modestly in accordance with their understanding of their faith is growing in the United Kingdom and around the world, most notably among the three Abrahamic faiths, Judaism, Islam and Christianity. It is especially among young women that modest dressing is on the rise, and they, more so than their mothers or grandmothers, are combining modest dress with mainstream fashion styles and shapes directly linking faith identities to the modern individuating practices of the fashion system. A young generation has grown up with consumer culture and expects to express all aspects of identity via participation in modes of consumption and display.

For this digital generation, as well as for older women, the Internet has proved indispensable in sourcing fashionable solutions to modesty requirements. The rise of online brands selling modest apparel has been accompanied by the development of a lively blogosphere devoted to modest styles, which have foregrounded women both as entrepreneurs and commentators. Dating to the early 2000s, this new and fast-growing field of online activity is characterized by rapid changes in modes of address and interaction typical of markets and communications online. For the modest dressing sector, often prompted by religious motivation, the increasing overlap and fluidity between commerce and commentary is of particular significance, opening up new routes to prominence for women within and between faith communities and between religious and secular participants.

The Internet has provided the means for the development of a niche market—now rapidly expanding, diversifying and segmenting—that serves modest dressers around the world. My focus has been on English-language e-commerce and related mediation arising predominantly from within Christian, Jewish and Muslim communities based mainly in North America and the United Kingdom.[1] As well as reaching consumers outside of brands' communities of origin, virtual marketing makes possible unique modes of crossover between commercial and religious missions. The Internet provides a platform for an interactive dialogue in which new conventions of modesty are created, communicated, contested and co-opted by practitioners from different denominations and religions. It brings manufacturers and consumers into ever more direct relationships with each other and fosters the development of new forms of fashion mediation in blogs and social media that in turn create new roles and forms of authority for women as arbitrators and advisors on both style and morality (Lewis 2013a). Deterritorialized and dematerialized, online modesty commentary (and commerce) facilitates cross-faith and interfaith dialogue that is less likely to occur offline and brings nonreligious or secular women more evidently into the frame of modest self-presentation.

Building on my previous study of new protocols in the recently emerged Muslim lifestyle print media (Lewis 2011), this chapter explores two areas of challenge for the new online modest fashion media. First, how the increasing commercialization of the blogosphere and social media poses particular challenges to the presumption of spiritual integrity that secures religious credibility in the independent modest blog sector, at the same time as opportunities for promotional tie-ins can benefit blogger profile and content. Second, how the incorporation of the reader style photo, now a genre standard, requires bloggers to make overt their definitions of modesty despite the sector netiquette of respecting multiple modesty codes. I conclude by considering new professional media opportunities for people of faith.

THE PERILS OF COMPANY TIE-INS: BLOG PRODUCT REVIEWS

In the modest fashion sector, the division between corporate and independent can be blurred when bloggers and brands alike may regard their activities as part of a spiritual mission. Like all early fashion bloggers, the first cohort of modest fashion bloggers was initially independent, with many coming online in the same years of the mid-2000s that saw the dramatic increase in blog writing and reading (especially among women) (Pew 2005). Modest blogging spanned the gamut of emergent blog genres, from topic-based reportage to personal style blogs featuring blogger self-portraits. Early adopter success stories include Jennifer Loch of JenMagazine.com (2004), Jana Kossaibati of Hijabstyle.co.uk (2007) and Elaine Hearn of Clothedmuch.com (2007), to name just a few, all of them searching out garments that could be adapted/styled to meet different modesty requirements and all characterized by coverage of wider issues to do with modest dress, politics and cultures. Successful bloggers attract large numbers of followers with active comments streams from international respondents from a variety of faith and/or secular positions. As in other sectors of the blogosphere (Kline and Burstein 2005), an A-list of star modest fashion bloggers has emerged from the first generation of bloggers. Increasingly, the most well-known are sought for collaborations with brands and some of them have started their own brands or e-shops. This coincides with the rapid expansion of designers and entrepreneurs entering the modest market and the increase each year in the numbers of independent and company-related blogs. The end of the decade saw an increase in modest blogs of all sorts: corporate blogs, often presented as if they are the output of a single person, as well as composite blogs made up of groups of modest fashion aficionados. The modest blog sector continues to expand and experiment. It is now possible to talk of a second generation of modest designers and mediators, often characterized by a less functionalist attitude to website design, visual representation (especially regarding the female form) and digital communications.

Like other early modest fashion bloggers, when Jana Kossaibati launched Hijabstyle in 2007 she looked high and low to find modest brands to announce to her readers and begged for promotional offers. Four years later, the market for modest fashion has increased, bloggers are wooed ever more effectively by brands with dedicated promotional campaigns, and Kossaibati has more offers than she can schedule for her monthly giveaway slot. Modest bloggers have rapidly found themselves negotiating a new territory in which they must arbitrate between the demands of companies and the evermore discerning needs of their readers. Facing an onslaught of PR demands—'Can you post, do a post about our sale, do a post about a collection, you know, we're a new company, we've just started, post about us'[2]—Kossaibati now restricts editorial commentary on her blog to things she feels are 'really going to be of interest', using Twitter for more mundane (sales, product line) announcements. Otherwise, 'I've kind of felt that's got a little bit out of hand and the blog's become a bit of an advertising kind of thing, a platform for just companies trying to disseminate their information'—with readers quick to complain.

Whilst the increase in modest fashion products is generally welcome, the increase in brand PR attention means that, like their nonreligious counterparts, modest bloggers face generic issues about autonomy and impartiality as their links with the industry develop. New York modern orthodox Jewish blogger Nina of Alltumbledown.com posted in June 2010 about her dilemma reviewing a free sample dress that arrived late and in poor condition (Plate 38):

> The dress finally arrived at the beginning of last week, unlabeled and completely enclosed in a plastic sleeve. I was dismayed to find a slight tear/pull in the fabric and a blue mark— it looked like someone had snagged a pen on an area near the collar. What to do? The dress was free, so they didn't owe me a return, and yet I couldn't endorse their product.[3]

Her contact at the company, whose response she quoted, appeared to blame the delivery service and suggested that she write a product review without 'dwelling on this "smudge"' or simply 'doing a general post':

> I'm not quite sure how to parse that email. Are they really blaming a defect in the fabric on [the delivery service]?...I am not comfortable (as you can tell) ignoring the defect, and cannot recommend a company that is irresponsible in shipping in a timely fashion, repeatedly assured me that the dress was in the mail when it clearly wasn't, and then asked me to ignore the defect when showing the dress to my readers.

By including the disputed service history into her blog post alongside a (positive) product review, Nina made methodological questions about blogger integrity part of her dialogue, asking readers:

> How do you deal with the unseemly side of reviews? Can a free product make up for poor service? As a reader, do you prefer candor, even if it means a company/product is held to a negative light?

Reader response was approving, with those who also blog admitting to the similar dilemmas: Vicki wrote, 'i have not come across this [particular] problem before but i have been sent products to review that do not suit me or that I would not wear and then I am stuck on what to do!? Xo'. And Nic shared, 'One time I was sent a free product I couldn't endorse, so I just threw the product away and told them why I did. I felt deceitful. You've given me the courage to let my readers know the truth about the product—we/they really do deserve to know!' One commenter, Fashion Theorist, interjected:

> My experience in journalism tells me this: when you're given an item for review, it's *not* a bribe for a good review. It's the company doing its best to get some low-cost press—giving a free item to a journalist (or blogger) is cheaper (and often more effective) than an ad campaign. With that in mind, I think you handled this very well. You related your experience with the company truthfully and accurately, neither glossing over the order fulfilment/QC issues nor dismissing any of the dress's positive features.

Writing an honest but unfavourable review may go down well with readers, but in relations with brands it can have consequences offline as well as online. For Kossaibati with (by June 2011) 2,500 daily visitors and upwards of 2,000 subscribers, it is of little significance if a poor review simply means that her write-up won't be featured on the company website. What she might lose in cross-promotional tie-ins, she gains in continued respect from her readers. But she also found herself 'expressing mutual outrage' when counselling a newer blogger, with far fewer followers, who was intimidated and even felt 'threatened' by a brand over of a negative review because, as Kossaibati saw it, they felt they could; the new blogger has less clout and less evident support. Modest fashion can be a small world, connected by community contacts that can be both advantageous (see below) and discomfortingly exposing.

Becoming savvy in her dealings with companies was a priority for personal style blogger Elaine Hearn, a member of the Mormon Church of Jesus Christ of Latter-day Saints (LDS). She 'realised more and more that reviews and giveaways are the best advertising strategies for companies . . . [and that] nobody was going to advertise on my blog [if] they already have a way to [reach the] market that freely' and decided to turn down promotions unless the brands were willing also to be sponsors.[4] Like Kossaibati, Hearn, a leading LDS blogger, responded informally to many requests for guidance before launching the Modest Bloggers Network, which is open to all LDS bloggers: 'I realised a lot of blogs [were] just popping up and I wanted a network so that we can rely on each other and support each other and so they can feel like we're all friends'. Another lead LDS blogger and editor of digital JenMagazine.com, Jennifer Loch, similarly helps out on requests for blog and website advice, and both she and Hearn have self-trained to be able to take on a small number of paying clients for website guidance and blog makeover services. For modest fashion bloggers who see their work as spiritually fulfilling rather than purely commercially driven (few yet earn more than a token amount), there is a widespread commitment to helping others. Whilst not uncharacteristic behaviour among 'secular' digital pioneers, in the modest sector the display and sharing of technical know-how can create new roles of potential prestige within religious organizations and communities (Thumma 2000; Campbell 2005), as well as generically enhancing individual reputations. In a world where reposting and retweeting secures status, other forms of mutually beneficial cross-promotion include new ratings mechanisms that validate digital modesty as a recognizable sphere of activity and endorse the social media sites of the organizers. For example *Top 100 Muslim*

Women Facebook Fan Pages, compiled by American Muslim Mom in 2011, was widely and rapidly circulated (with Kossaibati's Hijabstyle coming in seventh).[5]

Just as modest fashion brands are seeing an increase in cross-faith (and secular) customers, so too do blogs and social media demonstrate an increasing engagement across faiths. Online modest fashion discourse is now sufficiently established for postings quickly to migrate across platforms and faiths (a report on my Modest Dressing project in the UK *Jewish Chronicle* had been reposted within hours on several Muslim modest blogs and Facebook pages).[6] Assisted by key words and Google alerts, the zone of modest mediation also extends into related popular websites, fora and blogs, such as those concerned with craft and with parenthood. Achieving modest fashionability on a budget with how-to tips and original patterns, women mix discussions of styles and textiles with debates about multiple modesty codes, the regulation of female sexuality and women's role within conventional and 'alternative' religions.[7] The range and rapidity of these connections demonstrates the potential of fashion and its mediation to generate new types of spiritual, social and religious discourse. Often characterized by (and moderated to ensure) respect for multiple definitions of modesty, discussion can become heated and hostile, challenging the delicate habits of tolerance that characterize much online modesty discourse (Cameron 2012). For modest style bloggers, the need to anticipate and arbitrate potential tensions comes to the fore when dealing with reader photo posts.

DELICATE SITUATIONS: MODERATING MODESTY IN READER SUBMISSIONS

Brands have to make careful commercial decisions about what they will sell and how they will sell it, often facing, as with the print media, vociferous criticism if their visuals transgress presumed community codes of dress and visual representation. The ability to move beyond literal modes of reading is essential for the development of any minority media, but the etiquette needed within the religious sphere can be especially delicate. For bloggers, this comes up especially in relation to their handling of reader photos, by now a key component of the fashion blog genre but potentially explosive in the modest domain where circulating images of women's bodies in public can be negatively regarded, and judged, by religious and community regulators.

Surprised by how many photos she received, Kossaibati runs a very popular readers' style feature (Plate 39) but sometimes has to turn down photos of readers whose version of modesty do not meet her minimum requirements. Whilst it is her unspoken prerogative to define modesty as it appears under her banner, she wears it lightly, not announcing injunctions or regulations:

> I just think that if I set rules for myself about what I show on the website in terms of what I think is modest, so for example I won't put skinny jeans up or whatever, because for me I don't believe that's a good enough criteria, then I felt that I have to apply the same standards to readers' photos as well, because okay, sure that's the way they want to dress and that's fine, but at the end of the day it's on my website and people look at it as if this is what I am promoting personally, even if I'm not, but people still do. So what I have had to say a few times, I love your style and whatever, but I just want to promote what I feel is the best sort of standard for hijab that I believe in. And actually people have been pretty understanding about that.

Made cautious by critical responses to previous visuals, Kossaibati aims to project modesty broadly defined and to protect her potential contributors. Kossaibati does not feature her own image on her blog, but designer and entrepreneur Hana Tajima-Simpson always has and specifically used her blog StyleCovered.com (Plate 40a) to create publicity prior to the launch of her company, Maysaa, in 2010. Like other second generation modest designers able even by the late 2000s to presume on a more fashion forward audience (Lewis 2013b), Tajima-Simpson has always adopted and adapted the visual language of the secular fashion industry. She uses three blogs (reduced to two in 2012) to produce a differentiated Web presence, 'so in one way or another, what I want to say will get out there':

> For *StyleCovered* I have to make sure that there is elements within everything that I post that is relevant to people who do cover…The *Maysaa* blog [Figure 14.3b] is really difficult to write because it has to maintain like a business angle, [but] it has to be interesting, and personal as well…[Whereas] *Tumblr* [Figure 14.3c] is much more personal and much less writing…like a cross between a blog and Twitter so you can reblog other people's things…it's very much like a community type thing and because you're following other people and they're following you.[8]

Tajima-Simpson's 'You Wear It Well' feature on StyleCovered started slow but 'now [November 2010] every day I'll get two or three people sending me pictures'. Like Kossaibati, Tajima-Simpson must act as an arbitrator of both style and of morality.

> It's really difficult. I mean people can wear whatever they like, I'm not at all fussed, but for me to put something on the blog I have to also be aware that other readers might make comments that aren't necessarily nice…I don't want them to come under any negative scrutiny because of me, so I have to kind of be really careful about the kind of pictures. Like sometimes I'll crop it so you can't see a certain bit, something like that.

Unlike other fashion blogs, reader submissions to modest fashion blogs face evaluation on grounds not just of style but of modesty, and appear in a segment of the blogosphere likely to come under potentially hostile surveillance from community members rarely simpatico to fashion. If personal style blogs are understood generally to widen the range of images of women seen in fashion media (Rocamora 2011), modest bloggers who post their own or readers' images find themselves articulating alternative versions of modish modesty against a ground not just of fashion but of competing religious and community expectation. Elaine Hearn was not surprised to receive some criticism after she featured herself in skinny jeans: '[I knew that for some] LDS people skinny jeans would also be immodest, but I feel like a lot of it came from different Christian sites'. These anonymous posts were especially painful 'because I am also Christian and we're not taught to say negative things like that and so it was very hurtful for me to realise the lack of Christian fellowship.' Women designers/entrepreneurs and bloggers alike express a need to intervene in community definitions of modesty (whether over particular types of garments or the use of bright colours and patterns), to wrest the power to define modesty away from 'conservative' women (Lewis 2013a). In light of these intra- and interfaith concerns, it is not surprising that when, as is now common in the fashion industry, small companies start to invest in professionally managed digital communications they seek operatives with sufficient religious or community literacy to negotiate these suprafashion dilemmas.

NEW PROFESSIONAL MEDIA ROLES FOR FAITH COMMUNITIES

For the generally small-scale modest fashion manufacturers, even those that started online, initial media presence was handled in-house. Increasingly, companies are hiring specialist staff or outsourcing their Internet and social media communications. Just as minority ethnic marketers are now able to commoditize themselves with additional value in the global ethnic marketing business (Halter 2000), so too do the religious backgrounds of marketing and media personnel acquire new value. Just as new communications technologies impact on the form and content of the religions that adopt them, so too does religious utilization change the media. The twentieth century saw the development of syndication by US Protestant radio and televangelism (Allner 1977) whilst in the present, radical Islam combines digital language and forms to render calls to jihad in text speak (Bunt 2009: 12). In the modest domain, fashion-literate bloggers and respondents mix contemporary digital communications with religious terminology and ethnic slang to form a new discourse of modesty made vibrant through the immediacy of text speak, abbreviations and emoticons. Commercial marketers need to be familiar with all three: communications technologies, religious doctrine and faith-based cultures. Teaching executive or corporate team bloggers to display the authenticity that Scoble and Israel (2006) identified generically as the crucial commodity of the early corporate blogosphere in 2006 (typos welcomed as a sign of immediacy) requires particular skills from those providing professional media services to the modest sector.

Like other businesses seeking faith-based consumers (foods, finance), the modest fashion sector is creating demand for faithful professionals to act as such. Recruitment often follows community contacts: ultraorthodox Jewish clothiers H2O Pink Label in New York called in Brian Wallace's media company NowSourcing after he had 'done quite a bit of social media work within different [primarily Jewish] religious organisations'.[9] Wallace, an advocate of interactive marketing—'It's really about reaching people where they want to be reached'—distinguishes cultural competency from simply learning religious regulations as a necessary adjunct to media skills.

> It's one thing to be a practitioner but if it's actually part of your lifestyle [you] can instantly understand inside the mind of the consumer, because if I practise orthodox Judaism, I know what the standards of modesty are and I know how that works in terms of the Jewish religious calendar and all of the different nuances with that. That would be quite a steep learning curve if you were outside of that sector.

Interactivity is maximized and search engine algorithms activated when messages resonate with community culture and preoccupations ('Packing for Pesach' or naming a Twitter account #Frumchat; Figure 14.1). Able to presume from H2O customer profiles that target readers participate in orthodox clothing cultures, Wallace and his team of orthodox blog writers can keep posts pithy as per best marketing practice: 'For instance, there are certain holidays where it's appropriate to have new clothing or there are other holidays where it's appropriate not to buy any clothing at all. [Our Web site] assumes that anyone who is coming to purchase off of our site is already well familiar with the rules'.

In Utah, ModBod has also recently expanded and outsourced their Web and social media presence, also appointing a company known from local LDS community links. For ModBod founder Shellie Slade, 'I think it does help...I mean [the two web designers] understand the reasoning behind the product', even though as nonfashion-industry men their lack of fashion literacy and gendered cultural competencies is sometimes evident.[10] Relying on friends and family for contacts

H2O Pink Label: Modest Womens Clothing
How the People of the Book Learned to Tweet

How the People of the Book Learned to Tweet

Last week at #Frumchat was a lot of fun with Judy Wallace and @socialmediamom talking about shabbos. There was a consensus among the group that we can add to the peace of world by adding to our keeping of shabbos kodesh. This week we'll be discussing the significance of chinuch/education! We are the "People of the Book"! Prizes are going to be in high demand with gift certificates to the useful January 2011...
Source: H2O Pink Label Blog
Published: **2010-12-15 22:10:01 GMT**

 Like · Comment · Share · 15 December 2010 at 14:17 via RSS Graffiti

👍 Judy Wallace likes this.

H2O Pink Label: Modest Womens Clothing
Shabbos: The 25hr/Week Social Media Unplug

Shabbos: The 25hr/Week Social Media Unplug

(Source) We hope you all had a wonderful Chanukah. Now back to reality; we are relaunching our weekly #frumchat This week's topic is particularly pertinent to all you frum social media enthusiasts out there. How do we religious people differ from everyone else? We have Shabbos. Don't get me wrong, I am eternally grateful for it, but sometimes I wonder if I'm at a disadvantage?...
Source: H2O Pink Label Blog
Published: **2010-12-10 11:35:33 GMT**

 Like · Comment · Share · 10 December 2010 at 03:38 via RSS Graffiti

👍 Rishi Cohen, Judy Wallace and Michelle Singer Hazani like this.

 Duhh Winning i like
12 December 2010 at 06:30

14.1. 'How the People of the Book Learned to Tweet', H2O Pink Label, Facebook entry, 15 December 2010. Reproduced by kind permission of H2O

is not uncommon for small start-ups in any sector, and when New York fashion company Eva Kurshid similarly ramped up its Web site and digital marketing, it was these connections that led them to their new marketing director and pair of blog writers. One blogger, sister of cofounder Nyla Hashmi, had the ideal voice because she is 'really passionate about women's rights, especially in Muslim women and she's very much of an activist'.[11] Just as these companies have sought to fill media posts from within their community, so too are more people of religious persuasion getting corporate work in the secular fashion blogosphere. Modern orthodox Jewish fashion student (and intern at Eva Kurshid) Arielle Salkin writes for an e-magazine blog within the industry just like many of her student peers at Parsons.[12] As more religious people enter art and design education so too will they be represented in the blogging/posting/tweeting activities that are now essential components of early career formation.

Bloggers are being incorporated into the fashion media and public relations industries, acting as the ambassador or face for brands and requiring their own (status enhancing) banks of bookers and agents (Burney 2011). Advocated by some as the new 'influencers' who should be positioned on a par with stylists and photographers (Kurutz 2011), others, more cynical about the uneven degree of professional fashion knowledge in the blogosphere, predict that the 'blogger agent bubble should be bursting quite soon' (Rubin 2011). A-list bloggers recruited to the catwalk front row are aware that increasing industry links can compromise the independence conventionally attributed to bloggers. As they seek to preserve the historic integrity that is now commodified as the basis for their enhanced market value, new protocols for declaring freebies to readers emerge: 'I would never endorse a brand I didn't believe in'; and, 'Look, you might see an ad next to what you're reading, but that's my next rent payment there.'[13] For the smaller modest style sector this declarative strategy may be and remain effective, but in the mainstream fashion blogosphere where the opportunities for remuneration (in cash or in kind) are so much bigger, I suspect that the sorts of unspoken compromises long embedded in the functioning of the fashion media will transfer to the blogosphere. Just as many readers of fashion magazines are not aware of the open secret that global luxury brands secure editorial coverage directly proportionate to their advertising spend (Coleridge 1988; McRobbie 1998), so too will many readers of fashion blogs not entirely grasp the nuanced processes that secure access to shows in return for sufficiently favourable reviews. What will be the price of inclusion for modest mediators mandated to keep the faith?

NOTES

1. This research was carried out as part of the project Modest Dressing: Faith-based Fashion and Internet Retail, funded by the AHRC/ESRC Religion and Society Programme, 2010–11, with further support from the London College of Fashion, 2011–12. I am indebted to the contributions and insights of my project colleagues, Emma Tarlo and Jane Cameron. See http://www.fashion.arts.ac.uk/research/projects-collaborations/modest-dressing/.
2. This and all other quotations: R. Lewis (2011), personal interview with Jana Kossaibati, 17 June.
3. This and all other quotations: Alltumbledown (2010), 10 June, alltumbledown.blogspot.com, accessed 7 July 2011.
4. This and all other quotations: R. Lewis (2010), personal interview with Elaine Hearn, 22 November.
5. See http://americanmulsimmom.com/top-100-muslim-women-facebook-fan-pages, accessed 7 July 2011.
6. I thank Sue Ryan for bringing this to my attention.
7. My thanks to Laura Lewis, Melissa Esplin and Janine Goodwin for sending me links.
8. This and all other quotations: Hana Tajima-Simpson personal interview, London, 17 June 2011.
9. This and all other quotations: R. Lewis (2010), personal interview with Brian Wallace, CEO NowSourcing, 28 July.
10. R. Lewis (2011), personal interview with Shellie Slade, 17 June.
11. R. Lewis (2010), personal interview with Nyla Hashmi and Fatma Monkush, 12 July.

12. R. Lewis (2010), personal interview with Arielle Salkin, 16 July.
13. Bloggers Sasha Wilkins (Liberty London Girl) and Susie Lau (Style Bubble) in Burney, 2011.

BIBLIOGRAPHY

Allner, M. (1977), 'Religion and Fashion: American Evangelists as Trendsetters and Fashion Innovators in Marketing and Communication', *Modes and Modes,* 2/1: 145–55.

Bunt, G. R. (2009), *iMuslims: Rewiring the House Islam,* London: Hurst.

Burney, S. (2011), 'Blog Party', *The Sunday Times,* 17 July: 16–17.

Cameron, J. (2012), 'Modest Motivations: Religious/Secular Contestation in the Fashion Field', in R. Lewis (ed.), *Mediating Modesty,* London: I.B. Tauris, 137–57.

Campbell, H. (2005), *Exploring Religious Community Online: We Are One in the Network*, New York: Peter Lang.

Coleridge, N. (1988), *The Fashion Conspiracy,* London: Heinemann.

Halter, M. (2000), *Shopping for Identity: The Marketing of Identity,* New York: Schocken Books.

Kline, D. and D. Burnstein, eds (2005), *Blogs! How the Newest Media Revolution Is Changing Politics, Business, and Culture,* New York: CDS Books.

Kurutz, S. (2011), 'Fashion Bloggers, Posted and Represented', *The New York Times,* 26 September, www.nytimes.com/2011/09/29/fashion/fashion-bloggers-get-agents.html, accessed 20 December 2011.

Lewis, R. (2011), 'Marketing Muslim Lifestyle: A New Media Genre', *Journal of Middle East Women's Studies,* 6/3: 58–90.

Lewis, R. (2013a) 'Fashion Forward and Faith-tastic! Taste Making as Virtual Virtue: Online Modest Fashion and the Development of Women as Religious Interpreters and Intermediaries', in R. Lewis (ed.), *Mediating Modesty,* London: I.B. Tauris, 41–66.

Lewis, R. (2013b), 'Insider Voices, Changing Practices: Press and Industry Professionals Speak', in R. Lewis (ed.), *Mediating Modesty,* London: I.B. Tauris, 190–219.

McRobbie, A. (1998), *British Fashion Design: Rag Trade or Image Industry?,* London: Routledge.

Pew Internet and American Life Project (2005), *Data Memo: The State of Blogging,* 2 January, http://www.pewInternet.org/Reports/2005/The-State-of-Blogging/Data-Memo-Findings.aspx, accessed 2 October 2011.

Rocamora, A. (2011), 'Personal Fashion Blogs: Screens and Mirrors in Digital Self-portraits', *Fashion Theory: The Journal of Dress, Body, Culture,* 15/4: 407–42.

Rubin, J. (2011), 'Is the Fashion Blogger Bubble about to Burst', www.styleite.com/media/fashion-bloggers-agents/, accessed 20 December 2011.

Scoble, R. and S. Israel (2006), *Naked Conversations: How Blogs are Changing the Ways Businesses Talk with Customers,* Hoboken, NJ: John Wiley and Sons.

Thumma, S. (2000), 'Report of Webmaster Survey', Hartford Institute for Religion Research, http://hirr.hartsem.edu/bookshelf/thumma_article3.html, accessed 7 July 2011.

15

FASHION'S DIGITAL BODY
SEEING AND FEELING IN FASHION INTERACTIVES
eugenie shinkle

INTRODUCTION

For many years, the photograph has been fashion's primary media form. Over the past decade, however, the dissemination of fashion has grown to encompass much more than still images: it now includes films, podcasts, Web sites, sound works, online magazines and other forms—all increasingly articulated around virtual bodies and located in virtual spaces. These days, the launch of a collection by a major fashion house is accompanied by a cross-platform media experience: 'streamed as a YouTube runway show; accompanied by a fashion film; promoted via an interactive website, Facebook page, iPhone/iPad app, official blog, Flickr photo gallery; and discussed on Twitter' (Khamis and Munt 2010: 1). We can now try on clothes and discover the latest fashions online, interact with models in remote settings and style our outfits on a smart phone. As fashion photography moves away from the straightforward depiction of clothing to focus on 'existential, social, and cultural themes' (Lipovetsky 2002: T8), the 'fashion interactive'—digital content which users can select and control via a computer interface—seems poised to supersede the still photograph as fashion's key media form.

In fact, all visual media are interactive to some extent, in that they involve certain, often medium-specific, bodily actions and disciplines. Viewing analogue photographs, for instance, demands particular actions and conventions such as turning album pages or handling images by the edges to avoid damage. Digital media, however, place different and often unique cognitive and physical demands on the user (see, for example, Grodal 2003; Hansen 2006; Shinkle 2008).

Though computation has been thought of predominately as a representational medium, human–computer interaction assumes and requires an embodied user. In the following chapter, I examine the way that the relationship between representation and embodied action is played out in a number of recent fashion interactives.

Embodiment—a notion that is the basic building block of phenomenological philosophy—is a key term in the following study. Embodiment is a necessary condition of our being in the world. It is part of the fabric of human subjectivity: our very existence as human subjects, our ability to create and share meaning, depends upon the fact that we have bodies. Without bodies, phenomenologists argue, we couldn't be human subjects at all: we don't just have bodies; we *are* bodies (see, for instance, Lakoff and Johnson 1999; Merleau-Ponty 2000). Embodiment is the foundation not just of being but of meaning as well: meaningful action and interaction in the world is possible only because we are embodied subjects. The world, in turn, is meaningful because of the possibilities for action—the range of affordances—that it presents to us as embodied subjects.[1]

Just as the body is a necessary condition of interactivity, so it is of fashion itself. As human subjects, we are not just bodies, we are clothed bodies: fashion and clothing are meaningless without a body. Dress, as Entwistle argues, 'cannot be separated from the living, breathing, moving body it adorns' (2000: 9). Jennifer Craik describes fashion as a 'body technique'—a form of acculturation which '[regularizes] and [codifies] the display of the body and its comportment' (1993: 9). Craik goes on to argue that the body is not a biological given but is actively constructed through such normalizing techniques. It is certainly the case that fashion media participate in the normalization and codification of the body, but recent studies (see, for example, Massumi 2002) remind us that bodies are also biologically given. As well as discursive constructs, bodies are also fleshy, material things, and as such, they play a key role in the production of meaning. The allure of fashion media lies, in part, in the way they conjure the tactile, sensual associations of being dressed—the feel of fabric against the skin, the weight and drape of clothing as it moves with the body. If the address to the corporeal body is key to the way that fashion media become meaningful, then (how) is this privileged relationship with the body extended and enabled by fashion interactives?

Recent theories of human–computer interaction can help us to answer this question. The work of media theorist Mark B. N. Hansen examines the various ways that digital technology augments the capabilities of the human body and expands the scope for embodied interaction with media forms. So-called first-generation virtual reality (VR) theory explored the possibility of fully immersive VR experiences that excluded the corporeal body from the virtual domain. The second generation of VR theory has taken a different route, examining mixed or augmented reality (AR) interfaces, which merge real-world experience with computer-generated sensory inputs. Here, the virtual is understood less as a 'body-transcending space than as a new, computer-enhanced domain of affordances for extending our . . . interface with the world' (Hansen 2006: 27). The majority of fashion interactives fall into the latter category.

Fashion is a body-centred discipline that has traditionally been defined and delimited by the visual and dominated by a critical understanding of the fashioned body as a signifier. Roland Barthes's account of 'written clothing' in *The Fashion System* has marked out the terrain of much subsequent criticism. The body, Barthes claimed, 'cannot signify: clothing guarantees the passage from sentience to meaning' (Barthes 1985: 258). Fashion theorists such as Ulrich Lehmann, Patricia Calefato, Paul Jobling and others have built on this notion of the body as a signifying surface. For Lehmann, the fashioned body is 'a nonbody that only exists as a constantly updated simulacrum' (2002: T14); for Calefato, 'fashion has turned the body into discourse, a sign, a *thing*' (1997: 72).

Such assumptions are in need of questioning. Fashion's recent shift of focus from clothing to the transformation of the body itself has coincided roughly with a surge in the possibilities and new contexts for interaction offered by new technologies. A new generation of AR interactives ostensibly combines the best of both real and virtual worlds: the emancipatory possibilities of the latter and the sensual involvement of the former. In the context of fashion, such interactives also promise a more dynamic relation between the body as a signifier and the body in-depth—between the surface of the fashioned body as a representation and the deeper, more visceral sensory responses or 'affections' that describe the experience of being clothed. By positing virtual space as intimately linked to bodily action and by challenging the dominance of vision in the experience of digital media, Hansen's work (here, specifically, his notions of machinic vision, body image and body schema) enables us to examine how—and, indeed, whether—fashion interactives address and engage the body alongside more conventional modes of display. There remain some knotty questions, however, around fashion's readiness to leave behind the imperatives of seduction and spectacle and to welcome the extended interfaces and unruly affects that AR interfaces invite.

VISIBLE BODIES: THE BURBERRY INTERACTIVE

June 2010 saw the launch of Burberry's much-hyped 'fully immersive' and 'interactive' campaign. The campaign included fourteen interactive still images and six videos that sought to capture the energy associated with live fashion events. Users were invited 'not just to see images, but to feel a part of what we have created; connecting people through technology, music, the collections, the attitude, and the emotion captured' (Anakin 2010). Clicking on a still image caused the model to display the handbag or shoes in a different pose. Each video featured a group of models wearing items from the collection, walking from the back of a set towards the user.

The videos, in particular, offered the user an unusually broad range of affordances, opening a typically closed data space to human negotiation. By clicking the mouse, the user was able to start and stop a video, speed it up, slow it down and reverse its motion, thereby controlling the movement of the models within the shallow three-dimensional space. Clicking and dragging at various points on the screen allowed the user to move a short distance 'into' the image, to zoom in visually and to navigate 180 degrees around the models to see the clothes from different angles. The user thus occupied a privileged and infinitely variable point of view within the video image—a more-than-human perspective that Hansen terms 'machinic vision' (Hansen 2001: 61).

Machinic vision is a form of technologically enhanced seeing in which 'the task of processing information, that is perception, necessarily passes through a machinic circuit' (Hansen 2001: 61). Machinic vision expands the range of perception beyond the limits of the human body by replacing human vision with computation. It enables users to position themselves in ways that would be impossible in real life and to occupy points in virtual space that bear no relation to their position in the real world. Machinic vision is distinct from human vision, which is, by contrast, 'tied to embodiment and the singular form of affection correlated with it' (Hansen 2001: 61).

For Hansen, the notion of affection is key to understanding how the body is implicated in the perception and experience of digital media. Drawing on Henri Bergson's understanding of perception, Hansen posits the digital image as a process that is bound up with the activity of the body and linked to bodily capacities or affections such as proprioception, tactility and movement:

> [Our] body is not a mathematical point in space . . . its virtual actions are complicated by, and impregnated with, real actions, or, in other words . . . there is no perception without affection. Affection is, then, that part or aspect of the inside of our body which we mix with the image of external bodies. (Bergson cited in Hansen 2001: 61)

Digital images, Hansen argues, cannot be understood simply in terms of their surface appearance. Users also perceptually complete such images by bringing their own sensory memories and physical presence to bear on the act of perception. The actions of the perceiving body, in other words, play a significant part in the perception of all images, but new media images foreground—indeed, they demand—this innate interactivity.

Affordance, then, refers to more than what the user is able to do inside the virtual space of the digital image. It also concerns how, and by what means, users are engaged corporeally and affectively as part of the act of perception. Armed with this knowledge, we might ask again what sorts of affordances are offered by the Burberry interactive videos. It is certainly the case that the videos offer a range of otherwise unavailable viewpoints within virtual space. However, the infinitely variable point of view in the video is not that of an embodied user. It is the eye of a virtual camera—a mathematical abstraction, its movements produced by the screen-and-cursor manipulation of data. The effects of this manipulation are unsettling, producing an awkward, unnatural illusion of movement in the models, who track back and forth mechanically along a predetermined path. The impression is of something that is more than a still image, yet not quite a moving image: an animated photograph with an extended and malleable surface. Despite the campaign's insistence on feeling, there is no part of the user's body which is mixed with the image of the onscreen bodies—no intentional relation between the user's gestures in the real world and their effects in the virtual one.

It is worth recalling here Lev Manovich's observation that 'interaction' doesn't just refer to clicking, selecting links or other forms of data manipulation (Manovich 2001: 57). It also refers to psychological processes such as recall and identification that, along with tactile and haptic associations, also have a part to play in making images of clothing meaningful. If fashion, as Nick Knight observes, is meant to be experienced in motion (Khamis and Munt 2010: 11), then the interactive videos, which allow the user to control the movement of both models and garments, offer a good deal more than a still image. But the ability to survey the dataspace is based in a divergent relationship between bodily action and meaning: the user's body is instrumentalized, deployed as a tool for carrying out a range of onscreen actions. What is missing in this scenario is any sense of the intimacy or feeling of being clothed and, consequently, any sense of identification with the clothed bodies on display. Indeed, the models behave more like animated surfaces than living, feeling bodies; they are the virtual personification of Lehmann's 'constantly updated simulacrum'. Though the Burberry interactives invest the garments with more information, by decoupling the act of seeing from the user's body, they posit representation and embodied action as separate acts taking place in distinct spaces. The dialogue between the body as a signifier and the body in-depth—so vital to the experience of being clothed—is replaced here by a kind of excessive and exclusive visibility: the user's body is invisible; those of the models, untouched and untouchable.

Plate 33. A typical flapper, whose long lean lines epitomized fashion in the 1920s; *Vogue*, October 1926

Plate 34. Maurizio Baldassari, image from the catalogue, 2007

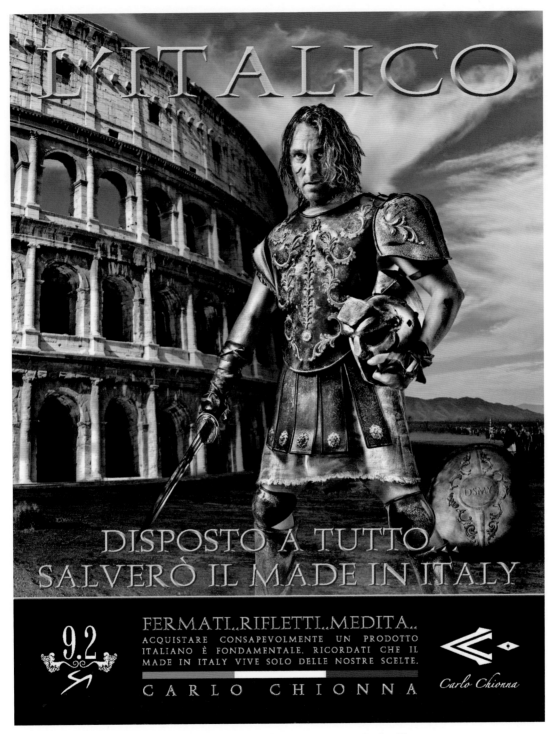

Plate 35. Maurizio Chionna, the Roman Gladiator. Courtesy Carlo Chionna

Plate 36. Dior Shanghai Dreamers. Image by Quentin Shih

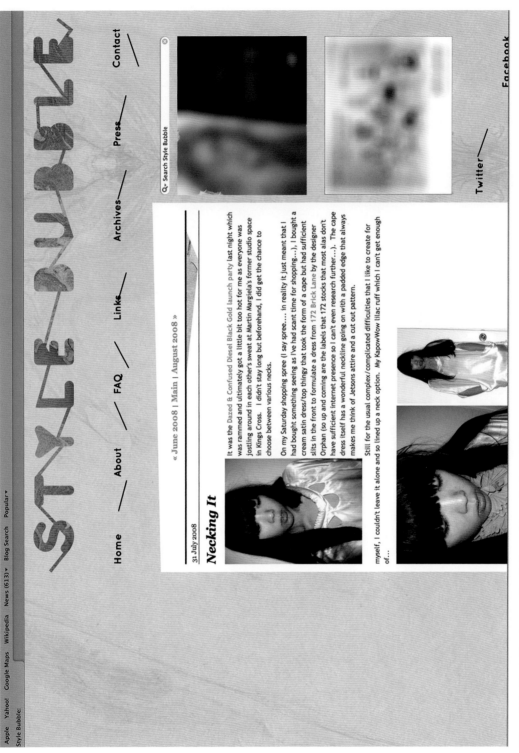

Plate 37. Susie Lau's popular fashion blog, Style Bubble

about   modesty   inspiration   sponsor   shop

1 0 . 0 6 . 2 0 1 0

Princess Peach

Hi there. I'm Nina, and I get dressed. Every day. In addition to brightly colored pencil skirts, glittery nails and sweater tights, I love puppies, stovetop popcorn and the printing press.

A few months ago, I was contacted by the folks at eshakti to have a custom dress made for a review. Since I have a hard time finding dresses that have longer sleeves and hemlines, I was quite excited. I chose to lengthen a silk tunic dress and sent in my measurements. After 4 weeks, I emailed to find out what was holding up the dress and was told it would arrive imminently. It didn't. I emailed back a while later, was told the same thing, and waited another 3 weeks. The dress finally arrived at the beginning of last week, unlabeled and completely enclosed in a plastic sleeve. I was dismayed to find a slight tear/pull in the fabric and a blue mark— it looked like someone had snagged a pen on an area near the collar. What to do? The dress was free, so they didn't owe me a return, and yet I couldn't endorse their product. I decided to email the woman with whom I had been in contact to discuss options.

Plate 38. Alltumbledown, blogpost, 10 June 2011. Reproduced by kind permission of Nina Cohen

Muslimah Style: Ghaida

Reader's Contribution

Plate 39. Ghaida, winner of the autumn/winter 2009/10 Muslimah Style feature competition. Reproduced by kind permission of Jana Kossaibati and Ghaida Tsurayya

Previous page: chiffon dropped pocket tee &
This page: Sheer overlay maxi skirt coming soon to maysaa.com

Plate 40. (a) StyleCovered.com, blogpost, 26 January 2011. (b) *Maysaa* digital magazine, n. 2, September 2010. (c) Hanatajima.tumblr.com, blogpost, January 2011. Reproduced by kind permission of Hana Tajima-Simpson

AUGMENTING REALITY: THE VIRTUAL DRESSING ROOM

Meaning, in the digital realm, is produced not simply through sophisticated illusions, but 'through an extension of our "natural"—that is embodied, perceptuomotor—interface with the world' (Hansen 2006: 3). Virtual dressing room (VDR) applications promise a closer fusion between representation and bodily action. Such applications have been available for some time now, but recent years have seen a surge in their popularity. Software packages such as FaceCake's Swivel or Zugara's Webcam Social Shopper work with webcam and motion-detection technology, projecting a live video image of the user's body into a virtual setting and allowing her to select and manipulate items of clothing displayed onscreen by 'reaching' for them with the hands, rather than using a controller.[2] Once selected, the software digitally superimposes an image of a garment or accessory over the live video image of the user. Swivel's technology allows the user to move forward, backwards or sideways within a limited range and increases or decreases the relative size of the garment to match. Some applications allow the garment a limited degree of 'wrap' around the user's body, though none are yet able to give a convincing illusion of fit.

In technical terms, such applications can be classified as augmented reality interfaces which incorporate tangible interaction—controller-free data manipulation systems that distribute the points of interaction across both physical and virtual environments. Here, the interaction with data involves the physical management of a real body in space. Where the affordances offered by the Burberry interactive are restricted to 'disconnected observation and control', new VDR applications enable a productive coupling of body and technology—'inhabited interaction in the world' (Dourish 2001: 102). Rather than a metaphor for representation, the real world becomes the medium for interaction. The dressed body that appears when the VDR user selects an item of clothing, however, is a strange kind of hybrid—a superposition of live video feed and virtual clothing in which the image of the user is hidden behind a two-dimensional representation of a garment that appears to hover in the air in front of her. The VDR simulates the appearance, but not the feeling of being clothed.

This odd disjunction can be theorized in terms of the difference between body image and body schema. The former refers to a visual apprehension or specular image of the body. The latter, by contrast, is not a conscious representation but a sense—made possible by the system of motor capacities and responses that animate the body—of inhabiting one's own body, being present in the surrounding space, moving through and experiencing the world. The body schema is the basis of the subject's ownership of her body—an ownership upon which the specular image is built and which the latter confirms (Hansen 2006: 44).

'Body image boundaries', as Gallagher and Cole write, 'tend to be relatively clearly defined. The body schema, in contrast, can be functionally integrated with its environment, even to the extent that it frequently incorporates certain objects into its operations' (cited in Hansen 2006: 48). The idea of body schema changes the way that we think about interactivity: rather than simply using a tool that is understood as separate from the self, interactivity involves incorporating technologies into the body schema—seamlessly integrating them into the bodily awareness and embodied activity of the user.

In the real world, garments function to augment both the body image and the body schema. Not only do they allow the wearer to deploy the body as a signifier, garments are fully incorporated into the body schema: they become part of the wearer's sense of bodily awareness. Farren and

Hutchinson have observed that clothes not only provide a communicative interface between the wearer and the world, but they can also be understood as technological forms that extend the function of the skin and thus modify our relation to our environment (2004: 464). To be dressed (at least, to be dressed comfortably) is thus to fully incorporate the garment as an interface—to dissolve the boundary between oneself and one's clothes.

In an analogous manner, the VDR encourages the user to incorporate the interface by effectively becoming the controller. The gestures of reaching, touching and selecting garments have equivalent meanings in both real and virtual domains: the user's visual apprehension of his or her body on the screen matches up with the body schema and is confirmed by it. The VDR interface, in other words, invites the user to create a relationship between his or her own affectively sensed body and its onscreen image. It does this not simply by projecting an image of the user into a virtual space but by breaching the boundary between real and virtual domains: integrating the user's real-world actions into the virtual environment. The resulting correlation between body schema and body image acts to animate the user's onscreen representation—not only does the user see his or her own body, but he or she also *feels* it as her own body.

Animating the garments, however, is more difficult. In fact, selecting and putting on a virtual garment introduces a rupture between the body image and the body schema. Rather than acting as an extension of the body, the virtual garment intervenes between the felt body and its image. It cannot be worn in the proper sense of the word; it can only be applied like a decal, overlaid on the image of the user's body. Though the VDR interface may be successfully incorporated into the user's body schema, the garments themselves, which exist only as representations, cannot. Paradoxically, it is the very simulation of being clothed that points to the schism between the body's visible surface and its affectively sensed depths. The VDR interface offers an experience that goes beyond the machinic vision of the Burberry interactives. But although the technology itself may be incorporated into the user's body schema, the very items it is designed to showcase, the garments themselves, remain exclusively visual.

AFFECTIVE INTERACTION: WEARABLE COMPUTING

The fashion interactives examined thus far privilege a kind of pleasurable play between the eye and an image of the clothed body. Apart from their novelty, we might ask what they offer that a conventional photograph doesn't. However, the ostensible failure of such devices to fully engage the user as an embodied subject needs to be understood in the context of their use. At present, fashion interactives are used predominately as commercial tools, a means of capturing market share by making online shopping more engaging.[3] Increasingly, online retailers are turning to interactives as a way of signalling a more democratic brand image, 'to enhance brand identity and secure consumer loyalty' (Lee, Kim and Fiore 2010: 140). Digital media forms are seen as a way of transitioning ordinary consumers into 'brand "owners and advocates" who "voluntarily" incorporate fashion media within their personalized media flows of YouTube, Facebook and Twitter' (Khamis and Munt 2010: 15). Current fashion interactives are best understood, in other words, as innovative forms of advertising, designed to encourage a 'wired' consumer to buy without being physically present. As such, the target of the fashion interactive is not the body in-depth—it is an eye that is open to colonization by consumer desire. The VDR, in particular, can be seen as an instrumentalization of fashion's logic: though it operates through the medium of an individual corporeal body, it masks this body behind virtual garments of uniform size and shape. Today's fashion interactives sit comfortably within a range of more conventional media that use visual spectacle as a portal through which to shape, normalize and commodify the body.

Some of the most interesting fashion interactives are those that exist—at least for the moment—outside the determinations of the market. Wearable computers or 'cybernetic garments' (Farren and Hutchinson 2004: 463) are relatively new media forms, found at the frontier of experimental rather than commercial development. The embedding of wires and silicon chips into textiles has grown, since the 1990s, into a wide array of interactive forms or 'networking surfaces', which include 'computationally controllable fabrics including shape-changing polymers, e-textiles, and nanoscale electronics' (Ryan 2009: 309). Wearable computers, or wearables, dissolve the boundary between body and hardware, bringing the digital domain directly into contact with the surface of the body.

If the garment itself can be understood as a paradigmatic interface—both a signifying form and an extension of the embodied self—then the wearable foregrounds fashion's privileged relation to the body in a way that other interfaces cannot. Engaging the body affectively and as a communicative surface, wearables are incorporated into the body schema as both garment and technological 'prosthetic', extending the range of affordances in both real and virtual domains. By focusing less on the content of virtual environments than on the way that digital content is experienced, they foreground the dimensions of touch and movement, which are so vital to the meaning of clothing (and meaning more broadly). Rather than using a technological interface to simulate the clothed body, the garment itself becomes the interface, incorporating all the fluency and immediacy of clothing itself.

Integrating representation and embodied interaction, wearable computing remains open to less determined, less conventional and less easily commercialized modes of bodily investment. Drawing on technological processes as well as the more personal practices of identification and sensory memory that characterize dress, interaction with wearable computers invites users to personalize digital experience in a similar manner. For Birringer and Danjoux, the wearable experience is grounded in intimacy, in 'the desire and erotic sensuality attached to the clothes we wear on our skin, the frivolous, extroverted but also secretive (even antiaesthetic) dimensions of fashioning appearance' (2006: 43). Wearable computing is concerned less with the commodity aspects of fashion than with the idea of 'refashioning' the body—'not just 'controlling' surface functionality in the interface but challenging digital transformation of the materiality of the body' (Birringer and Danjoux 2006: 42). By invoking fashion as an active verb rather than an abstract noun, the wearable calls on users to transform their bodies on their own terms, rather than those dictated by corporate fashion. Here, the virtual is enacted as a quality of the human rather than the strictly technological—as 'that capacity, so fundamental to human existence, to be in excess of one's actual state' (Hansen 2004: 51).

Inviting reflection on the ways that we integrate machine intelligence into our understanding of the fashioned body, wearable computing serves a more philosophical function than commercial fashion interactives. It asks questions about the ways that digital media shape our experience of clothing and about the place and nature of the material body within the logic of fashion—and this curiosity is precisely why wearable computing, at least in its present form, is unlikely to find a place within commercial fashion media. As Birringer and Danjoux point out, the mediating technologies through which we communicate and experience our environment have profound cultural and political stakes (2006: 41). Computer interfaces are sites onto which a culture's historical and social values are mapped. Alongside more positive cultural legacies, interfaces incorporate the logic of modern capitalism, flattening out difference and enacting 'small but continuous gestures of domination' (Selfe and Selfe 1994: 69). And these small but continuous gestures of domination—the persistent imperatives to shape and reshape the body—are fashion's stock in trade.

At the heart of fashion lies a paradox: a desire for constant change posed against an equally pressing requirement for uniformity. And it is, in part, this paradox that underpins the compulsion to dictate not just how the fashioned body should look but how it should feel. Fashion has a stake in controlling the transformation of the material body, in ensuring that it is consistently and predictably adaptable to fashion's demands, and in endorsing a body image that conforms to clearly defined norms of size, race, age and appearance. Yet fashion's obsession with dynamism, with the new and with constant change, encourages fleeting significance at the expense of deeper meaning: corporate fashion has little to gain from allowing consumers to get too attached to their clothes.

Hansen regards the advent of AR interfaces as a signal moment in our understanding of the body and of perception—'an opportunity to revalue the meaning and role accorded the body within the accepted conceptual frameworks of our philosophical tradition' (2006: 7). Creative interfaces such as wearable computers have the potential to expand the scope for embodied human agency and thus to transform human experience. In the context of fashion, they present the prospect of a newly emancipated body that participates in media flows rather than simply observing them—and a subject who is free to challenge normative ideals. At present, however, this sort of autonomy is incompatible with fashion's logic, which requires that the garment—and, indeed, the body itself—remains a skin that is quickly and easily shed. By holding apart real and digital realms rather than inviting their alliance, current fashion interactives discourage the emergence of rogue affects and unexpected transformations. It is inevitable that fashion will embrace, in its own time, new concepts of the body and new forms of embodiment. For now, however, fashion's relationship with the digital body remains skin deep.

NOTES

1. 'The world is already filled with meaning. Its meaning is to be found in the way in which it reveals itself to us as being available for our actions. It is only through those actions, and the possibility for actions that the world affords us, that we can come to find the world, in both its physical and social manifestations, meaningful' (Dourish 2001: 116).
2. Facecake's Swivel can be found at http://www.facecake.com/swivel/, accessed 23 December 2011; Zugara's Webcam Social Shopper at http://webcamsocialshopper.com/, accessed 16 August 2013.
3. 'With Swivel's real-time virtual Try-on and personalised shopping advice, it's never been easier to sample a variety of head-to-toe looks without having to hunt through every department in a store. When we put Swivel in front of real shoppers during our recent mall tour, they tried on three times as many products as a typical dressing room, and a staggering 77 per cent shared their new looks with family and friends' ('Facecake Unveils Virtual Dressing Room' 2012).

BIBLIOGRAPHY

Anakin (2010), 'Burberry Launches Interactive Ad Campaign', *Luxuo: Luxury Blog,* 25 June, http://www.luxuo.com/events/burberry-interactive-digital-campaign.html, accessed 4 April 2012.

Barthes, R. (1985), *The Fashion System,* trans. M. Ward and R. Howard, New York: Hill.

Birringer, J. and M. Danjoux (2006), 'The Emergent Dress: Transformation and Intimacy in Streaming Media and Fashion Performance', *Performance Research,* 11/4: 41–52.

Calefato, P. (1997), 'Fashion and Worldliness: Language and the Imagery of the Clothed Body', *Fashion Theory,* 1/1: 69–90.

Craik, J. (1993), *The Face of Fashion: Cultural Studies in Fashion,* London: Routledge.

Dourish, P. (2001), *Where the Action Is: The Foundations of Embodied Interaction,* Cambridge, MA: MIT Press.

Entwistle, J. (2000), *The Fashioned Body: Fashion, Dress, and Modern Social Theory,* Cambridge: Polity Press.

'Facecake Unveils Virtual Dressing Room' (2012), *On Windows,* 17 January, http://www.onwindows.com/Articles/Facecake-unveils-virtual-dressing-room/6502/Default.aspx, accessed 2 August 2013.

Farren, A. and A. Hutchinson (2004), 'Cyborgs, New Technology, and the Body: The Changing Nature of Garments', *Fashion Theory,* 8/4: 461–76.

Grodal, T. (2003), 'Stories for Eye, Ear, and Muscles: Video Games, Media, and Embodied Experience', in M.J.P. Wolf and B. Perron (eds), *The Video Game Theory Reader,* London: Routledge, 129–55.

Hansen, M.B.N. (2001), 'Seeing with the Body: The Digital Image in Postphotography', *Diacritics,* 31/4: 54–84.

Hansen, M.B.N. (2004), *New Philosophy for New Media,* Cambridge, MA: MIT Press.

Hansen, M.B.N. (2006), *Bodies in Code: Interfaces with Digital Media,* London: Routledge.

Khamis, S. and A. Munt (2010), 'The Three Cs of Fashion Media Today: Convergence, Creativity & Control', *Scan: Journal of Media Arts Culture,* 8/2, http://scan.net.au/scan/journal/print.php?journal_id=155&j_id=20, accessed 9 November 2011.

Lakoff, G. and M. Johnson (1999), *Philosophy in the Flesh: The Embodied Mind and its Challenge to Western Thought,* New York: Basic Books.

Lee, H.-H., J. Kim and A.M. Fiore (2010), 'Affective and Cognitive Online Shopping Experience: Effects of Image Interactivity Technology and Experimenting with Appearance', *Clothing & Textiles Research Journal,* 28/2: 140–54.

Lehmann, U. (2002), 'Fashion Photography', in U. Lehmann and J. Morgan (eds), *Chic Clicks: Creativity and Commerce in Contemporary Fashion Photography,* Boston: Institute of Contemporary Art, T12–T18.

Lipovetsky, G. (2002), 'More Than Fashion', in U. Lehmann and J. Morgan (eds), *Chic Clicks: Creativity and Commerce in Contemporary Fashion Photography,* Boston: Institute of Contemporary Art, T8–T11.

Manovich, L. (2001), *The Language of New Media,* Cambridge, MA: MIT Press.

Massumi, B. (2002), *Parables for the Virtual: Movement, Affect, Sensation,* Durham, NC: Duke University Press.

Merleau-Ponty, M. (2000), *The Phenomenology of Perception,* London: Routledge.

Ryan, S. E. (2009), 'Re-visioning the Interface: Technological Fashion as Critical Media', *Leonardo,* 42/4: 307–13.

Selfe, C. L. and R. J. Selfe Jr. (1994), 'The Politics of the Interface: Power and Its Exercise in Electronic Contact Zones', *College Composition and Communication,* 45/4: 480–504.

Shinkle, E. (2008), 'Video Games, Emotion, and the Six Senses', *Media, Culture and Society,* 30/6: 907–15.

16

CURRENT ISSUES IN THE FASHION MEDIA
INDUSTRY ROUNDTABLE

This chapter is an edit of a roundtable discussion that took place at the London College of Fashion during the conference Fashion Media: Yesterday Today Tomorrow in October 2010. Chaired by Penny Martin, it highlighted the experiences and perspectives of some key fashion media players:

Laura Bradley, former fashion features editor at SHOWstudio, editor of *i-D* online (at the time of the conference), and now editor of Another.com and commissioning editor of *Another Magazine*

Katrina Dodd, editor at *Contagious*, a consultancy and magazine that advises agencies and brands on how to understand and navigate and exploit and anticipate the digital arena

Penny Martin, former editor-in-chief of SHOWstudio, professor of fashion imagery at the London College of Fashion (at the time of the conference) and now editor-in-chief of *The Gentlewoman* magazine

Matthew Moneypenny, founder and CEO of Trunk Archive, a New York–based image and licensing agency

Penny Martin: For the most part, online hasn't been a forum for aesthetic innovation. Why is that?

Matthew Moneypenny: Because I think traditionally—that is traditionally for something we've only been doing a couple of years—most of the dot-coms I've seen that go with a print component are really just taking print designers and applying their talents to the online arena, and I don't think many of them have been terribly successful.

Katrina Dodd: There are reasons for doing that; it's less expensive for one thing. Most of the traditional media that has moved online used this method. But I think where the real, faster-paced stuff is happening is on sites like Net-a-Porter, ASOS.com. They are the ones really who are trying to extend themselves in terms of moving image content.

Penny: We've been reading all the reports about Jeremy Langmead leaving his post as editor of *Esquire* to go to Net-a-Porter's men's version, which is called Mr. Porter, and there have been numerous articles devoted to the idea that this is the 'new editorial'. They say that retail has the power, the resources, the opportunity, the studio space to editorialize the shopping experience, more so than print, and that soon there will be no need for a much more digested editorial experience.

Matthew: I still think the online retailers are always going to suffer from the fact that they're so clearly just selling something. So no matter how beautiful [a film or piece of content may be], how interesting it is, there is something that always feels a little trite and cheap. I can't get away from the fact that I'm watching something solely for the purpose of being sold to. On the other side of that, these companies are becoming quite wealthy, and where there is a lot of money there is a lot more room for development. So you have publishing companies struggling to find new ways to drive revenue and keep their current business models afloat, and then you have these enormous retailers that have come out of the blue and are generating hundreds of millions of dollars in profit. And with that comes an enormous capacity to do stuff that maybe none of us can predict. But I don't think it's ever going to kill print. Net-a-Porter is never going to be *Vogue*; Mr. Porter is never going to be *GQ* or *Esquire*, but the race is on to see where the eyeballs go in the immediate future.

Laura Bradley: I think it's interesting to see what Nowness are doing. I think they are genuinely innovating. It's an LVMH-sponsored project, yet not explicitly so, and it works a little bit like a blog so there will be a different post each day. It works a little bit like *Another*—they've got a 'Love' section where viewers can interact and say they like it or don't like it, and that's linked to their Facebook account.

Matthew: I think Nowness has done brilliantly partly because they weren't relying on a print component to begin with; they could completely reinvent what a magazine should be digitally. They have new content every day; it's always exclusive to Nowness; the only way they will run something is if it has never run anywhere else in the world online. And you can interact with it on the day you get the email; it's very, very smart content.

Penny: One of the things curator and conference key note speaker Charlotte Cotton was talking about earlier was the big offer with the Red Epic camera; it's such a high-resolution movie camera that you can apparently select stills from the motion footage it captures, which can become stills for your campaign. So you no longer need two teams shooting the same subject matter; you can choreograph a piece of motion content, and then ostensibly you can pull out your campaign. There's a fantastic Prada Postcards project that the brand created to promote their spring/summer 2010 eyewear range that was one of the best uses of digital media I've seen yet as it was really focused and didn't overextend its brief. It was somewhere between a show experience and a piece of editorial: Lindsey Wixon spins around, modelling the glasses as a voice narrates them. I think they call the piece an audio-tale. They made something like thirty-six of those films—one for just about every single language. This is a point that Inez van Lamsweerde has raised: just because you're a brilliant model doesn't mean you look beautiful whilst you're speaking. They're casting all these women, and they look great, and they can act, but there's something about the way their face looks when they're speaking that may not make a beautiful shot. So it could be in using Red Epic, you've captured this piece of motion image and when you slow it down to select the stills, you haven't got one. But what they've done with the Postcards project is make these different soundtracks and each one—there's one in Chinese; there's one in Korean; there's one in Taiwanese—you understand and respond to every single one of them. It's a clever workaround that exhibits some understanding of the constraints and opportunities of the medium at last.

So let's move on from fashion film to social networking for a moment. Is it benefitting or damaging editorial? Laura, you probably use social networking sites the most out of all of us?

Laura: Yeah, Twitter and Facebook are the main sites that we use. I always thought a lot of our traffic was coming through Twitter, and interestingly it's coming through Facebook. We're finding that a lot of people aren't using Twitter. They're reading the words on Twitter, but they're not actually clicking to go into the article itself. Whereas on Facebook it's a much slower feed, and you're able to put the byline there and a picture, and people are then clicking in that way.

Penny: Jeremy Leslie—of the magazine review site magculture.com—was saying the response to blog functionality on their site is no longer used as all the conversations are happening in a parallel universe on Twitter.

Katrina: That's part of being a community, isn't it? If you want to feedback about an article that you've read, you will follow somebody on Twitter or Facebook. I think both of those very high-profile examples are a gift for anyone working on a magazine because you get to know what your audience cares about for a start, what they feel passionate about—people send you suggestions and ideas. They might pan something that you have written or take violent exception to your expression of an idea, but all that stuff feeds the debate and where you go with content. The 'Like' thing on Facebook is becoming a really, really weird and interesting tool for everybody. You've got situations now where Urban Outfitters, the fashion chain, is corralling its online offering of clothes and things for sale on the basis of what are the most liked items on Facebook. So if a particular dress is getting fifty 'likes' a day, then that moves it up to a more prominent position on their site, and bingo, they sell more of that dress because people 'like' it.

Penny: Matt, what about that online culture floating up into what was previously seen as a more elite form of journalism and image culture? You share a studio space with an agency that's just taken on the blogger Tommy Ton as an assignment photographer. He's now shooting for American *Vogue* and so on, and I wonder

	whether you think the street blogger and the straight-up photographer have replaced the rock-star fashion photographer?
Matthew:	No, they haven't. Tommy Ton is the exception to the rule. Tommy is also a great photographer. He does a really good job of showing up at the right places, capturing the right people; he's mostly doing studies of accessories. He, self-funding, flew himself to Paris, Milan, New York and London and sat outside fashion shows and looked at what he thought was really interesting and captured those moments in way that's really beautiful; so, I don't think that anybody with a camera can suddenly do what Tommy does or do what Inez van Lamsweerde does—there's a skill. The good photographers have an inherent skill in making imagery. I think the great thing about someone like Tommy Ton is that in this environment you can be an outsider. Tommy Ton is a 5 foot 4 [162 cm] son of Vietnamese immigrants from Toronto, Canada, who went from nothing or not known two years ago to being someone who is sought after by pretty much every major fashion magazine. He has huge traffic on his site, and he deserves it. So, what online did for Tommy was to allow him to be heard and to be seen. But for every Tommy Ton there are a million crappy photographers with crappy ideas about what they think is good or bad. The industry's still a meritocracy. I don't think Steven Meisel or Craig McDean or Inez van Lamsweerde or Bruce Weber are particularly worried about a huge wave of fashion bloggers suddenly getting their campaigns and their cover stories.
Penny:	But things have shifted. What are the changes, and who is making money out of fashion photography?
Matthew:	It seems that people have always been making money at fashion photography. The difference, especially in what we do at Trunk, is that it's now much more global than it used to be. Photography is on the same path that TV and film have been on for a long time. Anywhere you travel in the world, if you look at a movie theatre or look at what is going on in television there, more than 50 per cent of it is usually British or American because the media that the US and the British create is really good. It's actually America's number two export after aerospace. So now, at Trunk, we're licensing images in Korea, Singapore, Brazil, Chile, South Africa, Botswana, in places that we had never heard from before. So those photographers whose imagery we represent, maybe they're making a little bit less on their day rates because of the economy, maybe they're making less because editorial contracts are not what they used to be, but it's coming back in other areas because their work is now being consumed around the globe when it comes to fashion, celebrity, beauty, et cetera.
Katrina:	Also I think it's really important to say that the democratization of content production has been one of the defining characteristics of the rise of digital over the last ten years. Everybody can take a picture, whack it up online and show the world. Anybody can make a film, stick it on YouTube and cross their fingers and hope for good reviews. But the reality is that people do not watch or look at rubbish content. They move on very, very quickly indeed. It is a meritocracy because the mechanisms are there for the good stuff to rise to the top. The proliferation

	of fashion bloggers is one thing, but there still is really just a handful of people whose sites get regular interested visits from the same people coming back again and again and again. So that meritocratic quality filter is still in place; it's just applied to a much wider landscape of opportunities for people who want to make stuff and put it out there, I think.
Penny:	I'd like to return to something we've been talking about quite a lot in various different forms throughout the conference, which is fashion film. Obviously, Laura and I clearly remember posting copy on SHOWstudio five years ago about how the future of fashion image was going to be about film. Today, somebody used the quote we used to bandy around, that fashion 'was designed to move and fashion film gave you the opportunity for an immersive experience where you could see 360 degrees of the garment and hear the sound and the motion'. Do you think it's lived up to those claims yet?
Matthew:	Yes and no. I think my biggest problem with fashion film is that when we watch something online we tend to watch it relatively small. Even if wc blow it up to the size of the laptop screen or the desktop screen, it's still blurred; it's still pixelated. And yet, we are the dream factory. This industry is known for creating unrealistic images of beautiful people doing beautiful things in beautiful clothes that very few people can afford. Part of the trick in doing that is retouching and making those pictures even more perfect than when they were captured, for better or for worse. At some point, the resolution of the screens is going to get high enough so that you'll have the resolution of the video that matches the dreams that the brands are trying to sell, and it's hideously expensive to retouch twenty-four frames per second. A commercial job for a retouching company like Box in New York costs thousands of dollars per image. So if one second is the equivalent of retouching twenty-four frames, you can do the math; to make a motion image look as slick as it does in print—not that slick is always good—it is an enormously expensive endeavour. I don't see that being the way of the future, necessarily.
Penny:	That said, when we started at SHOWstudio in 2000—the end of a period characterized by highly retouched, fantasy images by people like Nick Knight, Sølve Sundsbø and Phil Poynter—we thought that the low production values at which we could execute the motion imagery would stand in the way of our being able to convince a high-profile photographer to contribute work. But then by 2005, there was total saturation of broadband in the Western world and YouTube and 2.0 came along, and there was a readjustment in people's expectations of resolution. Suddenly people were happy to consume information at the most unbelievably pixelated, crappy level.
Katrina:	I think you're right. I think people have very different expectations of moving-image fashion online or on their phone or on their iPad than of a beautiful advertising image in a magazine. It's just a fundamentally different thing. I think part of the huge issue with fashion and with video and the moving image is that it's a language the industry hasn't properly learned to speak yet. Fashion has had decades to get to grips with the still image, and my God they've made it into an

absolute art, but the video thing has really been a swift learning curve in the last five to six years. What I really get annoyed at is when the fashion industry thinks throwing money and big names at a problem is going to provide some amazing answer that everybody is going to flock to watch. It patently doesn't work like that, and I think part of the issue is approaching moving image in a very different way from what they're expecting. People are used to watching a certain kind of stuff online and the certain kind of stuff that gets passed around via email or via Twitter is a very small, digestible, snack-size clips of content. If somebody asks me to watch something that lasts more than two minutes on my screen at work, that's quite a big ask because usually they've lost me by the first fifteen seconds, and that's especially true of fashion film. We've all grown up with TV advertising, and the whole advertising industry stood or fell on its ability to get a message across in fifteen-, thirty-second or one-minute bites, and fashion has looked at the Internet and gone, 'Well we don't have to buy that media; it's free, and yeah, we can make something that's seven minutes long; it's going to be awesome, and everyone is going to watch'. And that's just not true.

Penny: What could be considered best practise in fashion films so far?

Matthew: The examples are few and far between. The Meisel trailer for this season's fall/winter Prada campaign is interesting; it's Angela Lindvall lip-synching a KD Judd song in a blues jazz bar. It's very fifties and girlie and demonstrates a return to a fuller figure.[1] They could've had this fun moment in a jazz club. Instead it's Angela under a spotlight, and it was very dour. They've re-edited it, and the one that's online now is much more the vibe of the collection—they have re-edited into something that is a little bit energetic.

Penny: What was effective about the Prada sunglasses rotating woman piece was that they'd really thought about its editorial purpose—there's a very short message: 'We're selling this one object; we're not going to try to turn it into a narrative and a mood.' It wasn't really about an experience. It was about a single idea, executed very economically. Laura, you represent a magazine and an organization that was about personal style that came out of a fanzine culture. Are you therefore looking for a different kind of film experience when you're commissioning material?

Laura: Since I've been at *i-D,* my focus has been making sure our articles are really good, really strong writing. And that limits the length to 300 words; we don't want to do any more than that because people don't have the attention online. I think the only way you can get away with a long article is by doing a Q&A. We haven't really looked into fashion film at all. The *i-D* Web site is very much like *i-D.* It's not flashy; it's about really good content and the right frequency.

Katrina: Somebody earlier in the day asked, What are fashion films for? And often I think if you go to brands, a variety of places in fact, there's a bit of haziness about that, and I think possibly that has been part of the problem in creating these things. If you start with a very definite idea, maybe a commercial purpose—I want to sell more of this handbag, this dress—you're automatically giving yourself a bit of an advantage when it comes to creating something that fulfils that need.

Penny: But isn't that because a lot of the major brands haven't really decided how they are going to approach advertising online?

Katrina: I just think you have to approach advertising online in a fundamentally different way than you would take advertising in a magazine or newspaper. You've got to consider how people use digital media. You've got to think about where people like to spend time online. What we are seeing increasingly is a move away from the big show-off destination Web sites. It's slightly different for brands like Prada because they are serious, heavyweight players, and I guess the online destination site is the equivalent of the flagship store in Beijing or in New York or in Paris. But in most other brands, what you're seeing is people losing that automatic affiliation—we must have a giant flashy, awesome site—and they are starting to work out what they can do to take their content and their ideas to a place where people are just hanging out anyway. They are trying to do something there that will catch their attention and feed a little bit of interest and engagement.

Penny: I just wanted to sketch out a tale of two fashion shows that occurred during this past London and New York fashion week. On one hand, in London we had Burberry—this big flashy show where they took 'the officially unprecedented step' of integrating e-commerce into the show experience. It was a really big Milan-type fashion show, staged down by Tate Britain, with live streaming and an opportunity for viewers to express preferences through interactive functionality. Burberry are putting a lot of emphasis on the fact that they are the most active company online in terms of their retail concepts and they're editorializing their e-commerce. But the show was universally panned. It was as if they had gone a step too far, and it was felt by the press and the people attending that it was a very cold, remote experience. And then at the other end, during New York Fashion Week, 100 people were invited by Tom Ford to come to a salon presentation where there was only one photographer, Terry Richardson; there are no look-book pictures. You can't see this collection until February, which is unheard of—every other collection on the calendar can be seen within seconds of it hitting the catwalk. But the show experience featured 'real women', with Tom Ford narrating the line order himself: 'And Ms Beyoncé Knowles is wearing.' In comparison with the mass, corporate experience that the modern fashion show has become, Tom Ford launches his womenswear line with this incredibly personal experience—it was deliberately positioned to hold two fingers up to this whole world of fast fashion.

Matthew: I've seen Tom Ford do other things. When he opened his haberdashery on Madison Avenue in New York, you had to make an appointment to go there. That policy very quickly changed, and suddenly, it was an open shop like everything else on Madison Avenue and, 'Please come in' and, 'Please give me your money', so I think it's an interesting way to start a women's collection, but I don't think it's a good business model. I think what Burberry did is absolutely brilliant. There's a reason that their share prices are approaching £1,000 a share, and if you look at the grid, it's a hockey stick. They gave the audience interactivity; an audience that likes to say, 'I like this piece; I like this colour.' They knew what orders they needed to do; they got how much of everything to order—amazing market data. It's a very healthy company,

	and it's an amazing British brand. What they've done, especially this last season, is put themselves in a position to wipe the floor with every other retailer in that category.
Penny:	One of the things we're talking about is how you can consume fashion as photograph, and I guess Tom Ford's point is if you're that visually literate and have that kind of access to the clothing and understand them and consume them and live them for three months before they're in the shops by the time you can get a hold of them, you're bored of them.
Penny:	Should we open up to questions before we take a break?
Audience 1:	When you talk about photographers, you talk about them by name; when you talk about some bloggers, some journalists, you talk about them by name; when you talk about fashion films, you talk about brands—which I thought was quite curious. Are there great fashion film directors? Do they exist? Will they exist?
Katrina:	I think you're absolutely right about the lack of authorship on fashion films, and I think that's probably a bit of a problem. I do wish the production of fashion films would move a little beyond the confines of the fashion and photography industry and get into the hands of the production industry, especially the younger filmmakers out there who are on their knees, begging for budgets and opportunities to make films. The London-based music video production industry is in dire straits at the moment. They can't get budgets to make films, and that has traditionally been the route for new directing talent to get into adverts, from where they go into longer, larger productions like feature films. I was on a music video panel not so long ago, and basically music video direction was described as a hobby because there is so little scope and potential for talent to break through, and it's a real problem, and it's such a damn shame because I feel like there's a gigantic fashion-shaped opportunity for them.
Audience 2:	It's sort of back to the Burberry/Tom Ford debate and the point that people aren't willing to wait the three months or six months from seeing the show to buying the product. What do you think of the alternative solution of shortening cycle time from show through to production?
Matthew:	You mean show in the season? That the shows that happen in July or August are for fall as opposed to spring the next year? I think that would be amazing, but the reality is that the production time doesn't make it possible. For Burberry, it was still eight weeks, and it was specific pieces that had been predestined with those factories, knowing that they were going to have a rush of orders; it was a very well-coordinated effort. It takes a while to make clothing of quality. That's still somebody at a sewing machine putting the clothes together, and there's not really a way to get around that.
Audience 3:	Can you give us an example of good tweeting please?
Katrina:	*Contagious* magazine probably. Our basic use of Twitter is as a content distribution channel, and I think that's how most publications or most media organizations use Twitter. They use it to inform followers about new articles that have been posted on the site, for example. It can link us to people we would like to work with in the future. It can give an immediate sense of the kind of organization we are because

they can link immediately to our content and get a good sense of who we are. There's a kind of trust relationship built into Twitter. If you follow somebody, you want to know that they are not going to bombard you with the equivalent of Twitter spam just for the sake of it. You follow people you know will provide you with a ready stream of interesting snip bits of information and things to read.

Audience 4: More and more magazines and advertisers are using augmented reality—these kind of markers that you can scan with your computer or phone to get exclusive content. How important do you think this is, or is it just a gimmick to get people interested?

Matthew: Like the Rihanna thing, where if you buy a bag of Doritos you get to see the Rihanna video? It sold a lot of Doritos. Is it a gimmick? Yeah. Did it work? Totally. I don't see anything wrong with it. Do I think it is particularly upmarket? No. But I think it's effective. The bottom line is that you can't have great content without some form of payment. The music industry is suffering from that. It's not feasible to give people amazing music or great television or great movies with the production values that everyone in this room is accustomed to seeing without somewhere along the line someone paying for it. It's now that everybody is downloading Rihanna's songs for free and not paying for them; Rihanna has had to find another way to make money, and she found it with Doritos. So I think as a new business model, it's really interesting. Totally gimmicky; completely cheesy, but it's going to allow Rihanna to maintain the same production values that we have come to expect from contemporary music.

NOTE

1. See http://www.luxist.com/2010/07/12/angela-lindvall-sings-for-pradas-fall-ad-campaign-video/, accessed 25 July 2013.

INDEX

fashion magazines
    blogs and, 159–62
    early history of, 1–2, 13–23
    emergence of, 13
    online, 120
    Other in, 2, 35
    see also French fashion magazines; socialist
        fashion magazines; *specific magazines*
fashion media
    British, 2, 22, 24, 35, 39
    changes in, 1, 5–6
    current issues in, 8, 184–92
    fire bombings as, 110
    forms of, compared, 4
    proliferation of, 1
    theory of, 109–16
    see also digital media; guerrilla media; new
        media
fashion plates
    Bidou and, 19
    in *La Gallerie des modes*, 17
    Von Heideloff's, 18
The Fashion System (Barthes), 53, 118, 176
Fashion Toast (website), 160
fashion week, 135, 190
    Berlin (2009), 115
    New York, 133, 138, 190
feminine ideal
    of body, 8
    challenges to, 25
Fernandez, Franc, 114, 115
film
    Bara in, 139, 140
    crime and, 103–6
    see also cinema; fashion film
flapper, 139
Ford, Tom, 190–1
Foxton, Simon, 105
French brands, 147, 149–50
French fashion magazines
    intellectual profile of, 13–14, 16
    Revolution and, 19, 20
    salons and, 15–16

taste in, 1–2, 13–23
    see also specific magazines
French Revolution, fashion magazines and,
    19, 20
Fuller, Loïe, 123
function, fashion and, 29–32
fur, Baker and, 26

La Gallerie des modes, 17–18
The Gallery of Fashion, 17–18
Gazette du Bon Ton: art, modes et frivolities, 2,
    18–19
gender
    Chanel and, 53–5
    Schad and, 5, 85–93
Germanotta, Stefani Joanne Angelina *see* Lady
    Gaga
Greuze, Jean-Baptiste, 16–17
Grisey, Géraldine, 158
guerrilla media
    Abramovic and, 3, 113–14
    body extensions and, 111
    bombings and, 109–10, 112, 116
    defined, 110
    fashion as art and, 112
    hybrids in, 112–13, 116
    Kovacevic and, 115–16
    meat dress and, 3, 5, 114
    media theory of fashion and, 109–16

H2O Pink Label, 171–2
Haigh, John, 104
Harper's Bazaar, 160
'Head for the Haberdashery', 27
headscarf *see* Muslim headscarf
Hearn, Elaine, 168, 170
Hermès, 150
hijab, 75, 77, 78, 82
Hijabstyle (website), 166–7, 169
Hindley, Myra, 99–101, 106
Hogben, Ruth, 122–3
Hollander, Anne, 80, 85
homosexuality, in portraiture, 90–1